The Politics of Recognition and Social Justice

Via a wide range of case studies, this book examines new forms of resistance to social injustices in contemporary Western societies. Resistance requires agency, and agency is grounded in notions of the subject and subjectivity. How do people make sense of their subjectivity as they are constructed and reconstructed within relations of power? What kinds of subjectivities are needed to struggle against forms of dominance and claim recognition? The participants in the case studies are challenging forms of dominance and subordination grounded in class, race, culture, nationality, sexuality, religion, age, disability and other forms of social division. It is a premise of this book that new and/or reconstructed forms of subjectivity are required to challenge social relations of subordination and domination. Thus, the transformation of subjectivity as well as the restructuring of oppressive power relations is necessary to achieve social justice. By examining the construction of subjectivity of particular groups through an intersectional lens, the book aims to contribute to theoretical accounts of how subjects are constituted and how they can develop a critical distance from their positioning.

Maria Pallotta-Chiarolli is Senior Lecturer in the School of Health and Social Development at Deakin University, Melbourne, Australia.

Bob Pease is Chair of Social Work in the School of Health and Social Development at Deakin University, Geelong, Australia.

Routledge Advances in Feminist Studies and Intersectionality

Routledge Advances in Feminist Studies and Intersectionality is committed to the development of new feminist and profeminist perspectives on changing gender relations, with special attention to:

- Intersections between gender and power differentials based on age, class, dis/abilities, ethnicity, nationality, racialisation, sexuality, violence, and other social divisions.
- Intersections of societal dimensions and processes of continuity and change: culture, economy, generativity, polity, sexuality, science and technology;
- Embodiment: Intersections of discourse and materiality, and of sex and gender.
- Transdisciplinarity: intersections of humanities, social sciences, medical, technical and natural sciences.
- Intersections of different branches of feminist theorizing, including: historical materialist feminisms, postcolonial and anti-racist feminisms, radical feminisms, sexual difference feminisms, queerfeminisms, cyberfeminisms, posthuman feminisms, critical studies on men and masculinities.
- A critical analysis of the travelling of ideas, theories and concepts.
- A politics of location, reflexivity and transnational contextualising that reflects the basis of the Series framed within European diversity and transnational power relations.

The Politics of Recognition and Social Justice

Transforming Subjectivities and New Forms of Resistance

Edited by Maria Pallotta-Chiarolli and Bob Pease

Routledge
Taylor & Francis Group
NEW YORK   LONDON

First published 2014
by Routledge
711 Third Avenue, New York, NY 10017

Simultaneously published in the UK
by Routledge
2 Park Square, Milton Park, Abingdon, Oxon OX14 4RN

*Routledge is an imprint of the Taylor & Francis Group,
an informa business*

Library of Congress Cataloging-in-Publication Data
   The politics of recognition and social justice : transforming
subjectivities and new forms of resistance / edited by Maria
Pallotta-Chiarolli and Bob Pease.
      pages cm. — (Routledge advances in feminist studies and
intersectionality ; 15)
   Includes bibliographical references and index.
   1. Social justice.   2. Group identity.   I. Pallotta-Chiarolli, Maria,
1960– II. Pease, Bob.
   HM671.P65 2013
   303.3'72—dc23
   2013023150

ISBN13: 978-0-415-81945-9 (hbk)
ISBN13: 978-0-203-78851-6 (ebk)

Typeset in Sabon
by IBT Global.

Contents

PART III
Validating Racialised Subjectivities

PART IV
Interrogating Privileged Subjectivities

PART V
Creating New Spaces of Resistance in Everyday Life

Figures

Foreword

Bronwyn Davies
University of Melbourne

Once you grasp the idea that the subject is multiply determined by social and discursive structures and practices, and that the subject exists not as a solid entity but as a set of fluid practices, how do you then think about social justice and social change?

Caught as we have been for the last three decades in the intense individualism of neoliberal forms of governmentality, our ideas of the centrality and significance of our individual selves has been significantly heightened. We have been 'persuaded' to become generic subjects in an intense competition with each other for limited goods. We have learned to shape ourselves to become what governments and employment institutions think they want. In many ways we have been made more vulnerable, which has served to ensure our continuing desire to compete and to conform. We have been persuaded that the only real value is the dollar, and with our base nature thus formed, we have also been persuaded of the need for ever-increasing surveillance of our fellow humans, who no longer have a set of values by which to guide their own action. It's a sorry story: a neoliberal epistemology has taken such a firm hold that even the collapse of market economies around the world has not broken its grip, not just on structures, but on individual selves.

It's as if we are trapped in a set of structures and practices that we know are faulty, but we don't know how to break out of them. The intense individualism—the belief in our own vulnerability in the face of intense competition and limited rewards—places us on the treadmill of a productivity we no longer really believe in. My own solution to this dilemma was to quit the institutional apparatus and to launch myself as an independent scholar almost four years ago. My adjunct position at Melbourne University gives me a virtual institutional location if I need it, and otherwise leaves me free to think, and to creatively evolve (in Bergson's 1998 terms)—to encounter multiple facets of the world in such a way that I am always open to being changed, to differentiating myself in Deleuzian (1994) terms. At least that's the ideal that I am working toward. I often find myself making decisions as if I were still caught in a neoliberal universe of meaning. Just as when I first took up feminism in the 70s and 80s, I would find myself still caught up, yet again, in a romantic storyline that I had so earnestly and so thoroughly deconstructed; or as a young mother I would hear myself sounding like my own mother, the one I had decided not to be like. Such repetitions sometimes seem tedious and overwhelming—somehow inevitable, however undesirable.

The thing is that none of us is simply a subject of will, able to decide, and choose, freed from the forces that shape us—forces that make action possible or meaningful (Davies 2010). Yet we do break out, and the world does change—to become more neoliberal over the last three decades for example—but also to become less homophobic, less sexist, less racist. Such changes do not take place all in a flash of the Paul-on-the-road-to-Damascus variety. They are far more complicated than that. We are willful subjects, often with very good intentions. But intentions are never enough. We are also subjects of thought, and thought (intersecting with desire, relationality, social context and history) changes in bursts and flashes alongside seemingly intractable contradictions and compulsions to stay the same—recognizably the same as we were yesterday, and the day before that. We are often tediously boring, insecure creatures . . .

This fascinating book takes us right into the heart of this conundrum of individual and social change. Each chapter takes us into one set of potential transformations, examining, for example, men confronting their own positions of power and privilege, and middle-class pedagogues questioning their unearned entitlements or the pedagogy and politics of privilege. The papers are situated in a wonderfully diverse array of settings. They examine privilege and disadvantage in tertiary settings, analyzing the way working-class women must struggle for recognition. They examine the way colonizers must confront their entanglements in relations of power when working with colonized people. They take us into the spaces of male dancers learning to be more graceful, working with choreographers to reconceptualize male dance, and feminist women raising their sons not to be sexist, working together to reconceptualize masculinity. We meet people working with the disabled, learning to see disabled people as fully human, sexual beings. We are invited into the space of transgender activism, and of women discovering ways of living with bisexual partners. We meet migrant Somali women daily crossing the borders between their home culture and their host culture, and we discover the impact of house-building on southern European migrants' sense of community. We discover the impact of prison on young Maori women's subjectivities, and the impact on women of childhood sexual abuse. In each study we discover something different, sometimes shocking and often confronting, about the struggle for recognition, the politics of privilege and of resistance, and the surprising conjunctions and disjunctions associated with social change.

Each of the fifteen papers presents a case study in the intersections between the specificities of individuals, and the social structures and practices within which their specificity is made recognizable, viable, and habitable.

We are dependent for our survival on being recognizable, which means, in Butler's (1997) analysis, fitting within the existing categories of human-ness. But those categories are also our undoing. Deleuze (1994) argues that difference is not about being in one category or another, but on our capac-ity to become different in each moment, to creatively evolve new ways of seeing and being—since that is where the vital force of life resides (Davies et al., 2013). And that is the complex space that this book enters into. Not that its theoretical framing is explicitly Deleuzian, but rather that this chal-lenge, which I identify as a Deleuzian challenge, is the one the editors and the various authors take up. Without denying the specificity of the indi-vidual, and without underestimating the power of the social and the discur-sive, how are we to think of social change? But more, this book wants us to think about how we might better contribute to that social change if we can understand this complex interface between the specificity of the human subject, and the cultural, social, historical and geographical forces at play in shaping that subject.

REFERENCES

Bergson, H. 1998. *Creative Evolution.* Translated by A. Mitchell. Mineola, NY: Dover Publications. First published 1911.

Butler, J. 1997. *The Psychic Life of Power: Theories in Subjection.* Stanford: Stan-ford University Press.

Davies, B. 2010. "The Struggle between the Individualised Subject of Phenom-enology and the Multiplicities of the Poststructuralist Subject: the Problem of Agency." *Reconceptualizing Educational Research Methodology* 1(1):54-68.

Davies, B., L. Claes, K. De Munck, E. De Schauwer, I. Van De Putte, and M. Ver-stichele. (2013). "Recognition and Difference: a Collective Biography." *Interna-tional Journal of Qualitative Studies in Education* 25(6): 680-690.

Deleuze, G. 1994. *Difference and Repetition,* Translated by P. Patton. New York: Columbia University Press.

Acknowledgments

We wish to acknowledge the passion and commitment of our contributors, who combine academia and activism, in their work for social justice.

Maria also wishes to thank Bob for his camaraderie and insights. After many years of being inspired by Bob's work and ways of going about that work, it has been a sheer pleasure collaborating on this project.

Bob would like to thank Maria for being such a supportive and engaged collaborator, whose enthusiasm for the project has never waned. It's been great to have worked together on such an important anthology.

1 Recognition, Resistance and Reconstruction

An Introduction to Subjectivities and Social Justice

Maria Pallotta-Chiarolli and Bob Pease

INTRODUCTION

The aim of this book is to examine new forms of resistance to social injustices in contemporary Western societies. Resistance requires agency, and agency is grounded in notions of the subject and subjectivity (Parker 1999). It is a premise of this book that new and/or reconstructed forms of subjectivity are required to challenge social relations of subordination and domination.

Subjectivity is primarily based on lived experience (Malone 2000). While subjectivity is sometimes used to explore individualistic strategies for personal meaning, we argue that subjectivity is central to political struggles against regimes of power (Elliott 2007). Thus, understanding how subjects are constituted is important in fostering the capacity of critical reflection and social transformation (Allen 2008).

Our aim here is to understand the relationship between subjectivity and the wider social order. The relationship between the psyche and society is one of the most challenging issues facing social theory (Emirbayer and Mische 1998; McNay 2000; Davies et al., 2013). While there is a variety of theoretical approaches to subjectivity, those that explore the links between the subject and society are the most promising in developing strategies for resistance. In this introductory chapter, we review and interrogate what we believe are the most important theoretical approaches to subjectivity, drawing upon Marxism, critical theory, feminism, postcolonialism and post-structuralism. Our aim in this book is not to develop a new theory of subjectivities. Rather, we are more concerned with investigating how diverse subjectivities are constructed and reconstructed.

Numerous writers on subjectivity challenge the notion of a unified subject. Frost and Hoggett (2008), for example, point out that post-liberal notions of subjectivity move beyond the idea of a rational consistent identity to locate the subject within power relations and inequality. Subjectivity is not transhistorical, but rather is connected to particular social and cultural contexts (McNay 2008). Once we move away from the notion of subjectivity as bounded, rational and autonomous, we embrace the idea of a socially situated and historically mediated subjectivity intersected by gender, race, class, sexuality and other social categories (Layton 2008). Indeed, positionality, intersectionality and the intersection of multiple positionalities are significant structures and processes that require multiple and diverse agentic negotiations and navigations (Anthias 2008; Lutz, Vivar and Supik 2011; Yuval-Davis 2006). *Positionality* refers to both structural social position and social positioning "as process, that is, a set of practices, actions and meanings" (Shinozaki 2012, 1811). Crenshaw (1989) coined the term "intersectionality" to foster the recognition of how multiple social divisions may simultaneously create discrimination and marginalisation (see also hooks 1981; Anthias and Yuval-Davis 1983; Brah and Phoenix 2004). Pallotta-Chiarolli (2004, 2010) adopts and applies the term "interweaving" to describe how these multiple axes of difference require multiple and interwoven strategies of resistance, resilience and agency. Thus, intra-group identities and the subsequent confluences and conflicts are able to be recognised and resourced for. It must be stated here that not all identifications cause disadvantage, and, indeed, within one person or community, an intersectional approach allows for the recognition of the continuum between privileged and ostracised identities and subjectivities. Likewise, in any research, resourcing or action, not all identities can be mapped, analysed or addressed at once and equally, and, as will be evident in this book's collection, some identities are more likely to come to the fore in certain contexts than others. Nevertheless, intersectionality is a framing device that keeps us mindful of the interactions and interweavings between identities, and their "criss-crossing and power-infused social relations and spaces- how we make sense of ourselves and mediate the contours of social life" (Yip and Page 2013). In this book, "the intimate interconnections, mutual constitutions and messiness of everyday identifications and lived experiences . . . linked to structural phenomena" will be exemplified (Taylor, Hines and Casey 2011, 2, 4).

Following the above discussion regarding multiple positionalities, it becomes apparent that subjective processes are both intra-psychic and socio-historical (Mama 1995). They are internalised from discourses (Venn 2002) and shaped by material conditions (Malone 2000). They change over time and can be multiple and contradictory (Walsh and Bahnisch 2002). Furthermore, subjectivity is best understood as being performed or actively constructed rather than being reflective of an essential core. It is embodied and reflected in one's engagement and practice in the world (McNay 2008). If subjectivity is constructed through practice, it is neither fully determined nor fully capable of being willed.

Layton (2010) points out how in the context of neoliberalism, many in the professional middle class in Western societies have adapted their subjectivities to individualistic norms that separate the individual from the social. Modern subjectivities in neoliberal market economies are constituted primarily through roles as workers and consumers (Burkitt 2008). Layton (2009) observes how the investment in individualised forms of identity encourage disidentification with the suffering of others and thus disables individuals from the capacity for empathy and responsibility, and for how one is implicated in their suffering. This is what happens when the psychic is separated out from the social. For Butler (2004), recognition is required for the vulnerability of others to be seen, understood and altered/reconstructed.

While subjects often accommodate to regimes of power, they have the capacity to re-imagine themselves as new political subjects. We need to understand more fully how external relations of power are psychically internalised to construct a particular sense of self. It seems clear that refusing to accommodate to dominant power relations will necessitate the creation of new forms of subjectivity (Allen 2008). Burkitt (2008) has previously raised the question of whether or not new forms of subjectivity that are not linked to domination and control are emerging. For example, many social movement activists are constructing collective identities that combine ant-sexism, anti-racism and anti-capitalism, among others (Layton 2009). Burkitt (2008) believes that these new forms of resistance have the potential to create a new democratic form of politics and that the subjectivities of individuals who resist domination and control should be researched. This book is in part a response to that imperative.

MOVING BEYOND STRUCTURAL DETERMINISM

In the compilation of the chapters in this book, we are returning to an age-old debate in critical theory and Marxism where the primacy of economic structures is cast against voluntarist models of change which emphasise changes in consciousness leading to changes in cultural norms as a catalyst for significant structural change. In early Marxist debates, this issue was framed in terms of ideology. Why did so many working-class people come to accept inequalities and injustices as legitimate (Gil 2008)? While the Marxist notion of false consciousness was appropriately understood as patronising and elitist, Marxists were trying to understand oppressed people's accommodation to dominant ideologies.

We need to explore ways in which individuals become both complicit in sustaining oppressive social relations as well as resisting them (Layton 2008; Freire 1972). Gil (2008) argues that the key task is working out how to understand subjectivity in ways that move beyond the intra-psychic to encompass the cultural, political and social. The challenge we face is how to locate the individual within the context of the social without reverting to a socially determinist conception of the self. At the same time, how do we understand human subjectivity without disconnecting the individual from their historical and social context (Layton 2008; Davies et al., forthcoming)?

Structural determinists would argue that individuals have no capacity at all for human agency (Robinson 2003–2004). Materialists argue that focusing on language and culture privileges agency and identity over structural inequalities. They question the extent to which systemic and structural forms of oppression can be addressed by forms of identity politics (McNay 2008). For many years now, the conflict between materialist and cultural analyses has translated into a tension between a politics focused on structural changes versus a politics emphasising the affirmation of marginalised identities. This is mirrored in the debate between cultural and materialist feminisms (McNay 2004). While some feminists have attempted to explore the interconnections between cultural and materialist approaches, many have continued to emphasise the superiority of one form of analysis over another. For example, Walby (2001) argues that the main sources of change will not come from individual action, but rather from the interaction between social structures. Hence, she places more emphasis on changes to the gender division of labour than changes within gender norms and ideologies.

Materialists believe that substantial structural change must flow from the macro level downward to the micro level. In discussing changes in women's lives, for example, McNay (2000) reminds readers that the gender division of labour, and the resulting material resources that flow from it, has been an important source of both subordination and emancipation. Similarly, in their study of cosmetic surgery as an increasingly "legitimized form of female empowerment" that simultaneously highlights women's increased access to material resources as well as women's ongoing disempowerment via the increased scrutinisation of their bodies, Doyle and Karl (2008, 84) argue that "the concept of choice needs to be critically examined within the context of popular post-feminist and neoliberal ideologies of the self which focus upon individual responsibility and consumer agency, thereby rendering invisible structural and social inequities."

One does not have to be a structural determinist, however, to acknowledge that there are material constraints on discursive change and that material conditions influence and shape subjectivities (Malone 2000). In the British context of the late 1990s and early twenty-first century, the politics of neoliberalism, with its endorsement of individual liberalism as promoted within New Labour's commitment to the ideology of *The Third Way*, sought "to reconcile the irreconcilable" by "combining elements of left social democracy with right neoliberalism" (McRobbie 2000, 100). A commitment to tackling social inequalities was accompanied by an endorsement of the free market economy and capitalism. Doyle and Karl argue that the focus on individual responsibility helped to "create the conditions for social acceptance of a reduction in state welfare and an increase in the rights and responsibilities of the individual consumer", which further entrenches white and middle-class constructs of consumerism and individualism (2008, 87). The discourse of individuality renders invisible the class-based structural mechanisms involved in its formation and operation (Skeggs 2004).

However, if we give priority to the transformation of economic structures as the basis of all significant change, then it leaves no room for changes in consciousness and subjectivity through the agency of individuals as a basis for social change. While ordinary people have no control over external objective sources of oppression in their lives (Robinson 2003–2004), they are able to work out how to relate to those structures (Malone 2000). Otherwise, they are posited as having no agency in the face of those structural forces. And, if we allow no space for agency and change within social relations without structural change, we end up with a reductionist position. With the rise of feminist materialism, and especially the work of Barad (2007), we see attempts to move beyond the binary of realism and constructivism. Barad has formulated the notion of agential realism which posits that agency is not an attribute of a subject or something that someone has, but is rather a relationship that is enacted in the world.

Whatever theoretical lens we use, we need to understand how to make relations of subordination and domination accessible to people's awareness as a precursor to questioning and resisting them. As Hoy (2005) observes, if we are able to acknowledge the way in which our thoughts and actions are shaped by external constraints, these constraints are less likely to be effective in limiting our agency. We need to understand systemic constraints in order to "cross boundaries, crack codes, and bring back a store of secret information that society would like to use to keep us *all* in thrall" (Queen 1991, 20–21).

THE POLITICS OF RECOGNITION

Recognition has increasingly become a key concept in the social sciences. Honneth (2003) identifies misrecognition as a form of disrespect. Recognition of one's humanity by others is a basic requirement to avoid the distorting of one's subjectivity. One is unable to flourish as a person in the absence of affirmation of subjectivity. Honneth (2003) regards recognition as a key component of social justice. It thus constitutes an injustice if people are stunted and deformed through misrecognition. Allen (2008) argues that our desire for recognition is so powerful that we prefer recognition that reinforces our subordination over and above not getting recognition at all. This is why we can so easily become psychically invested in various forms of subordination.

Honneth (2003) says that recognition politics provides greater opportunities for agency and resistance. Certainly, what is of value in Honneth's conception of recognition is his consideration of the role of emotions as a catalyst for political action. The emotional consequences of the experience of misrecognition can provide an impetus for recognition struggles (McNay 2008), whereby various social movements in relation to gender, Indigenous people, disability and sexuality and so on seek to reaffirm marginalised identities (Yuval-Davis 2011). Such movements were sometimes pitted as alternatives to the more traditional politics of the left which focused on redistribution of resources.

Several theorists have coined terms to articulate these notions of recognition, resistance and reconstruction in relation to identity politics. In her work with same-sex families, Finch builds upon Butler's notion of performativity and describes what she has termed "displaying" as the process by which individuals, and groups of individuals, "convey to each other and to relevant audiences" that their actions and identities constitute legitimacy and, indeed, deserve recognition (2007, 67). In the context of our book, we argue for the "need for display" to ensure recognition, acknowledgment and subsequent reconstructive action. However, we must also keep in mind that if we look at display and agency in terms of Butler's ideas on enacted identity and recognition, "the social norms that constitute our existence [and actions] carry desires that do not originate with our individual personhood" (2004, 1), meaning our perceived agency, what we display and how, is predicated on the constraint of social norms. This also illustrates Foucault's (1988) construction of subject-hood as produced through the intersection of how we operate on ourselves (the technologies of self) to respond to how society operates on us (the technologies of power/domination).

This notion of "situated agency" (Foucault 1988; Butler 2004) can also be applied to the term "resist-ances" coined by Grace and Benson (2000) to describe direct actions informed and enacted in the intersection of the personal, the political and the pedagogical. Likewise, Hill (1995) coined the term "fugitive knowledge" to describe oppositional knowledge produced by queer persons to inform queer discourses, recognition and resistances in educational and other socio-cultural spaces. Similarly, Britzman (1995, 235) speaks to the possibility of using "suspicious discourses" that "exceed practices of normalization." Another example is the work of Maxwell and Aggleton (2010), who propose the notion of "agency in action" as a new way of understanding agency beyond that which stresses agentic practice as resistance or the challenging of dominant expectations and understandings. Instead, "agency in action" offers two new ways of understanding agency: either through "reacting into action" and *taking power back* or by "starting from" a *powerful* position.

In relation to the above theorisations of "situated agency", particularly in relation to Foucault and Butler, Davies et al. (2013) grapple with the "paradoxical tension" regarding how specific acts of recognition may paradoxically require subjection to existing discourses which were not chosen but are depended upon in order to initiate and sustain agency: 'The result is an autonomous, repressed subject—one who is subjected but longs to escape the terms of subjection' (Davies et al. 2013, 681). The challenge is how to combine what Davies et al. call this "melancholic Foucauldian/Butlerian framework", which positions the constitutive act as "repressed" and the individual "subjected to prior terms or categories" that must be taken up as one's own, with the work of Barad (2007) and Deleuze (1994). This "Baradian/Deleuzian framework" locates the constitutive act as "an ongoing entanglement of mutual agencies through which life/art/being is generated in each present moment" (Davies et al. forthcoming, 5). Recognition is thus envisioned within a Deleuzian both/ and framing: *both* a repetition of the already familiar *and* the possibility of the "new-as-yet-unthought", also described as the Deleuzian "line of flight" or Baradian "intra-action" of "entangled agencies" (Davies et al. 2013, 6; see also Barad 2007; Deleuze 1994). Identity and subjectivity are simultaneously vulnerable to existing discourse, as evidenced in the neo-liberal systems of rewarding individual agency which uphold and conform to structural discourses of achievement, success and citizenship, as well as this vulnerability enabling the person to unfold, evolve and create. The above border zone between the personal and the political may be useful to those critics who have argued that identity politics has neglected key political and institutional issues and has become too focused on personal identity and personal solutions to structural problems. For them, there is too much concentration on the self, which is seen to be regulated by dominant discourses (Elliott 2007). Fraser (2003b), for example, argues that because recognition politics is more concerned with the cultural struggles focused on identity, it neglects the importance of structural and economic inequalities. McNay (2004) also argues that cultural analyses fail to locate the recognition of identities within the context of access to material resources. Walby (2001) similarly argues against the concept of recognition because, in her view, it is too accommodated to the existing social order and insufficiently concerned with structural change.

For McNay (2008) the concept of misrecognition with its emphasis on everyday interactions obscures the ways in which structural dynamics of power infuse subjectivity. Misrecognition, she argues, is grounded in culture and disconnected from the economy and the political order. In McNay's (2008) view, subjectivity cannot be separated from structural forces because it is shaped by social relations of power.

Thus, the emphasis on doing and performing subjectivities has been criticised for overemphasising the face-to-face interactions of individuals and groups at the expense of structural analyses of power relations. McNay (2008) argues that the politics of recognition is premised on a simplification of the sources of identity and agency in the formation of subjects. While she agrees with the importance of subjectivity as emphasised in the work of key recognition theorists, she believes that the current understanding of recognition does not do justice to a sociological understanding of power relations.

This tension between recognition and redistribution is sometimes framed dichotomously as the affirmation and revaluation of aspects of subordinated groups which are marginalised versus the transformation of structural relations of power which marginalize them (Fraser 2003b). Fraser (2001) has pointed out that progressive politics has been divided for some time between political struggles focused on redistribution of resources and political struggles focused on respect for difference and affirmation of non-culturally dominant identities. These two forms of political struggle have at times been in conflict and there has been little cooperation or overlap between them. Fraser argues that this is a false dichotomy. In her view, social justice requires both recognition and redistribution. She is thus concerned with creating an overarching conceptual framework to encompass both forms of politics rather than subsuming one under the other.

The key difference between Honneth and Fraser is that while Honneth (2003) argues that struggles over redistribution are a reflection of a wider struggle over recognition, Fraser (2003b) argues that redistribution politics and identity politics are separate and unconnected arenas of political struggle. She argues that while both forms of struggle are essential for social justice, neither one can be reduced to the other.

The dialogue between Fraser and Honneth (2003b) has made a significant contribution to understanding subjectivity and agency in the context of power relations. However, this dialogue has not resolved the dichotomous frame of recognition and redistribution as oppositional to each other. When is the source of oppression a result of misrecognition by others through interpersonal interactions and when is it structurally and systemically based? How do we understand the relationship between the two forms of oppression?

BOURDIEU AND THE EMBODIMENT OF SUBJECTIVITIES

McNay (2008) suggests that habitus may provide a way through the polarisation of objectivism in redistribution politics and subjectivism in recognition politics. The work of Bourdieu (1977) is helpful in explaining how various forms of inequality are reproduced and internalised. He formulated the term "habitus" to explain how a system of stable psychological positions leads people to see the world from a particular perspective. One of the benefits of habitus is that it enables us to understand the notion of embodied subjectivity. Bourdieu's (1977) notion of habitus enables us to see how social inequalities are sustained through the dispositions of individuals and through embodiment. Unlike Marxist and radical humanist views, which outline how people's ideas and consciousness are shaped by dominant ideologies, Bourdieu emphasised how dominant ideologies are also incorporated into the body so as to influence behaviour at an unconscious and habitual level. They are then experienced as a form of second nature.

Bourdieu (2001, 95) argues that such dispositions are "beyond the grip of conscious control and therefore not amenable to transformations or corrections". For Bourdieu choice is understood within a structure that is not of individuals' making. Bourdieu (1977) believes that while we come to believe that we are freely choosing various courses of action, we do not recognise the extent to which our choices have been narrowed and constrained.

Bourdieu (1999) draws attention to the psychic injuries caused by social injustice. He uses the language of social suffering to convey the ways which people's experience of oppression is reflected not only in access to material resources but also in their feelings of resentment, anger and despair (Bourdieu 1999). Frost and Hoggett (2008) point out how this suffering is internalised and creates hidden injuries of class, race and gender among other forms of hurt. This can also be understood as internalised oppression.

Bourdieu of course has been criticised for being overly determinist in relation to the ways in which individuals accommodate to social structures (McNay 2008). Bourdieu (2001) is critical of the idea of consciousness raising because it suggests that individuals can easily transform their consciousness and their capacity to act. For individuals to have agency in Bourdieu's terms, they would have to first develop awareness of their habitus and how it was shaped by socio-cultural forces. For Bourdieu (1990), reflexive sociology is a mechanism for fostering such critical resistance.

FOUCAULT AND THE DISCURSIVE CONSTRUCTION OF SUBJECTIVITIES

Misrecognition can be understood as a form of positioning in dominant discourses. Foucault (1979) is also interested in how individuals accommodate themselves to social injustices. Positioning theory has been used to explore the mechanisms of accommodation to dominant discourses (Willig 2000; Pease 2000). Discourses make positions available for individuals, and these positions are taken up in relation to other people. When taken up, the world is seen from the standpoint of that position, and this process involves, among other things, positioning oneself in relation to categories and storylines. It also involves locating oneself as a member of various subclasses of categories as distinct from others. Thus, one develops a sense of oneself "as belonging to the world in certain ways and thus seeing the world from the perspective of one so positioned" (Davies and Harre 1990, 46–47). These dynamics of positioning reflect differential power and often a lack of reflexivity about the harm that is caused by such acts (Davies 2008). Through this process, people can become fixed in a position as they are shaped by "the range of linguistic practices available to them to make sense" of the world (Potter and Wetherall 1987, 109).

The individual is thus constituted and reconstituted through a variety of discursive practices and changing material circumstances. Multiple subject positions resulting from the involvement in different discourses lead to individuals being composed of a set of contradictory subjectivities. This multiplicity of discourses leads to internal conflict and contradiction.

As discourses compete with each other for the allegiance of individual subjects, however, the accommodation of subjects to particular discourses is never final and is open to challenge and change (Pease 2000). Hoy (2005) argues that while Foucault emphasises how individuals become complicit in the processes of internalising dominant ideologies, they can develop awareness of these processes and have the capacity of individual agency to resist them. In other words, Foucault (1988) has theorised about "the technologies of power", which he terms "governmentality". He has also theorised about the "technologies of the self" which operate with the technologies of power:

> to effect by their own means or with the help of others a certain num-
> ber of operations on their own bodies and souls, thoughts, conduct,
> and way of being, so as to transform themselves in order to attain a
> certain state of happiness, purity, wisdom, perfection or immortality.
> (Martin, Gutman and Hutton 1988, 18)

Critical reflexivity involves the self questioning what is held to be "universal, necessary, obligatory." This kind of interrogation opens up a space for experimentation; reality is confronted with liberty and possibility: "We can never be ensnared by power: we can always modify its grip in determinate conditions and according to a precise strategy" (Foucault 1988, 123). The self must "grasp the points where change is possible and desirable, and to determine the precise form this change should take" (Foucault in Rabinow 1984, 46). Thus, an analysis of personal agency must not dispense with the analysis of normative and normalising ascriptive structures in identity formation and recognition. Situated agency acknowledges that even critical skills and practices of resistance are themselves socially produced and constrained by cultural discourses. They are not simply the result of some inner space that transgresses the outer world. Questions arise in understanding how individuals select certain actions and strategies individually and collectively, and why they believe they need to undertake these actions. What are the various sociocultural, legal and political discourses that frame the kinds of strategies individuals and groups undertake, and their belief in the need for specific types of strategies? How do they utilise the gaps, silences and distances between their various worlds, each with its own "regimes of truth" (Derrida 1981), to construct border zones within which they can construct new "truths"?

REMAKING SUBJECTIVITIES

What are the possibilities for resistance and the remaking of subjectivity? In engaging with this question in this collection, we are mindful of the work of theorists such as Butler (2004) and Sabsay (2012), who problematise who has the power to define what agency is or not; what constitutes 'correct' forms of agency and resistance; and who has earned the right to be recognised. For Butler (2004), some lives are rendered "unliveable" due to the lack of recognition because existing norms allocate recognition "differentially". She asks what might be done to produce "a more egalitarian set of conditions for recognizability . . . in order to produce more radically democratic results?" (2009, 6). Otherwise, "normative restrictions" based on hierarchies of power delineate between "personal choice" defined as upholding autonomy and "compulsory choices" defined as based on coercion: "it seems that certain choices, such as wearing a hijab and also working in commercial sex, could not be choices at all" (Sabsay 2012, 617). Sabsay points out that only certain kinds of personal choices are regarded as "a legitimate expression of sovereign autonomy", while other choices are understood as "oxymoronically, 'compulsory choices' . . . [which] serve as evidence that such subjects lack sovereign autonomy altogether" (Sabsay 2012, 617).

An example of research being undertaken at these intersections of "personal choice" and "compulsory choice" is the work of Ingrey (2013). She is interested in how individual students enact their own gendered subjectivity or agency through clothing choices as a basis for reflecting on possibilities for troubling gender binaries in schools. She concludes that they are engaged in their own subject-hood (personal choice) while they are also inculcated by the forces of consumerism, or acted upon (compulsory choice). Her work is premised on that of Davies (2006), who draws on Butler (1995), in a theorisation of subjects possessing a "conditioned agency" and being engaged in this "double directionality" (Davies 2006, 428).

Gil (2008) is another theorist who is sceptical of concepts like agency, choice and autonomy. He argues that the celebration of agency in the face of limited scope for political activism may create false hopes about the possibilities of change. The concept of agency can all too easily accommodate to neoliberalism's emphasis on the individual as rational, calculating and self-regulating, whereby they are fully responsible for life options whatever the structural constraints. Certainly, one can see how neoliberalism can easily redirect empowerment and choice to its political agenda. However, is the concept of agency also inevitably infused with neoliberal ideology, as Gil (2008) argues?

McNay (2008) argues that in most discussions of subjectivity, there is little scope for people to resist and transform dominant forms of subjection and constraint. Just because individual subjectivities are socially constructed, it does not mean that they are incapable of critically reflecting on that social construction and exercising some response to it. In this book, following Allen (2008), we challenge the pessimism so often expressed in social theorising about subjectivity that individuals are unable to critically reflect on their social positioning. While we acknowledge the cultural construction of subjectivity, we argue that individuals are able to recognise the ways in which they are socially constructed and are able to critique these processes. As Robinson (2003–2004) argues in the context of a discussion about white supremacy, ordinary people can choose the extent to which they reproduce or challenge white structural oppression.

We do not underestimate the power of structural forms of oppression to shape the experiences of ordinary people. Of course, there is no automatic transition from oppositional political consciousness to individual and social action. Beyond recognising injustice, one must also be able to identify the systemic sources of injustice, devise strategies of resistance and have the moral courage to act in the face of dominant interests (McNay 2010).

Hoggett (2001) says that our capacity for reflexivity is shaped in part by our difficulty in facing our anxieties and fears. Allen (2008) argues that sometimes, resistance to power may mean refusing to be what we have become through the processes of subjection. As Robinson (2003–2004) says, simply by saying "I refuse", individuals name the reality of their experience and they challenge the notion that structural forces can completely determine their choices and their capacity to resist.

Whether we are exploring subjectivity though the lens of Marx, Foucault, Butler or Bourdieu, we are interested in exploring processes internalising the social that go beyond consciousness. If Cho and Lewis (2006) are correct in their view that oppressive social relations construct libidinal responses, then we may need to interrogate the unconscious as a key factor shaping subjectivity. Although beyond the scope of this book, we raise the issue that psychoanalytic frameworks may need to be incorporated into our theorising of subjectivity. When oppressive power relations become embedded in the psyche, we need different strategies to engage people in resistance. For Cho and Lewis (2006), this may involve "critical unconsciousness raising".

While the concept of agency offers a sense of hope in our capacity to transform structurally-based inequalities (London Feminist Salon Collective 2004), we need to consider whether or not this is a false hope. How do we avoid both the dangers of structural determinism on the one hand and the illusion of free-floating individualism on the other? Archer (2000) has identified the dilemma quite well. Writing from a critical realist perspective, she emphasises the need to avoid both the oversocialised conception of personhood in which individuals are totally formed by discourse with no agency whatsoever and the free-acting individualism which ignores any social and cultural influences on the construction of subjectivity. To this view, and in a further development of the Deleuzian "both/and" strategies put forward by Davies et al. (2013), we offer the tripartite construction of agency as put forward by Emirbayer and Mische (1998): first, "iteration" requires the selective reactivation of past patterns of thought and action; second; "projectivity" requires the imagination of future trajectories of action and reconfigurations of structure; and third, "practical evaluation" depends on the capacity (i.e. economic, cultural, educational etc capital) to make practical and viable decisions from the available possibilities.

BORDER DWELLING: AGENTIC POSITIONING AND BEING POSITIONED

In order to facilitate an understanding of the interconnected machinations of agency and social determinism, this book puts forward a framing as constructed by Pallotta-Chiarolli (2004, 2010) which examines the very processes of positioning within, between and beyond this dichotomy. The term "ascription" is used to refer to the assignation of a label, quality or character to a person or group. This frame reveals the significance of three interwoven forces of socio-cultural structure and agentic subjectivity: *social ascription* being the labels and actions (both affirming and negating) imposed on the individual by the sites of power in the wider society such as the law, media, popular culture, education, religion and medical institutions; *community ascription* being the labels and actions one's significant others, such as members of religious, ethnic, gender and sexual communities, affirm or disapprove; and *self-ascription* being the individual resisting, selecting and determining necessary or desired labels and actions from the constructions available (situated agency), or attempting to devise an alternative subjectivity (personal agency).

"They Say, Therefore I Should Be": External Ascription

Social ascription is very similar to positioning theory in relation to positioning in discourses. It refers to the labels, classifications and actions imposed on one by the powerful central discourses within a society as upheld by institutions such as the media, religion, education and the law. As will be presented throughout this book, where individuals have responded with non-compliance, the consequences have been marginalisation, pathologisation and sometimes criminalisation. Mason calls this wider societal code the "discourse of silence" that renders some realities, relationships and ways of being "both unseeable and unknowable" (1995, 87).

Foucault (1979) uses the panopticon model as symbolic of this power of the wider social order. The panoptical prison placed one guard in the centre who surveilled all the prisoners night and day. One effect of constantly being watched was that prisoners began to watch themselves, whether the guard was there or not. In other words, the external guard's gaze began to be internalised in each prisoner. The panoptical gaze is the self-surveillance of those who have been conditioned to being watched, evaluated and regulated. Hierarchical, continuous and functional surveillance, as felt by many individuals discussed in the following chapters, is organised as multiple, automatic and anonymous power. Disciplinary power is therefore exercised through its invisibility; at the same time it imposes on those whom it subjects a principle of compulsory visibility which assures the hold of the power that is exercised over them. The panopticon is "at once surveillance and observation, security and knowledge, individualization and totaliza-tion, isolation and transparency" (Rabinow 1984, 217). Power is made visible not by public display of its source and origin, but by the objectifica-tion of those on whom it is used, and through the formation of a body of knowledge about these individuals. This may lead to individuals scripting performances of normativity: scissoring, simplifying and homogenizing their selves and their lives, finding the "ready-made code and having to accommodate oneself to it" (Trinh 1991, 136).

Nevertheless, within this system, panopticonic conformity to social norms is a form of agency. It can be beneficial, gratifying, profitable and pragmatic. Conformity to a set of norms is a means of maintaining status. Panopticonic conformity can also be called 'passing': self-regulation and normative performativity as an agentic strategy of assimilation to social ascriptions in order to avoid discrimination and harassment that may come from misrecognition and discursive appropriation (Kroeger 2003). Thus, passing can be as agentic as non-compliance, as people may "pass in order to bypass being excluded unjustly in their attempts to achieve ordinary, honorable aims and ambitions" and in order "to be more truly themselves" (Kroeger 2003, 2). If a person is not "passing by default" but, instead, "passing deliberately," passing can become a subversive act (Samuels 2003, 243), an act of defiance, a performance on the very stage of social scrutiny and surveillance.

Passing can also become a strategy for action because, if it permits a person to gain some "standing" and stability, including economic stability, on the outside, these spaces can then provide sites within which to nur-ture strength and gain access to future "power to be an agent of change" (Kroeger 2003, 133). Thus, although passing may sometimes be and feel like a "dissonant interjection", it may serve the "purpose of smoothing a path of transition to a new and desired position or location" or reconstruc-tion and therefore be a "dissonant smoothing" (2003, 210).

Anzaldua (1990) uses the metaphor "haciendo caras" as a performance strategy of deliberately provoking misrecognition in order to protect the self and points out both the ascribed and agentic elements of this strategy:

> *haciendo caras*, "making faces" means to put on a face . . . Some of us are forced to acquire the ability, like a chameleon, to change color when the dangers are many and the options few . . . Between the masks we've internalized, one on top of another, are our interfaces . . . We begin to acquire the agency of making our own *caras*. (xv–xvi)

Thus, people are social performers who know the lines in the "dominant" drama and are able to "take licence with the play" via script switching, script evasion and juxtaposition (Cohen and Taylor 1976, 64). Useful insights and understandings may come from having to deal with, resist and negotiate social ascription and panopticonic policing. Hence, bordering external ascription and self-ascription becomes a site from which we see the instability of social categories, their temporal and spatial shifts and fluctuations. And it is on this border where resistances, recognition and reconstruction can occur.

"They Say, Therefore I Must Be": The Politics of Community Ascription

It is seen as necessary and desirable for members of marginalised groups to adhere with one another and celebrate a common culture, heritage and experience. This grouping is usually referred to as a 'community'. Part of this learning can be problematic as individuals negotiate the identities with which they have come into the community, deciding what needs to be shed and what needs to be adopted. Rigid conformity and uniformity become internally coercive as a means of achieving recognition and resisting external social coercion (Pallotta-Chiarolli 2010). For many marginal groups, the existence of the marginal-within-the-marginal is often problematic as it can be seen to counteract their need for a united homogenous front in order to provide security and support for its members and a location to plan and implement strategies of resistance to the centre, mainstream power. Difficulties and contradictions will manifest themselves within a community in relation to recognition: how will it present itself to the wider society, how will it deal with internal differences and the positioning of personal agency within that community? Goffman (1963) uses the phrase "concern with in-group purification" to describe the efforts of stigmatised persons to "normify" their own conduct and also "clean up" the conduct of others in the group. Yuval-Davis (2011) discusses how we need to understand the sometimes contradictory performances required of minority groups, and members of those groups, who seek recognition.

Thus, for many individuals, the sanctuary of recognition and belonging offered by a community or collective may also be a prison. The "multiple within" realities call for the following questions to be addressed: how does one use the word 'community' without meaning homogeneity, and where and how are the boundaries of exclusion and inclusion of a community drawn (Martin and Pallotta-Chiarolli 2009; Pallotta-Chiarolli and Martin 2009)?

"I Say, Therefore I Am": Personal Ascription

As we have put forward in this chapter, people are, and always have been, active agents in the constitution of their unfolding social worlds. Framed by panopticonic regulations, socially ascribed meanings and community rules for belonging and recognition, subjectivity is "an emergent, situated, negotiated one where considerable variation becomes possible" (Plummer 1975, 50). If agents were unable to originate new forms of activity then "it would be impossible to account for the extraordinary variation in social conduct that has been exhibited in the course of human history" (Cohen 1987, 291).

Stigma management (Goffman 1963) is a form of agency. Stigmatised people's lives are characterised by a constant focus on intertwined processes of concealing, passing, information control and revealing. "Disidentifiers" such as props, actions or verbal expressions are used to distract and fool those who would scrutinise and ostracise so that they believe border dwellers do not have the deviant stigma. Both resisting and desiring identification and membership of various worlds, border dwellers are forced or desire to construct new identities and new 'homes' that allow them to journey between, within and beyond these worlds. These strategies of personal agency exemplify Foucault's belief in "the plurality of resistances": "resistances that are possible, necessary, improbable; others that are spontaneous, savage, solitary, concerted, rampant, or violent; still others that are quick to compromise, interested, or sacrificial" (1978, 96).

"Polluting" is used as a metaphor by the anthropologist Mary Douglas (1966) to articulate recognition, strength, agency and empowerment, and it is not intended to imply negative, insidious, harmful or underhanded machinations. Indeed, it is only through polluting existing and residual systems and structures that emergent and empowering systems and structures can evolve and reconstruction occur. It is via non-compliance, innovation and resistance to their dominant worlds that far-reaching, empowering political, social, cultural and legal outcomes are initiated. There is always a polluting excess, a supplement beyond fixed and normative poles that can never be subsumed. Pollutants are agentically "embracing ambivalence, contingency and uncertainty and thus transcending boundaries" (Marotta 2002, 40). In this way, they are agents in the reconstitution of the social order.

In summary, being on the borders allows for agency in relation to acknowledgment, action and community allegiance. This construction of agency transcends both "thoroughgoing determinism and unqualified freedom, while preserving all possibilities between these extremes" (Cohen 1987, 285). Passing (normalisation), bordering (negotiation) and polluting (noncompliance) happen simultaneously and in interwoven ways. Being located in the borderland involves a straddling of various identifications and social groups, drawing the best from each into a personal behavioural and interpersonal system and remaining detached enough to be able to critique and challenge these very locations and groupings. Being located in the borderland means acknowledging that while one is actively pursuing personal agency, choosing from the sexual, interpersonal, political, legal, economic, gendered, social and cultural options available to one at a particular historical, economic, political time, there are external forces and discourses from both power-challenging minority communities and the powerful centre of the wider society constantly trying to pinpoint, locate, fixate, label, construct and ascribe an identity that is acceptable and useful to them.

As the following chapters will reveal, there are particular circumstances that tend to influence the level and nature of agency. Individuals need to have: access to knowledge of their social, gendered, sexual, economic and other locations; the modes, economic or otherwise, of articulating and utilising this knowledge; and the means of disseminating this knowledge to others, such as their support networks and activist groups, who validate and respect their knowledge, as well as plan collective strategies to act upon it.

AN OVERVIEW OF THE CHAPTERS

The book is divided into five parts. Part I offers three studies that explore the misrecognition and reconstruction of gendered subjectivities. First, Julie Peters utilises her autoethnography of non-normative gender performance, such as transgenderism, to examine and critique the differing life strategies, resistances and non-compliances in terms of their impact on her personal agency, recognition/misrecognition, bordering and passing, as well as the importance of her ongoing activism. In the second chapter, Jack Migdalek discusses the influences that pervasive discourses of patriarchy, heteronormativity and gendernormativity had on ways in which he came to operate and embody as a male dancer and choreographer. Referring also to ethnographic fieldwork with educators, he speculates on what it takes to challenge habitual perceptions, positioning and modes of practice in cultures that are not easily accepting of difference, both in regard to the embodiment of gender in the performance arts and in the theatre of the everyday. In the third chapter on gendered subjectivities, Sarah Epstein's interviews with feminist mothers of sons demonstrate how, through feminist maternal practice, sons are held accountable to non-normative masculinity practices, and mothers can reposition their sons' masculine subjectivities. In this interaction, agency is conceptualised and the mother and son relationship becomes a site for social transformation.

The two contributions in Part II call for the recognition of resistant sexualities. First, Russell Shuttleworth calls for the reconceptualisation of disabled sexual subjectivities. This recognition and reconstruction is necessary in order to retain a crucial space for agentic subjectivity that can work in productive tandem with a diversity of differently embodied disabled people to transform negative perceptions about their sexualities. In the second chapter, Maria Pallotta-Chiarolli draws from her research with women who are in non-coercive and consensual relationships with bisexual-identifying and/or bisexual-behaving men. The subjectivities, agency and resistance of these women and their male partners are presented through an exploration of how they 'design' their long-term mixed-orientation relationships. Strategies of negotiation, construction and reconstruction are explored.

Part III undertakes the work of validating racialised subjectivities via three chapters which engage with diverse ethnic and Indigenous communities.

First, Georgia Birch presents her ethnographic work with older Somali women. The Somali women live in the 'white' dominant culture of Australia, yet constantly cross the borders between their traditional Somali culture and the dominant culture, juggling each value system and developing strategies for resistance. The chapter also highlights how the research process also transformed the researcher's subjectivity. The second chapter in this section by Mirjana Lozanovska explores how the physical adaptation, remaking and maintenance or building of the house, plays a significant role in elderly southern European immigrants' sense of belonging to a community. She illustrates how practices of individual or collective house-building extend the migrant's subjectivity such that migrants previously identified as unskilled labourers are transformed into subjects capable of skilled productions and imagination. Finally, Sophie Goldingay and Tania Mataki explore the Indigenous subjectivities of young Maori women serving time in age-mixed women's prisons in New Zealand. It presents how they developed alternative constructions of what constitutes integrity and worth by drawing on New Zealand Indigenous values and worldviews.

After the above thorough explorations of the agency and resistance of marginalised and subjugated subjectivities in regard to gender, sexuality, ethnicity and Indigeneity, the three chapters in Part IV interrogate a range of privileged subjectivities that are complicit in or responsible for that marginalisation and subjugation, asking, as Bob Pease does in the first chapter, what would it mean and how could the oppressors and the privileged be reconfigured and transformed? What potential is there for privileged activists to contribute to progressive social change? The chapter outlines the emergence of a pedagogy for the privileged which provides a conceptual and pedagogical framework for engaging members of privileged groups about their unearned entitlements. In the next chapter, Clare Land presents a specific example of the theoretical and pedagogical framework provided by Bob Pease. Drawing from interviews with non-Indigenous supporters of Indigenous struggles in southeast Australia, she asks how do people positioned as 'colonisers' who critique colonialism make sense of their subjectivity as they reckon with their entanglement in relations of power? The third chapter in this part by Stephen Fisher critically analyses existing pedagogical frameworks for training men to become advocates for gender equality. While many programs advocate a developmental approach to working with potential allies, Fisher contends that there is a need for greater attention to the practical and political issues of men who are in a position of gendered power and privilege.

The final part of this book takes us from the larger stage of structural politics, as discussed and exemplified in the preceding parts, to the politics of the everyday, the politics of the personal, as lived within these structures. It presents how individuals create new spaces of resistance in everyday life. In the first chapter, Tina Kostecki explores how older Australian women who have experienced childhood sexual abuse have constructed their identities and some aspects of their lives. Their diverse and nuanced insights demonstrate how the women resist and reconstruct oppressive patterns in their everyday lives. The second chapter by Norah Hosken presents an autoethnographic engagement with how working-class women struggle for recognition in tertiary education settings. She argues that the misrecognition and disciplining of working-class girls into lingering doubt is a form of symbolic violence normalised in Western colonialist patriarchal society. Emancipatory potential includes relational and connected ways of knowing where realisations of complicity can form feelings, places and ways to produce the empathy, collective aspiration and agency needed to progress social justice. The third chapter by Heather D'Cruz is also set within tertiary education settings. As a social work academic, she critically examines many of the incidents that emerge almost daily as examples of the politics of privilege and inequality. Through an autoethnographic approach, she asks what are the meanings of agency and subjectivity, and, therefore, how activism and resistance may be constituted. The final chapter by Mark Furlong presents interpersonal relationships as a performance stage, where the politics of respect and recognition are dramatised, and where the impact of the process of individualisation is very evident. Via the use of two vignettes, Furlong then demonstrates that reciprocal and ethical relationships can be approximated.

As can be seen from the overview, this book is an eclectic and diverse collection of theory- and research-based chapters which exemplify, analyse and indeed interrogate the theoretical machinations we have outlined in this introduction. It is our privilege to be able to present these passionate engagements with recognition, resistance and reconstruction in a range of intersectionalities and subjectivities that highlight multiple ways of working toward social justice. These case studies are far from exhaustive of the possibilities for encouraging the development of alternative subjectivities. We hope that this collection inspires others to contribute to this larger project of constructing subjectivities that contribute to the transformation of unjust social relations and oppressive structures.

REFERENCES

Allen, A. 2008. *The Politics of Ourselves: Autonomy and Gender in Contemporary Critical Theory*. New York: Columbia University Press.

Anthias, F. 2008. "Thinking through the Lens of Translocational Positionality: An Intersectionality Frame for Understanding Identity and Belonging." *Translocations: Migration and Social Change* 4 (1): 5–20.

Anthias, F., and N. Yuval-Davis. 1983. "Contextualizing Feminism: Gender, Ethnic and Social Divisions." *Feminist Review* 15:62–75.

Anzaldua, G., ed. 1990. *Making Face, Making Soul: Hacienda Caras*. San Francisco: Aunt Lute Press.

Archer, M. 2000. *Being Human: The Problem of Agency*. New York: Cambridge University Press.

Barad, K. 2007. *Meeting the Universe Halfway: Quantum Physics and the Entanglement of Matter and Meaning*. Durham, NC: University of Chicago Press.

Bourdieu, P. 1977. *Outline of a Theory of Practice.* New York: Cambridge University Press.

Bourdieu, P. 1990. *In Other Words: Towards a Reflexive Sociology.* New York: Stanford University Press.

Bourdieu, P. 1999. *The Weight of the World: Social Suffering in Contemporary Society.* Cambridge: Polity.

Bourdieu, P. 2001. *Masculine Domination.* Cambridge: Polity.

Brah, A., and A. Phoenix. 2004. "Ain't I a Woman? Revisiting Intersectionality." *Journal of International Women's Studies* 5 (3): 75–86.

Britzman, D. 1995. "'The Question of Belief': Writing Poststructural Ethnography." *Qualitative Studies in Education* 8:229–238.

Burkitt, I. 2008. "Subjectivity, Self and Everyday Life in Contemporary Capitalism." *Subjectivity* 23:236–245.

Butler, J. 1995. "Contingent foundations: feminism and the question of 'postmodernism'". In Benhabib, S., J. Butler, D. Cornell, and N. Fraser (eds) *Feminist Contentions. A Philosophical Exchange.* New York: Routledge.

Butler, J. 2004. *Undoing Gender.* New York: Routledge.

Butler, J. 2009. *Frames of War: When Is Life Grievable?* London: Verso.

Cho, D., and T. Lewis. 2006. "The Persistent Life of Oppression: The Unconscious, Power and Subjectivity." *Interchange* 36 (3): 313–329.

Cohen, I.J. 1987. "Structuration Theory and Social Praxis." In *Social Theory Today*, edited by A. Giddens and J.H. Turner. Oxford: Polity.

Cohen, S., and L. Taylor. 1976. *Escape Attempts: The Theory and Practice of Resistance to Everyday Life.* London: Allen Lane.

Crenshaw, K. 1989. "Demarginalizing the Intersection of Race and Sex: A Black Feminist Critique of Antidiscrimination Doctrine, Feminist Theory and Antiracist Politics." *University of Chicago Legal Forum: Feminism in the Law: Theory, Practice and Criticism* 139–167.

Davies, B. 2006. "Subjectification: the relevance of Butler's analysis for education." British Journal of Sociology of Education. Special issue. Troubling identities: reflections on Judith Butler's work for the Sociology of Education, 27(4), 425–438.

Davies, B. 2008. "Re-Thinking 'Behavior' in Terms of Positioning and the Ethics of Responsibility." In *Critical Readings in Teacher Education*, edited by A. Phelan and J. Sumsion. Rotterdam: Sense Publishers.

Davies, B., L. Claes, K. De Munck, E. De Schauwer, I. Van De Putte and M. Verstichele. 2013. "Recognition and Difference: A Collective Biography." *International Journal of Qualitative Studies in Education* 25(6): 680–690.

Davies, B., and R. Harre. 1990. "Positioning: The Discursive Production of Selves." *Journal for the Theory of Social Behaviour* 20 (1): 43–63.

Deleuze, G. 1994. *Difference and Repetition.* Translated by Paul Patton. New York: Columbia University Press.

Derrida, J. 1981. *Positions.* Chicago: University of Chicago Press.

Douglas, M. 1966. *Purity and Danger: An Analysis of Concepts of Pollution and Taboo.* New York: Ark.

Doyle, J., and I. Karl. 2008. "Shame on You: Cosmetic Surgery and Class Transformation in *10 Years Younger.*" In *Exposing Lifestyle Television: The Big Reveal*, edited by G. Palmer. Hampshire, UK: Ashgate Publishing.

Elliott, A. 2007. *Concepts of the Self.* 2nd ed. Cambridge: Polity.

Emirbayer, M., and A. Mische. 1998. "What Is Agency?" *American Journal of Sociology* 103:962–1023.

Finch, J. 2007. "Displaying Families." *Sociology* 41 (1): 65–81.

Foucault, M. 1978. *The History of Sexuality, Volume 1: An Introduction.* New York: Pantheon.

Foucault, M. 1979. *Discipline and Punish: The Birth of the Prison.* New York: Vintage.

Foucault, M. 1988. *The History of Sexuality, Volume 3: The Care of the Self.* New York: Vintage Books.

Fraser, N. 2001. "Recognition without Ethics?" *Theory, Culture & Society* 18 (2–3): 21–42.

Fraser, N. 2003a. "Distorted beyond all Recognition: A Rejoinder to Axel Honneth." In *Redistribution or Recognition? A Political-Philosophical Exchange,* edited by N. Fraser and A. Honneth. London: Verso.

Fraser, N. 2003b. "Social Justice in the Age of Identity Politics: Redistribution, Recognition and Participation." In *Redistribution or Recognition? A Political-Philosophical Exchange,* edited by N. Fraser and A. Honneth. London: Verso.

Fraser, N., and A. Honneth. 2003a. "Introduction." In *Redistribution or Recognition? A Political-Philosophical Exchange,* edited by N. Fraser and A. Honneth, London: Verso.

Fraser, N., and A. Honneth. 2003b. *Redistribution or Recognition? A Political-Philosophical Exchange.* London: Verso.

Freire, P. 1972. *Pedagogy of the Oppressed.* Harmondsworth, UK: Penguin.

Frost, L., and P. Hoggett. 2008. "Human Agency and Human Suffering." *Critical Social Policy* 28 (4): 438–460.

Gil, R. 2008. "Culture and Subjectivity in Neoliberal and Postfeminist Times." *Subjectivity* 25:432–445.

Goffman, E. 1963. *Stigma: Notes on the Management of Spoiled Identity.* Harmondsworth, UK: Penguin.

Grace, A.P., and F.J. Benson. 2000. "Using Autobiographical Queer Life Narratives of Teachers to Connect Personal, Political and Pedagogical Spaces." *International Journal of Inclusive Education* 4 (2): 89–109.

Hill, R.J. 1995. "Gay Discourse in Adult Education: A Critical Review." *Adult Education Quarterly* 45:142–158.

Hoggett, P. 2001. "Agency, Rationality and Social Policy" *Journal of Social Policy* 30:37–56.

Honneth, A. 2003. "Redistribution as Recognition: A Response to Nancy Fraser." In *Redistribution or Recognition? A Political-Philosophical Exchange,* edited by N. Fraser and A. Honneth. London: Verso.

hooks, b. 1981. *Ain't I a Woman: Black Women and Feminism.* Boston: South End Press.

Hoy, D. 2005. *Critical Resistance: From Poststructuralism to Post-Critique.* Cambridge: MIT Press.

Ingrey, J.C. 2013. "Troubling Gender Binaries in Schools: From Sumptuary Law to Sartorial Agency." *Discourse: Studies in the Cultural Politics of Education* 34(3): 424–438.

Kroeger, B. 2003. *Passing: When People Can't Be Who They Are.* New York: Public Affairs.

Layton, L. 2008. "What Divides the Subject? Psychoanalytic Reflections on Subjectivity, Subjection and Resistance." *Subjectivity* 22:60–72.

Layton, L. 2009. "Who's Responsible? Our Mutual Implication in Each Other's Suffering." *Psychoanalytic Dialogues* 19:105–120.

Layton, L. 2010. "Irrational Exuberance: Neoliberal Subjectivity and the Perversion of Truth." *Subjectivity* 3 (3): 303–322.

London Feminist Salon Collective. 2004. "The Problematisation of Agency in Postmodern Theory: As Feminist Educational Researchers, Where Do We Go from Here?" *Gender and Education* 16 (1): 25–33.

Lutz, H., M. Vivar and L. Supik, eds. 2011. *Framing Intersectionality: Debates on a Multi-Faceted Concept in Gender Studies.* Farnham, Surrey, UK: Ashgate.

Malone, K. 2000. "Critical Psychology, Subjectivity and the Politics of the Lost Signifier." In *Critical Psychology: Voices for Change*, edited by T. Sloan. New York: St. Martins Press.

Mama, A. 1995. *Beyond the Mask: Race, Gender and Subjectivity*. London: Routledge.

Marotta, V. 2002. "Zygmunt Bauman: Order, Strangerhood and Freedom." *Thesis Eleven* 70:36–54.

Martin, E., and M. Pallotta-Chiarolli. 2009. "'Which Sexuality? Which Service?': Bisexual Young People's Experiences with Youth, Queer, and Mental Health Services." *Journal of LGBT Youth* 6 (2–3): 199–222.

Martin, L.H., H. Gutman and P.H. Hutton. 1988. *Technologies of the Self: A Seminar with Michel Foucault*. Amherst: University of Massachusetts Press.

Mason, G. 1995. "(Out)Laws: Acts of Proscription in the Sexual Order." In *Public and Private: Feminist Legal Debates*, edited by M. Thornton. London: Oxford University Press.

Maxwell, C., and P. Aggleton 2010. "Agency in Action: Young Women and Their Sexual Relationships in a Private School." *Gender and Education* 22 (3): 327–343.

McNay, L. 2000. *Gender and Agency: Reconfiguring the Subject in Feminist and Legal Theory*. Cambridge: Polity.

McNay, L. 2004. "Agency and Experience: Gender as a Lived Relation." *Sociological Review* 52 (2): 173–190.

McNay, L. 2008. *Against Recognition*. Cambridge: Polity.

McNay, L. 2010. "Feminism and Post-Identity Politics: The Problem with Agency." *Constellations* 17 (4): 512–525.

McRobbie, A. 2000. "Feminism and the Third Way." *Feminist Review* 64:97–112.

Pallotta-Chiarolli, M. 2004. "From 'Difference' to 'Diversity': Exploring the Social Determinants of Youth Health." In *Understanding Health: A Determinants Approach*, edited by H. Keleher and B. Murphy. Melbourne: Oxford University Press.

Pallotta-Chiarolli, M. 2010. *Border Sexualities, Border Families in Schools*. New York: Rowman and Littlefield.

Pallotta-Chiarolli, M., and E. Martin. 2009. "'Exclusion by Inclusion': Bisexual Young People, Marginalisation and Mental Health in Relation to Substance Abuse." In *Theorising Social Exclusion*, edited by A. Taket, B.R. Crisp, A. Nevill, G. Lamaro, M. Graham and S. Barter-Godfrey. London: Routledge.

Parker, I. 1999. "Critical Reflexive Humanism and Critical Constructionist Psychology." In *Social Constructionist Psychology*, edited by D. Nightingale and J. Cromby. Buckingham: Open University Press.

Pease, B. 2000. *Recreating Men: Postmodern Masculinity Politics*. London: Sage.

Plummer, K. 1975. *Sexual Stigma: An Interactionist Account*. London: Routledge and Kegan Paul.

Potter, J., and M. Wetherall. 1987. *Discourse and Social Psychology*. London: Sage.

Queen, C. A. 1991. "The Queer in Me" in L. Hutchins and L. Ka'ahumanu (ed) *Bi Any Other Name*. Boston: Alyson Publications.

Rabinow, P. 1984. *The Foucault Reader*. London: Penguin.

Robinson, R. 2003–2004. "Human Agency, Negated Subjectivity and White Structural Oppression: An Analysis of Critical Race Practice/Praxis." *American University Law Review* 53:1361–1420.

Sabsay, L. 2012. "The Emergence of the Other Sexual Citizen: Orientalism and the Modernisation of Sexuality." *Citizenship Studies* 16 (5–6): 605–623.

Samuels, E. 2003. "My Body, My Closet: Invisible Disability and the Limits of Coming-Out Discourse." *GLQ: A Journal of Lesbian and Gay Studies* 9 (1–2): 233–255.

Shinozaki, K. 2012. "Transnational Dynamics in Researching Migrants: Self-Reflexivity and Boundary-Drawing in Fieldwork." *Ethnic and Racial Studies* 35 (10): 1810–1827.

Skeggs, B. 2004. *Class, Culture, Self.* London: Routledge.

Taylor, Y., S. Hines and M. Casey, eds. 2011. *Theorizing Intersectionality and Sexuality.* Basingstoke: Palgrave.

Trinh, T.M. 1991. *When the Moon Waxes Red.* New York: Routledge.

Venn, C. 2002. "Refiguring Subjectivity after Modernity." In *Challenging Subjects: Critical Psychology for a New Millennium*, edited by V. Walkerdine. Basingstoke: Palgrave.

Walby, S. 2001. "From Community to Coalition: The Politics of Recognition as the Handmaiden of the Politics of Equality in an Era of Globalization." *Theory, Culture & Society* 18 (2–3): 113–135.

Walsh, M., and M. Bahnisch. 2002. "Political Subjects, Workplaces and Subjectivities." In *Challenging Subjects: Critical Psychology for a New Millennium*, edited by V. Walkerdine. Basingstoke: Palgrave.

Willig, C. 2000. "A Discourse Dynamic Approach to the Study of Subjectivity in Health Psychology." *Theory and Psychology* 10 (4): 547–570.

Yip, A., and S. Page. 2013. *Religious and Sexual Identities: A Multi-Faith Exploration of Young Adults.* Farnham, Surrey, UK: Ashgate.

Yuval-Davis, N. 2006. "Intersectionality and Feminist Politics." *European Journal of Women's Studies* 13 (3): 193–209.

Yuval-Davis, N. 2011. "Beyond the Recognition and Re-Distribution Dichotomy: Intersectionality and Stratification." In *Framing Intersectionality: Debates on a Multi-Faceted Concept in Gender Studies*, edited by H. Lutz, M. Vivar and L. Supik. Farnham, Surrey, UK: Ashgate.

Part I
Reconstructing Gendered Subjectivities

2 Normative Gender Coercion and Its Subversion

An Autoethnography of a Quest for Recognition

Julie Peters

WRITING ABOUT A LIFE LIVED BEYOND THE 'LOSE/LOSE' OPTIONS

In our Western culture, a non-normative gendered life is often seen, even by the individual themselves, as problematic, morally bankrupt or sick (American Psychiatric Association 2000). Terms such as 'transsexual' or 'transgendered' carry so much stigma (Goffman 1963; Leonard et al. 2012) that most who might be so labelled, go to extraordinary lengths to avoid this labelling and recognition. Their strategies include secrecy, seeking a ghetto, passing to seek misrecognition and seeking a *cure*. The social pressures to conform to biologically determined binary gendered roles led me to see two 'lose/lose' options—either ignore my deepest inner feelings on how I wanted to live and conform to an *appropriate* gender role, or live as I wanted and be ostracised and stigmatised. By presenting events, experiences and periods in my life, this chapter will demonstrate that I, as subject, both in the sense of being subject to the culture I live in and also because of my self-conscious awareness, was able to gain some understanding of the limits that our culture has over my performance of gender. I will use phenomenological autoethnography to examine my own socially situated subjectivity intersected by non-conformist practices of gender. My subjectivity is examined by exploring the multiple and often contradictory links between myself as subject, my internal agentic voice and the ever-changing society I was living in.

The aim of phenomenology as a method is to describe the temporal flow of what is experienced by the consciousness of the subject—in this case my subjectivity—and to describe those phenomena free from any theoretical abstractions. On phenomenology, Thomas Kando (1973, 133) notes, "Objectivity, here, means the accurate rendering of the subject's subjectivity." Autoethnography (Ellis 1999, 2013; Holman Jones and Adams 2010) is ethnography of the self or one's own group and, as Deborah Reed-Danahay (1997) notes, the method synthesises ethnography with a defined subject position. Tami Spry (2001) suggests good autoethnography must be emotionally engaging as well as critically self-reflective. To that end, I use my poetry, photography and prose to emotionally engage the reader. So the phenomenological awareness helps gather un-abstracted data which are then analysed (auto)ethnographically, using a variety of sociological frames, which are introduced in body of the chapter as needed.

THE AUTOETHNOGRAPHY

As a child, starting to develop a sense of myself as a subject, I had no clear concept of living in a dichotomously gendered world, and no concept of myself as a gendered subject. I was happily living in an amazing world where all adults seemed to think I was important. So when people told me I was a boy it didn't really mean much. A few years later, but before I started school, I thought my parents had simply made a mistake. I couldn't see any reason I couldn't be a girl. I was sure that all they had to do was acknowledge I was a girl, buy me girls' clothes, stop cutting my hair and I would be a girl. I can clearly remember demanding Mum to tell me why I wasn't a girl. She said that God made me a boy. I then said I was going to grow up to be a lady and she told me that every single boy grows up to be a man. I was horrified.

REALISATIONS AND EARLY ATTEMPTS AT RESISTANCE

Once I realised the majority of the world thought I was a boy, I consciously chose to not tell them they were wrong. Neil Hao (2011) notes that strategic silence can be a source of personal agency. My silence was also a strategy for managing the stigma (Goffman 1963) of being labelled

Figure 2.1   Julie Peters, 1957, age six.

as a boy who wanted to be a girl. My silence may have kept me safe, but it didn't solve my problem. People still thought I was a boy and expected me to behave like one. A social consequence of my silence was a complete lack of recognition by family, school or health professionals that I was having problems finding a place in the gendered world. Considering the socio-historical situation in which I found myself—1950s and 1960s Catholic working-class Australia—disclosure would have only attracted criticism and punishment, and no practical solutions or empowerment. Nancy Fraser (2001, 24) argues for recognition as meaning to have the social status to participate "as a peer in social life" and misrecognition then meaning social subordination preventing such participation. In this context I was not able to participate in social life as a girl or as a gender non-conforming boy. Over the next few decades, my silence became habitual to the extent that I became so scared of expressing an opinion, on almost any subject, that I denied myself a voice. But on the positive side, my silence gave me the opportunity to become an acute observer of social behaviour. This would become a valuable social skill later in my life. Anzaldua (1987, 101) notes that the border dweller copes "by developing a tolerance for contradictions, a tolerance for ambiguity." This consciousness eventually helped me see beyond the paradigm of dichotomous biologically determined gender performativity.

Parallel to my strategic silence was a growing awareness that my parents could not control what I was thinking. Daydreaming I was a girl became one of my earliest strategies of resistance to the dominant power relations which reinforce the biologically determined gender duality. Foucault (1982, 780) describes this asserting my right to be different against the social authority to constrain my identity as an "antagonism of strategies." This struggle can also be framed by Barrett's (1958, 19) suggestion that "every thinker . . . puts some portion of the stable world in danger as soon as he begins to think."

In early primary school, I had two or three favourite dreams that I dreamed whenever I found a spare moment. This is one from early primary school age:

> I dived deep into the water of the boys' swimming pool, found an underwater cave, swam through it and found myself in the girls' pool. I swam up. A beautiful lady dressed me in a girl's swimming costume. I was now a girl and played with the other girls.

Because I felt my dream life was so much better than my real life, I was not socialising outside of the family. I saw no point joining in games at school because I had to play boys' games. I was disengaged and did virtually no schoolwork during the seven years of prep school and primary school. My dreams of being a girl were pleasant enough, but I was starting to become frustrated that I wasn't a girl. This lack was more sharply defined as I started high school, where all the students and teachers were male. Our headmaster, a Christian Brother, was determined to "make men of us" and used physical violence as a pedagogical method, in many ways not dissimilar to the disciplinary management of prisoners described by Foucault (1975).

As an eleven-year-old, I had grown to almost the same height as my mother. I suddenly realised that her clothes would fit me. When I was in the house alone, I found a dress, shoes and lipstick and used a scarf to hide my boy's haircut. I looked like a girl, and it felt just right. And now that I was in high school, I was allowed to stay up late on Friday or Saturday night and watch a late movie. So when everyone else had gone to bed, I would dress as a girl and watch my movie.

Once I had had this joyous taste of being a girl, I wanted more. I needed people to see me as a girl for me to be a girl. So very late at night—to avoid social surveillance (Foucault 1975)—I would sneak out the back door, catch trains or walk. I loved it when someone looked toward me and saw a girl. On some nights, I couldn't get out until after the last train (after midnight). On these nights I would go for longer walks. I soon discovered that local streets, which were very ordinary streets by day, were red-light streets by night. Very soon men were trying to entice me into their cars. I was petrified that I would be discovered. In my little high heels I couldn't retreat quickly, but I did get to a quieter street and tried to just enjoy the walk. But then another car started to follow me—and at walking pace. I determined to ignore it. Getting no reaction from me, the car eventually sped off. To my horror, as the car passed me, I could see it was a police car. I could

Figure 2.2   Julie Peters, dress collage, 1963, age eleven.

only guess they were testing my motive for walking alone so late. This very literal "policing" of my behaviour led to self-policing as described by Foucault (1975). I stopped walking late at night even though I was pleased they thought I was a girl. I didn't stop dressing as a girl. But I started searching for safer opportunities.

This early period can be framed using the gender/agency analysis of Lois McNay (2000). As a child, when I started to understand I was living in a gendered world, much of my inherent agency was stripped from me, because the world was convinced I was a boy, expected me to behave like one. But I did gain some agency dreaming of being a girl. In early high school, I also demonstrated creativity in searching for autonomous agency, by secretly being a girl.

In year nine we studied *Twelfth Night*. I was amazed to learn that boys played girls in Shakespeare's time:

> In the play Olivia (played by a boy) fell for Viola (a boy playing a woman who was pretending to be a boy) because Olivia thought Viola was an attractive man. But Viola fell for Orsino, but couldn't tell him how she felt, because Orsino would think a boy was in love with him and neither of them wanted to be homosexual. But then, it all became a bit confusing when Orsino became annoyed with Viola (still disguised as Cesario) because Olivia, who he fancied, had fallen for him, Cesario . . . I mean her, Viola!

Figure 2.3   Twelfth Night, Penguin USA.

As a thirteen-year-old, I loved this farce on gender and sexuality confusion and sub-textually gender crossing and same-sex attraction. And what amazed me the most was that we were studying this in a very conservative working-class Catholic school. I saw that theatre might be a socially acceptable way of breaking gender rules and still be considered sort of normal. Or in more theoretical terms, theatre and theatricality on stage—but not in the everyday—could be a safe place for a gender border dweller (Anzaldua 1987). Even though I could see that if you were 'theatrical', you could play a girl, I had also seen that the pretty boy who read Viola in class was being sexually abused by our English teacher. This convinced me not to publicly declare my love of theatre and performance. I realised there were consequences to standing out, being seen by the panopticon of unseen observers (Foucault 1975), and this also resulted in self-surveillance of both my wanting to be a girl and my interest in theatre.

PUBERTY AND DESPERATE TIMES

In early high school, I had just taken my first positive steps toward having some agency, by experimenting with being a girl secretly, when something terrible happened. My body turned traitor on me. It was like an evil spell had been cast:

> MACBETH'S WITCHES:
>> Spirits evil gather near,
>> Spell to make this life go queer.
>> Eye of toad, testes of quails,
>> Slugs'n snails'n puppy dogs' tails.
>> Your voice of boy, oh so sweet,
>> Drop octaves manly very deep,
>
> ME:
>> Drops my voice so drops my heart,
>> My soul and head as friends depart.
>
> MACBETH'S WITCHES:
>> Command thee, I, black hairs to sprout,
>> W'signs so manly encrust without,
>> Pock and mark this girly skin,
>> Deep blacken scar the soul within.
>
> ME:
>> Their evil, evil spell comes true,
>> Black hairs on face and legs push through.
>> Their scheme so cunning, I do fear
>> Will make, to all, me male appear.

(Peters 2011)

The feeling of sadness and pointlessness that overwhelmed me didn't happen overnight; it grew in proportion to the hair on my pimply face. I soon despaired of ever being a girl. By the time I turned fifteen, I had dropped from top of the class to twenty-first in our class of forty-five. I was still desperate to be a girl, but every day my body was looking more and more male. Society, community, everyone I knew was ascribing maleness to me. I knew that if I gave in and admitted their ascription of maleness, my life would be so much easier. But my deep self-ascription was, somehow, that I was really female. This internal conflict required a huge daily commitment of mental and emotional energy to safely get through each day. The more I followed the social mores for masculine behaviour, the more depressed I felt. I was far too scared to be seen to be a feminine male, and this led me to expend a great deal of energy in self-surveillance (Foucault 1975). By my late teens, this continual shifting between trying to adopt masculine mores and hiding my femininity was flipping me between depression and powerlessness.

In late high school, I stumbled across an acceptable way of passing as a male that gave me some agency but didn't require particularly masculine behaviour—performing 'the eccentric'. Weeks and James (1995) note that eccentric behaviour is *just* within the bounds of being acceptable and normalised transgression. And so it allows a degree of resistance and subversion. The characteristics they list for 'eccentrics' include being non-conforming, creative, strongly motivated by curiosity, idealistic, intelligent, opinionated and outspoken, non-competitive, a mischievous sense of humour and usually single and the eldest or an only child. In examining their list, I note that both as an adolescent and now I possess most of these characteristics.

My social ascription as 'an eccentric' was instigated by my move from a working-class high school at the end of year ten to a middle-class high school on a scholarship in year eleven. Academically, I was close to the top of my class, even in this middle-class school. But I had decayed teeth, was dishevelled and obviously poor. None of these seemed to even be noticed in working-class Port Melbourne. Being good at science, I was soon labelled 'the mad professor'. This ascription of being 'an eccentric' was an effective agentic avenue to avoid more debilitating labelling. Even though being seen as eccentric helped me get through high school safely, it continued my misrecognition (Fraser 2001), in that I was not recognised as someone who could not perform gender in the way society expected.

At the start of 1969, at seventeen, I had a very short burst of high self-esteem when awarded a Commonwealth Scholarship to Melbourne University. I was too scared to read humanities, because humanities students needed to express opinions. With a belief that I needed an extreme investment in self-surveillance to just survive, I didn't want anyone knowing what I really thought about anything. So at university, I read electrical engineering—a field where I imagined there would be right and wrong answers and I would never need to express an opinion. Being accepted into a prestigious university meant my extended family was, for the first time in my life, complimentary. But my burst of self-esteem didn't last. I was at a university with seven thousand undergraduate women. Their presence reminded me that I had failed in my dream to be one of them. I was also shocked at the misogyny, as expressed in jokes and drunken songs, of my fellow engineering students. I understood their hatred of women to mean they also hated me and this increased my self-surveillance.

By mid-winter of 1969, my first year at university, I was incredibly depressed. I wasn't looking after myself. Rotten teeth made it painful to eat. I felt lost. In our small cracked bathroom mirror, if I half closed my eyes, I almost didn't look like a male. Being a boy was bad enough, but being a man was horrible. I couldn't see the point of shaving because I still looked like a man afterward. I had soft skin and strong hairs and hundreds of pimples. "Mirror, Mirror on the wall, who's the ugliest one of all?" Me of course! I was aware that some people thought I was a good-looking man. But all I could see was an ugly hairy woman. That mirror shouted "Man!" at me, every morning. So I stopped looking. I stopped shaving. Not shaving was a desperate attempt to not remind myself I looked like a man. I saw the mirror as a source of misrecognition, ascribing maleness

Figure 2.4   Julie Peters, 1970, age nineteen.

to me. Reading engineering and looking unkempt all but guaranteed my misrecognition; no woman could see me as an equal. On my bad days, both men and women saw me as someone with problems, someone to be avoided. But neither did I want the stigma of being recognised as mentally ill. I started to avoid socialising, because every social occasion seemed to reinforce my misrecognition.

Early 1971 marks the nadir of my self-esteem, agency and certainties. I dropped out of university and started working in television. I had started drinking heavily and at a deep level I realised that if I didn't do something soon I would crack. I started to hate myself for not being a woman. My alcohol abuse and driving while drunk, Menninger (1938) would count as chronic suicide—behaving in such a dangerous way that one is likely to be 'accidentally' killed. This period of my life is consistent with the findings of Leonard et al. (2012), who note that trans people suffer significantly more psychological distress and anxiety and have poorer mental health and resilience than the general population.

At this incredibly low point, I remembered having high self-esteem as a child, and this memory allowed me to believe it was possible to have high self-esteem again. I didn't know how, but I believed it was possible. Manically, I started doing anything I could succeed at. I learned electronics for work and practiced the operational skills I needed on camera and vision mixing. I had stumbled across a strategy that worked for me. I found that if I gained self-esteem in one area of my life, it washed over my whole life. This gradual accumulation of esteem would eventually enable me to face my real problems. But in my early twenties, I felt I was on the edge of cracking every day. When I felt scared, I went off and did something I was competent at and I got a morsel of esteem. That meant I didn't crack that day, and so I woke up the next day.

I was able to use creative autonomous agency (McNay 2000) for resistance and for delivering some self-esteem and personal agency, and I started to discover a liveable life (Butler 2004). And even though I was still being socially ascribed as male, I started to have a sense of self-recognition (Fraser 2001) beyond maleness, a claim to equity, a claim at participating as a full partner in society.

TRANSGRESSION, PASSING AND THE QUEST FOR IDENTITY AND RECOGNITION

After I had dropped out of university and a few months of having a job and an income, I moved out of home, shaved my beard and tried being a woman on my days off from work. When I first shaved, I was shocked. My face had changed under the beard, and I didn't recognise myself. I felt desperately sad because I didn't look like the girl I imagined I would. But driven by desperation to be a girl, I devoted all my spare energy studying femininity skills and trying to be a woman in the social world. For the first time in years I felt some joy.

This developing of performance skills clearly fits the concept of gender as performance as described by Goffman (1976/1979) and Butler (1990). My first attempts were not very successful, and I was seen as a transgressive male. This bordering the binary of gender performance challenged people's categorisations and brought disapproval. Fortunately, I was able to read the social circumstances well enough to avoid physical violence. I found being transgressive stressful and tried to remove as much stress from my life as possible, for example, running in the morning and getting enough sleep. I still had a day-to-day working life, where I tried to develop an eccentric persona to deflect gibes. But deep down I was still not myself. I started to become obsessed with the idea that if I could just recognise the right-named identity—or possibly a named psychiatric disorder—then I would know what to do, who to see, how to behave, and this would maximise my personal agency. I read everything I could on gender non-conformity. I went out of my way to meet transsexuals, transvestites and drag queens, wondering if I was one of them. After reading a number of medical, biographical and feminist texts, I firmly concluded I was not transsexual. I could not live the very secretive life a number

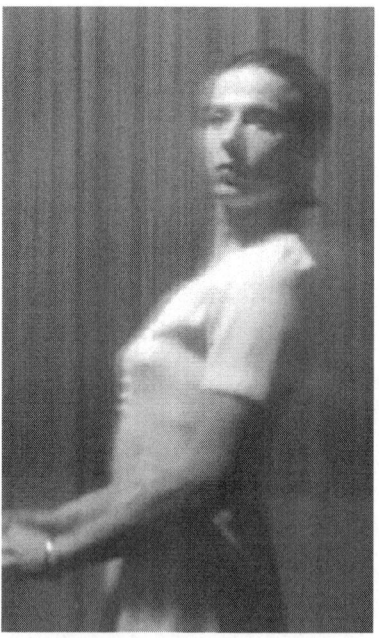

Figure 2.5   Julie Peters, 1974, age twenty-three.

of transsexual women I met led. I also read widely on philosophy, psychology, biology and fashion. I started catalogues of Image, Archetype, Dress and Colour. I collected hundreds of fashion magazines, did classes in makeup, dance, sewing, pattern drafting, acting. And I practiced these skills as often as I could.

Intuitively I had realised gender was performative. I was not to know it then, but this quest for self-recognition, or identity quest, was to last almost twenty years—from when I was about twenty-two to forty. Keeping busy with all these activities, at the time, gave me a sense of achievement, moving ahead. I did gain some agency (McNay 2000) by allowing myself to transgress dichotomous gendered norms. But living in a constant state of non-compliance on the borders sapped my agency. On the downside of seeking a named identity, Connell (2009, 108) suggests, "to weld one's personality into a united whole (an identity) is to refuse internal diversity and openness. It may also be to refuse to change."

Figure 2.6   Julie Peters, 1976, boy bumps/girl bumps.

By my late twenties, I was taking just enough oestrogen that I looked androgynous rather than masculine or feminine. This enabled me, with a slight change of dress and attitude, to control whether I was taken for male or female. I still didn't believe I could ever be a woman, but I had definitely proven I could be androgynous in behaviour (Singer 1976), dress and body. But I was trying to make 'androgyny' work as a named identity rather than a way of transcending the limits of gender, and consequently it was limiting, just like all named identities. In an embodied sense, I kept this androgynous look for almost a decade. As I turned thirty, I went back to university and finished a Bachelor of Science degree. The degree gave me a hit of self-esteem and an opportunity of starting a new career as a woman. But the self-esteem was in the doing it. When I graduated, I felt incredibly sad I wasn't a woman. My confidence in being androgynous came unstuck and I increased my dosage of oestrogen. As I approached forty, most people read me as female. I liked that! This border dwelling challenged people's commitment to the dichotomous nature of gender (Anzaldua 1987).

Figure 2.7   Julie Peters, 1989, a 'model' woman?

Over 1988 and 1989, I took thousands of photos of myself. These photos had multiple purposes, having fun dressing up, feedback on what worked and what didn't and photographic proof the female me actually existed. I experimented with the high femininity of being a 'model' woman. I thought that if I could successfully do high femininity, I could perform the full spectrum of femininities and so could then pitch it where I chose to.

Figure 2.7 shows me performing a number of the photographic advertising poses, so well documented by Erving Goffman (1976/1979). In this particular photo I am displaying delicacy using the dimension of feminine touch (p. 29), ritualised subordination (p. 40) and sexual availability to the gaze of the viewer by sitting in a nightdress. To fantasise that I could be a model, even for the split second it takes to expose a photograph, gave me a huge boost in self-esteem. But the sense of achievement was short-lived. Yes, I achieved it, but these images did not answer any of my existential questions, and I moved on to my next gender project (Connell 2009).

TRANSITION AND THE ART OF LIVING IN A GENDERED WORLD

In 1990, at the age of thirty-nine, a major disruption in my thinking occurred. I realised I could no longer cope with my ongoing and accelerating quest for self-recognition, my identity quest. I understood I could never be biologically female. But I could also see that gender—and so 'being-a-woman'—was primarily a set of social relations (Goffman1976/1979; Connell 2009), which I knew I could perform. So when I asked myself why not live as a woman, I didn't have a good answer. I then examined the likely consequences of living as a woman. I knew I could easily deal with the joy, and I thought I had enough resilience to deal with any negativity from family, community and colleagues.

Not long after I had transitioned—with the help of oestrogen and still two years before surgery—one of the men at work said to me, "You ought to have transsexual tattooed on your forehead, so blokes like me aren't tricked into being poofters[1]." He felt it was important to police the borderlands. He could see that my passing-as-a-woman hid my non-compliance with the gendered norms he believed were important. He realised he was attracted to my performance of femininity, but he believed I was male so he felt he needed to police my gender non-compliance to prevent him misrecognising himself as homosexual.

My transition resulted in me having real agency. I was able to find a way to live as a woman that increased my respect for self and gave me my first glimpse of a life where I could transcend social and self-surveillance.

It was only after living as a woman for many years that I understood that I needed external recognition of my gender non-conformity to obtain appropriate legal, medical and social changes which I required in order to

Figure 2.8   Julie Peters, 1999, age forty-eight.

achieve equity. Gender non-conformist individuals often suffer violence, vilification and discrimination in employment (Leonard et al. 2012). I lobbied politicians and educated health care professionals as a strategy to gain social recognition. I felt legal recognition was important. I had changed my name legally to Julie Peters, but my birth certificate listed me as male. In this instance I saw that society was not recognising my lived reality. In 1996, I ran for the House of Representatives, on an environmental and social justice platform. I was not elected, but because of my openness and being comfortable in my own skin, I was able to reform a number of politicians' views on gender non-conformity. My running for public office helped achieve a degree of recognition of transgender issues. For me this confirms Lisa Dowling's (2008) view on political action, noting Foucault's belief that power is diffuse and resistance can be effective by voicing dissent or reversing discourse from a marginal position.

After a few years of being a public 'transsexual', I started to feel uncomfortable. Initially I was very pleased to have a political voice and be listened to. But I soon realised that I was not making significant progress beyond my initial impact. I found the press seemed to be always after the same basic story and rarely asked a challenging question that could deepen public knowledge on the operation of gender in society. So in 2001, I withdrew from doing press and started to look for a more effective way of being politically active.

I started to ask myself how to live in this gendered world. The existentialist view (Flynn 2006) variously names our lack of control of the world we live in as facticity, historicity, in-situation or force-of-circumstance but emphasises that what is important is not so much the situation you find

Figure 2.9   Julie Peters, 2002, age fifty-one.

yourself in but how you live responsibly in that world. I found myself living in a gendered world, where people expect you to have one of the two approved genders, preferably determined by one's biology, and to have one of the two sexualities, preferably heterosexuality.

One day I saw it.
People created gender.
Arbitrary rules.

I discovered that
Cultural limits are mere mists.
The cage is unlocked.

The choice is mine.
Life as skilled execution,
With agency sublime.

What an incredible thought, to think that it might be possible to live a life where cultural limits are "mere mists" and I can choose my own path. The thought was both terrifying and exhilarating. To try to put it into practice seemed utopian. In examining Nietzsche, Thomas Flynn (2006, 40) describes "free spirits" or "true individuals" who are challenged to assume "life affirming moral and life enhancing aesthetic values . . . [that] coalesce in the project of making one's life a work of art". Lisa Downing (2008, 2), noting a new direction in Foucault's later works, is intrigued with the idea of "(giving style) to one's character—a great and rare art" as an agent of resistance.

CONCLUSION

In this chapter I have explored the multiple and sometimes contradictory links between my internal voice, subjectivity and daily social practices over the arc of my lifetime. The selected narratives have shown that my personal agency has varied considerably, from incredibly low to very solid, depending on the strategy I was adopting at any particular time.

The examples I have documented have shown an important 'catch-22'. People can only make sense of their subjectivity within relations of power and the struggle against domination if they have made enough progress in their resistance to gain the self-esteem and clarity of thought needed to realise they can actually resist. What I have shown in this chapter is that I stepped outside the negative feedback loop by achieving in other non-gendered areas of my life. This then gave me the self-esteem to tackle my primary area of subjugation—binary gender.

I believe ongoing social activism is essential. Connell (2012) notes that gender is onto-formative, in that it is both formed by the performance of gender and the performance of gender creates new practices of gender. And so performing gender imaginatively is activism. I have tried a number of different types of activism (Peters 1999, 2005, 2011) and am looking at Action Research and Performance Ethnography as tools to try to debunk the myth that normative gender coercion is unstoppable. Kirby (1979, quoted in Alexander 2005, 423) suggests that autobiography, autoethnography and performance art have at their focus "a critique of self and society, self in society, and self as a resistive and transformative force of society." Stacy Holman Jones (2007) suggests torch singing—a musical form sung by women, which on the surface is about desire, unrequited love and often being a victim—demonstrates the radical potential of performance, noting it can be an effective tool in resistance and inspiring change and that it can operate on a continuum from covert commentary to overt protest.

But ultimately living in a gendered society is a delicate balance. Today, I am non-compliant to dichotomous restrictions on gendered behaviour. I negotiate bordering in all my important relationships, activism and in academia. And I pass as an ordinary woman when the social relationships are normally anonymous, such as in the street or when shopping.

But there is still one question I would like answered—where did the desire to be a girl come from? Was it an individual or social desire, or a combination of the two?

For most of my life I have deliberately misrepresented myself to avoid recognition as a gender non-conformist, but now I understand the importance of recognition. And while academics continue to work on the social, medical and systemic questions around the operation of gender in society, it is imperative we all claim equity in recognition, which Fraser (2001) takes to mean allowing all individuals the social status to participate as full partners in social interaction.

NOTES

1. Poofter is Australian slang for a male homosexual.

REFERENCES

Alexander, B. 2005. "Performance Ethnography: The Reenacting and Inciting of Culture." In *The SAGE Handbook of Qualitative Research*, 3rd ed., edited by N.K. Denzin and Y.S. Lincoln. Thousand Oaks, CA: Sage Publications.

American Psychiatric Association. 2000. *DSM-IV-TR—Diagnostic and Statistical Manual of Mental Disorders of the American Psychiatric Association*. 4th ed. (text revision). Arlington, VA: American Psychiatric Publishing.

Anzaldua, G. 1987. *Borderlands/La Frontera: The New Mestiza*. San Francisco, CA: Spinsters/Aunt Lute.

Barrett, W. 1958. *Irrational Man: A Study in Existential Philosophy*. New York: Doubleday.

Butler, J. 1990. *Gender Trouble*. New York: Routledge.

Butler, J. 2004. *Undoing Gender*. New York: Routledge.

Connell, R.W. 2009. *Gender: in World Perspective*. 2nd ed. Cambridge: Polity.

Connell, R.W. 2012. "Transsexual Women and Feminist Thought: Toward New Understanding and New Politics." *Signs* 37 (4): 857–881.

Downing, L. 2008. *The Cambridge Introduction to Michel Foucault*. New York: Cambridge University Press.

Ellis, C. 1999. "Heartfelt Autoethnography." *Qualitative Health Research* 9 (5): 669–683.

Ellis, C. 2013. "Crossing the Rabbit Hole: Autoethnographic Life Review." *Qualitative Inquiry* 19 (1): 35–45.

Flynn, T.R. 2006. *Existentialism: A Very Short Introduction*. Oxford: Oxford University Press.

Foucault, M. 1975. *Surveiller et Punir*. Translated by A. Sheridan as *Discipline and Punish*. Harmondsworth, UK: Penguin.

Foucault, M. 1982. "The Subject and Power." *Critical Inquiry* 8 (4): 777–795.

Fraser, N. 2001. "Recognition without Ethics?" *Theory, Culture & Society* 18 (2–3): 21–42.

Goffman, E. 1963. *Stigma: Notes on the Management of Spoiled Identity*. Englewood Cliffs, NJ: Prentice-Hall.

Goffman, E. 1976/1979. *Gender Advertisements*. New York: Harper and Row.

Hao, R.N. 2011. "Rethinking Critical Pedagogy: Implications on Silence and Silent Bodies." *Text and Performance Quarterly* 31 (3): 267–284.

Holman Jones, S. 2007. *Torch Singing: Performing Resistance and Desire from Billie Holiday to Edith Piaf*. Lanham, MD: Altamira Press.

Holman Jones, S., and T.E. Adams. 2010. "Autoethnography is a Queer Method." In *Queer Methods and Methodologies: Intersecting Queer Theories and Social Science Research*, edited by K. Browne and C. Nash. Farnham: Ashgate.

Kando, T. 1973. *Sex Change: The Achievement of Gender Identity among Feminized Transsexuals*. Springfield, IL: Charles C. Thomas.

Leonard, W., M. Pitts, A. Mitchell, A. Lyons, S. Patel, M. Couch and A. Barrett. 2012. *Private Lives 2: The Second National Survey of the Health and Wellbeing of Gay, Lesbian, Bisexual and Transgender (GLBTI) Australians*. Monograph Series Number 86. Melbourne: Australian Research Centre in Sex, Health & Society, La Trobe University.

McNay, L. 2000. *Gender and Agency: Reconfiguring the Subject in Feminist and Legal Theory*. Cambridge: Polity.

Menninger, K. 1938. *Man against Himself.* New York: Harvest Books.

Peters, J. 1999. "i DREAM therefore i AM." *Home Page, Julie Elizabeth Peters.* Accessed December 2, 2012. http://home.mira.net/~janie/dream/index.htm.

Peters, J. 2005. "Gender as Performance, Not Gender Theory." *Gay & Lesbian Issues and Psychology Review* 1 (3): 98–101.

Peters, J. 2011. "A Transgendered Life." In *Polari Journal*, special issue "Trans-Verse," edited by D.J. Baker and S. Kentlyn. Bellingen, Australia. Accessed December 9, 2012. http://www.polarijournal.com/resources/Peters-Transgendered_Life.pdf.

Reed-Danahay, D. 1997. "Editorial Introduction." In *Auto/Ethnography: Rewriting the Self and the Social*, edited by D. Reed-Danahay. New York: Berg.

Singer, J. 1976. *Androgyny: Towards a New Theory of Sexuality.* New York: Anchor Press/Doubleday.

Spry, T. 2001. "Performing Autoethnography: An Embodied Methodological Praxis." *Qualitative Inquiry* 7 (6): 706–732.

Weeks, D., and J. James. 1995. *Eccentrics: A Study of Sanity and Strangeness.* New York: Kodansha America.

3 "Mincing, Striding, Stomping, Gliding"

Messing with Gender Choreographic Taboos

Jack Migdalek

A dance teacher admonishes a male student: "You're moving like a girl! Broaden your shoulders. Open your chest. Put some power into it. Command the space around you."

In this chapter I discuss the influences that pervasive discourses of patriarchy, heteronormativity and gendernormativity had on ways in which I came to operate and embody as a male dancer and choreographer, and I parallel these with the positioning and agency of individuals, as subjects categorised by biological sex in broader social and cultural contexts. I pose questions concerning what it takes to become aware of and challenge inequitable aspects of our own practices and positioning. My concerns are for the social and emotional well-being of those who are not inclined to perform according to restrictive and differential modes of what is commonly considered fitting and/or normal for those who are recognised as male or female.

Through charting the ways in which my dancer body was trained and choreographed, as well as the ways in which I choreographed and directed the bodies of others, I question the delicacy of the relationship between personal and social control over how we come to embody and understand gender. Addressing the "astonishing gap between what bodies can do and what they 'choose' to do" (Gard 2003a, 219), I challenge the notion that what we take to be normal and aesthetic embodiment for individuals according to biological sex is intrinsic and natural, as opposed to being constituted by societies and cultures to which we are exposed and within which we operate. This discussion raises implications concerning social attitudes, behaviours and practices in general.

Embodiment as I engage with it in this chapter, is the manner or "bodily technique" (Mauss 1979) in which a physical practice (choreography) is executed, and not body size, shape, colour or adornment. Where I refer to gender, I refer to socially constructed aspects of femininity and masculinity by which an action is performed and not to biological sex. While gender categories of masculine and feminine may be dependent on culture, setting and time, and as such difficult to define (Butler 2004), I feel compelled to use these terms. For the contexts of this chapter, my definitions for 'feminine' are gentle, graceful, delicate, soft, pliant; my definitions for 'masculine' are strong, forceful, powerful, unyielding.

HABITUS, ENCULTURATION, AGENCY AND TASTE

The proposition that we are unaware of gendered aspects of our perceptions and practices can be elucidated through theories of habitus (Bourdieu 1990) wherein non-consciously performed practices are "internalised
as second nature and so forgotten" (1990, 56). Notions of habitus, which
manifest in both perception and action, can be applied to habitual and
embedded ways of doing and perceiving that which is feminine and that
which is masculine. Indeed, a person's "disciplinary history" (habitual patterns of movement and corporeal commitments undertaken in day-to-day
life) will affect not only the person's body, but also their thoughts and ways
of being (Grosz 1994, 142; see also Kamler 1993). My disciplinary history,
as a male subject of mainstream worlds of dance, marked and formed me in
the past and still inform and resonate in who I am today. The same can be
claimed of the disciplinary histories of colonised subjects of other gendernormative worlds in which common culturally promoted norms of masculinity and femininity operate at a level of the subconscious and render other
expressions of gender as subordinate (Migdalek 2012b).

My male body was—and is—capable of performing in a feminine manner, yet it was never directed or choreographed to move in this way unless
for comic effect. As a male dance student, studying contemporary, classical
ballet and jazz styles, and as a male dancer performing in commercial musicals, film and television for mainstream audiences, I was coached to move
powerfully and strongly, and to occupy a large amount of space. I saw and

Figure 3.1   Jack Migdalek, dance: 'femininity and masculinity.' Photograph by Rob
Chiarolli.

understood that working male dancers moved with these qualities. Indeed, it was through taking on these qualities in my dancing that I became a working professional dancer myself. Through a process of practice, moving in ways demanded by the directors and choreographers with whom I worked became natural and also comfortable for my body to perform. This came to be my 'male dancer habitus'. The notion of mincing, gliding or dancing in a feminine manner congealed in my mind and male body as a distasteful concept, one steeped in internalised "femiphobia" (Ducat 2004) where male femininity was taboo.

My dance training ties in with a history of Western dance in which, to alleviate anxieties around the masculinity and sexuality of male performance artists, bodies of males have been frequently choreographed in hypermasculine ways (Buchbinder 2004; Gard 2001, 2006). The male dancer moving in a feminine manner has traditionally been deemed to be unattractive and suspect of homosexuality (Burt 1995, 2001; Foulkes 2001). Although there may have been variation between the dance styles of those who choreographed my male body, the choreography they produced on male dancers' bodies was ultimately athletic, expansive and masculine. My female counterparts were choreographed according to a broader spectrum of choreographic possibilities that included delicate, soft and feminine motion, modes of embodiment that were taboo for me.

Cultural theorist Angela McRobbie (2009) argues that even where we appear to have agency, what we choose to do is framed, regulated and contextualised to a large degree by cultural boundaries, influences and parameters. Where neoliberal sentiment may espouse a line of thinking in which individuals have agency to do anything, such lines of thought erase influences of systemic inequitable frameworks, such as patriarchal hierarchies of gender behaviour which envelop us (McRobbie 2009). It is impossible not to take into account cultural influences, such as media and popular culture, when contemplating ways in which individuals might choose, be inspired or come to embody. As such, agency as well as the capacity for resistance do not necessarily denote autonomy.

Just as the practices in the dance studios in which I trained positioned me in certain ways toward the embodiment of masculinity and femininity, so too are people in the everyday conditioned toward notions of appropriate gender performance. And this occurs from a very young age. DePalma and Atkinson (2008) argue that schools, for example, are sites of tacit instruction in the possibilities and limitations of gender and sexual identity (see also Kehily 2002; Renold 2005; Lingard, Martino and Mills 2009). These often hinge on embodied patterns of behaviour that are valued differently according to biological sex (Kamler et al. 1994; Gard 2003a; Shilling 2003).

My enculturation as a son and student enforced embodied norms for males and females. That those around me did not look positively on transgressions of these norms influenced me to conform to what I came to understand as being appropriate embodiment. I gave a good deal of credence to how I envisaged others perceived me, and this led to endeavouring not to project as feminine, which—even before being aware of social notions concerning homosexuality—I knew was not befitting successful boys and men. As a subject of panopticonic control (Foucault 1977), I self-regulated my behaviour and did not act upon any feminine inclinations I may have had. Indeed, whilst my inclination may have been toward feminine embodiment, I believe that my conceptions of the type of embodiment that was appropriate to males restricted how I may have otherwise operated. All this is contingent on taste, being the perception of that which is agreeable and/or aesthetic. Taste, like habitus, does not operate at the level of consciousness (Bourdieu 1990; Turner 1992; Shilling 2003).

Embodied femininity and masculinity on figures seen in mainstream television, cinema and theatre impacted on what I came to regard as agreeable, attractive and aesthetic for bodies that projected as male or female. In particular, I came to understand non-gender normative embodiment to be comic, ludicrous, deviant, suspect, repugnant and/or homosexual. The laughter evoked by male, larger-than-life caricatures who pranced around in an effeminate manner made it very clear to me that soft or feminine movement was not considered manly or appropriate for males.

Differential signalling of what is aesthetically attractive and unattractive for male and female forms continues to be enforced in the mainstream media. For example, public comments made by expert judges on the popular television program So You Think You Can Dance Australia (produced by Fremantle Media, 2008–2010) valorise masculine embodied movement for male dance performers ("dance hard and strong like a man"), whilst disavowing males who dance in a feminine manner for being "too girlie" and "too effeminate" (Migdalek 2009, 2012a, 2012b).

CHOREOGRAPHING THE BODIES OF OTHERS

I was inducted into heteronormative discourses and ideologies concerning stylisations of the body and aesthetic notions of embodiment deemed to befit male and female forms. This initiation influenced my work, not only as a dancer, but also as a dance teacher and choreographer. In directing and choreographing bodies of others, I habitually drew upon repertoires of motion, as artefacts of my enculturation, that seemed fitting—perhaps through their very familiarity—without thought of the restrictive and inequitable gender codes within. The inherent gendered way in which I directed/choreographed the bodies of male and female actors/dancers was significantly shaped by direction/choreography that, through a lifetime of exposure to and experience of mainstream examples, I perceived and took for granted as appropriate and natural to male and female bodies. This came to be my 'directorial-choreographic habitus'.

Drawing on my kinaesthetic experience, knowledge and aesthetic sensibility of dance, I did not direct or choreograph males to move in a feminine manner unless to project as comic, ludicrous or strange. It never occurred to me why female bodies that I choreographed to move in a feminine manner did not project in these ways. Despite my agency as a choreographer over the bodies of others, I was ignorant of the machinations of my directorial-choreographic habitus.

An early experience of choreographing bodies was in the 1980s, when a female friend and I choreographed our own male and female bodies to perform weekly at a popular Melbourne discotheque. How we choreographed our bodies was informed not only by ways in which our own male and female dancer bodies had been trained and choreographed by others, but also by what we perceived our employers and audiences wanted and expected of us: she moving slinkily; me moving powerfully. Our personal agency as choreographers worked in tandem with social controls and mechanisms. As testimony to habitus being non-conscious (Bourdieu 1990), it never occurred to us to move our bodies any differently.

Together with two other dancers, I choreographed and performed in a government-funded dance education company that toured to hundreds of Australian public and private schools during the 1980s. Our company included two male dancers and one female dancer. Aware that males performing in a feminine manner were received negatively or as objects of suspicion or ridicule by mainstream audiences (Burt 1995; Foster 2001; Gard 2003b, 2006), we aimed, like many male dancers before us, to alleviate anxieties around how audiences might read our masculinity and sexuality as male performance artists (see Burt 1995; Gard 2001, 2006; Buchbinder 2004). The choreography we created for the males in the company involved expansive steps that took power, space and a high degree of palpable athleticism. Any physical contact between the male dancers in our choreography was robust and on a par with sports (see Foster 2001; Gorely, Holroyd and Kirk 2003; Risner 2007). In trying to get by as male dancers, we worked directly toward combating students' gendernormative preconceptions of dance. However, in doing so, we unknowingly denied the artistry, validity and aesthetic qualities of male bodies that might also move in a soft, gentle or delicate manner (see Gard 2006).

In addition to choreographing for the stage, I taught jazz classes for adults at dance studios, gyms and community centres. As is often the case, most of the students who attended were female. I would prepare routines in advance of classes, and I recall how I automatically adjusted these whenever males joined my class. Where choreography may have been slinky and feminine, I adjusted it to be performed with straighter lines, wider stance, more force and less fluid hip and shoulder motion. I did so because I presumed that moving in the feminine manner of the choreography as I had intended to teach it would be uncomfortable and unbecoming for male students to execute.

These examples demonstrate how unaware I was of gendered ways in which I operated. Recent self-reflexive autoethnographic investigation has led me to question the force and ideology behind embedded and inequitable notions of what I felt was 'suitable' movement for male as opposed to female bodies. It has been ironic and frustrating to me to recognise that my choreographic habitus operated in such gender-conforming ways, given that my own embodied inclination and tendencies as a youngster had been gender non-conforming: (interviews with family members confirmed that I moved delicately and in a 'girlish' manner). My misrecognition of gender-conforming ways by which I came to operate is testimony to the force of my social conditioning. The ways in which I came to direct and choreograph male and female bodies simply reinforced oppressive gender norms that had themselves been oppressive to me. I believe that other choreographers—even liberal-minded ones who might hate to think of themselves as gendered—also unwittingly reinforce the same. Even though choreographers may be agentic, embedded habitual ways in which they do and view male and female bodies are so ingrained that they are likely to be unaware of how these affect ways in which they perceive, cast, direct and choreograph bodies on whom they work. It stands to reason that these practices will also impact on the understandings of gender of audiences, as well as those upon whose bodies choreography is taught. Developing recognition of inequitable aspects of one's habitus is a positive step toward resistance and reconstruction.

INEQUITABLE ASPECTS IN THE PRACTICES OF OTHERS

I wanted to ascertain gender conformity in the perspectives and practices of others. And so, under the auspices of a major Australian arts centre that offered practical professional development for performance artists, I conducted a day-long fieldwork session with approximately thirty fellow performance arts practitioners/educators. The session involved a series of practical drama, dance, music and design workshop activities, in which participants were encouraged to explore and deconstruct notions of embodied gender inequity within their art-forms and their own practices, as well as ways in which such inequities may impact on those with whom they work.

It surprised me to find that only very few fieldwork participants were open to questioning why, in directing/choreographing male and female forms, they made the aesthetic decisions that they did. Although fieldwork participants advocated directing and choreographing dance where male and female dancers are choreographed to their movement capabilities and not their biological sex, comments and creative output indicated a preference to see male dancers moving strongly and athletically and an aversion to males dancing in a feminine manner. My sense was that these performance arts practitioners/educators regarded what they found to be personally aesthetic for male or female embodiment to be organic and instinctive and not contingent on their enculturation. In much the same way that individuals overlook the proposition that their sense of taste is culturally framed or imposed (McRobbie 2009), so too is there a tendency for individuals to take that which they understand to be their "internal essence" as a given (Butler 2004). While most participants were clear on *what* they felt was aesthetically pleasing, only several appeared mindful to considering *why*. Despite some recognition of embedded gender inequities within performance arts disciplines, participants were on the whole resistant to interrogate gendered aspects of their own work as artists.

A group of participants expressed their discomfort with a workshop task in which they were asked to conceive practical activities for the performance arts classroom that might expose or challenge embodied gender inequities: "We wanted to be careful . . . that we weren't coming in with an agenda." This comment belies the existence of dominant societal agendas and implies the group members' political neutrality as educators (see Tierney 1997). It is likely that these educators did not conceive that the 'norms' by which they taught and operated could themselves be laden with agendas, precisely because these norms aligned with dominant ways of thinking. In coining the term 'authentic' to describe a state of innocence that they perceived in young children, fieldwork participants failed to recognise hidden but prevalent adult world assumptions and agendas, such as those of gendernormativity (Taylor and Richardson 2005) and the heterosexual matrix (Butler 1990), to which children are exposed even prior to attending school (see also Kehily 2002; Renold 2005; Paechter 2007; DePalma and Atkinson 2008). Participants' talk of focusing students' attention on inequities of gender embodiment as being the 'pushing of an agenda' struck and frustrated me, because I believe that the same educators would not hesitate to push agendas that would tackle a mind-set or mentality that discriminates against racism, sexism or ageism with their students as forms of discrimination not to be tolerated (see Kehily 2002). Is it that ideologies of gender embodiment are less worthy of being exposed or challenged, or is it just that they are so invisibilised/normalised that as a result they are overlooked?

A key issue for fieldwork participants who were resistant to delving into how they might challenge embodied inequities of gender may have been a fundamental discomfort concerning their personal submission to the same, or in other words, their own complicity in sustaining embodied inequities of gender through their personal, professional and/or everyday practices. It is unsettling to conceive that one's own habitual behaviour and practices may be a contributing factor to the continuation of a state of affairs that is inequitable. There is a tendency to discard disturbing subjects so that we do not have to deal with them (Trinh 1992).

A few fieldwork participants were more open to investigating inequitable aspects of their own positioning. One dance educator ventured to speak as a mother about her discomfort with her aversive reactions to the feminine way that one of her sons dances. In discussion, she began to question why her sense of aesthetics for male and female forms was so fixed. This kind of reflexive self-consciousness is a positive step toward exposing the discourses and ideologies that form and bolster what we take to be our own natural responses.

SELF-REFLEXIVITY AND CHANGE

Performance artists are unlikely to be aware of the relationship between their sense of aesthetics and their induction into performance arts disciplines, which to all intents and purposes feel natural and instinctive to them. So too are individuals in general unlikely to be aware of the relationship between ways in which they perceive and operate in their worlds and their enculturation. How then might it be possible to open ourselves up to recognising, questioning/resisting and reconstructing inequitable ideologies that are integral to how we habitually perceive and behave in the worlds in which we operate?

Through self-reflexive work, it is possible to take an inventory of the impacts of our own routine assumptions, positions, values, interests, attitudes, commitments, biases and social identity on our actions and understandings (see Lincoln 1995; Ollis 2008; Szarycz 2010). This work enables us to recognise and question connections between our enculturation to worlds in which we are raised and our own practices. Education researcher Helen Cahill (2010) argues that if we want to affect social change through shifting patterns of behaviour, we must make visible and unravel the discourses (which normally escape our attention) that pattern our thinking and assumptions about what is 'natural'.

Through autoethnography, rigorous self-reflexive investigation of my own practices, and practical choreographic experimentation, I have become mindful that, despite not thinking of myself as gendered, my dance and everyday habitus have been compliant with, limited by and reflective of dominant patriarchal and inequitable ideologies embedded-as-nature in the cultures from which I hail.

Methods of critical inquiry, such as the exploratory drama workshop, can serve to raise individuals' awareness of inequitable ways in which we read and perform gender differently according to the biological sex of the performer (Zeig 1985; Migdalek 2009). However, it may take time for such work to impact on the individual. To illustrate, I now refer to the experiences of one fieldwork participant, Tanya, who had grappled uneasily with issues raised in the workshops. Tanya, who had been a professional classical ballet dancer, threw herself into a physical improvisation activity that I conducted at the start of the session. In physically responding to the soft and lilting classical ballet music, it was clear that Tanya drew upon a repertoire of motion that was familiar to both her eyes and body as a result of years of exposure and experience as a female student and performer of classical ballet. In discussion, Tanya acknowledged that male and female bodies were positioned differently to one another in classical ballet. However, she did not regard this positioning as being gendered, claiming that "art aims to connect people to the deepest parts of themselves" and that "these go beyond gender."

In regard to the suggestion that habitual gender norms of embodiment be interrogated, Tanya questioned "Why the need to unravel?" It seems to me that Tanya did not conceive that her playing into a certain gender performativity, via a lifetime of enculturation into the patriarchal and gender inequitable conventions of the classical ballet, is very much connected to why, from deep within, she is comfortable embodying in a feminine manner. That such embodiment feels natural to her is something I doubt Tanya had ever questioned. Where an individual like Tanya might consider particular embodiment as more fitting to a male or female body as an essential or authentic truth, my feeling is that such an outlook is testimony of a blind spot to the force of enculturation as constructive of such sensibilities (see Fuchs 2001).

Although Tanya acknowledged that differences in representations of male and female bodies in the classical ballet may be gendered, she saw these differences as transparent and not relevant to contemporary issues of embodiment. She spoke of the classical ballet as "history", and did not acknowledge that representations of classical balletic and other bodies onstage may be inscriptive of gender behaviour for male and female bodies in the here and now of the everyday (see Dempster 1988), nor the potential negative impact of such representations on the sense of self of those whose embodied inclinations may not fit with established norms and orders of gender embodiment.

Tanya is a tall, white, fair-haired, able-bodied, non-masculine-embodying woman who, when she was dancing professionally, had the physical capital that would never have caused her to feel physically disenfranchised or misfit. Due to this privileged positioning (see Pease 2010), it follows that she would not be as aware or empathetic of what it is like to feel physically impoverished, as would those who struggle with and are tormented by such feelings. Tanya distanced herself from the problems of others by stating: "It's only if you have a problem with it, it becomes a problem. It becomes a problem if you the individual have a problem with it." Tanya's simplistic view that that which is problematic is only so because the individual has allowed it to become so is devoid of an understanding of context and systemic constraints and influences (see McRobbie 2009).

Tanya's outlook implies that problems of those inclined to perform masculinity and femininity against prescribed norms are not the concern of those who do not have such issues. Her standpoint brings to mind Connell's (1995) contention that it is not in the interests of empowered groups to change gender inequities that exist or to defend the rights of 'others' (see also Dyer 1997; Paechter 2007; Pease 2010). Indeed, those who are well positioned within empowered landscapes are not likely to respond well to implications that their own practices are an essential part of networks of oppression and privilege (Fruehling Springwood and King 2001). There is no vested interest for those whose performances of masculinity/femininity bear elevated physical capital or match dominant norms (such as Tanya's) to seek or affect change. When discussion centred on the well-being of individuals who did not walk or sit in gendered ways as prescribed for their biological sex, Tanya dismissed this by exclaiming that people should simply be grateful for being able to walk.

This line of thinking disengages and exonerates mainstream society from situations of the marginalised, absconding all responsibility and connection. What is overlooked here is the possibility that there may be something problematic within the fabric of society that, through sustaining gendered outlooks and attitudes toward other embodiments of masculinity and femininity, causes individuals to feel 'misfit' and experience oppression or marginalisation in the first place.

Interestingly, eight months after the fieldwork session, I received an apologetic e-mail from Tanya in which she reflected back on the day:

> "I just couldn't get my head around worrying about how men are perceived when some people can't even control their capacity to stand. It was just my own issues getting in the way. I do understand the need to be 'you' without too much imposing of stereotypes, I expect dance itself continues to do just that and I am certainly a culprit of continuing tradition. All in all I expect my view is one that is coloured and ignorant . . . I am sorry for that."

What strikes and inspires me is that over time, the material which was raised in the day-long fieldwork session stirred something in Tanya's consciousness and made some personal impact or connection, despite having been strongly resisted at the time it was raised. As hooks (1994) argues, pedagogy that involves the exposing of biases and old ways of knowing, may take months or years to be realised, and in bringing about social shift is likely to cause discomfort, confusion and pain along the way. In the eight months since the fieldwork, it appears that Tanya, through her discomforts, has become more open to questioning her own embedded assumptions and more sensitive to the situations of those who are marginalised in ways that she may not have experienced firsthand. It is heartening to see Tanya recognise that her previously expressed neoliberal sentiments on individual agency and empowerment may be a form of misrecognition and marginalisation. The link between the fieldwork session and self-reflexive processes that caused a shift in Tanya's outlook is testimony to the potential of arts-based professional development workshops as a form of intervention in uncontested normalised misrecognition and subsequent opportunities for reconstruction.

Bob Pease (2010) contends that where privilege is experienced as being 'natural' and 'normal'—such as by white, heterosexual, middle-class, able-bodied males—there is also likely to be a blindness on the part of the privileged to ways in which they themselves sustain and reproduce systems of oppression and social division. A further problem here is that those who sustain existing systems of oppression are also frequently members of the oppressed (Freire 1990) who, as a result of their conditioning, are often unable to look critically at, or recognise their capacity for resistance within, the social systems in which they are submerged and within which they are trying to gain some privilege. If oppressive and inequitable norms and attitudes are to change, then it is vital that those who maintain existing systems that support such inequities come to understand their complicity in sustaining those very systems of oppression (see hooks 2001; Pease 2010).

CONCLUSION

Self-reflexive investigation has led me to question the extent to which worlds in which I have been inducted, and habitual ways by which I have come to operate, uphold notions of equity in regard to the embodiment of gender.

Like most individuals placed in, and exposed to, particular social and cultural settings or fields (Bourdieu 1990), my body learned to play by the rules, such as those set by dance teachers and choreographers in dance studios and rehearsal rooms. My instruction and training as a dance student and young dancer have had a pervasive influence on my positioning toward embodiment in adulthood, not only in formal dance performance arenas, but also in the everyday. In both contexts, I was effectively blind to the inequitable status quo of worlds into which I was enculturated.

Looking back on my work as a choreographer, it is not without feelings of guilt that I reflect on the distinctively different ways in which I unwittingly directed and choreographed the bodies of those who presented as males and females respectively. My 'choreographic habitus' was reflective of, and dictated by, my already established sense of taste and aesthetic. This was deeply embedded in gendernormative, heteronormative and patriarchal ideologies, as informed by life inscription and induction to a cultural heritage that prescribes differing norms for male bodies and female bodies. The gendered machinations of my subjective choreographic practices were so entrenched and invisible that they not only appeared, but also *felt* perfectly 'natural'. I was so used to perceiving and operating in particular ways that I was unable to recognise connections between the ways in which I operated and ways in which I had been conditioned. It is precisely because the machinations of habitus and taste (Bourdieu 1990) remain largely invisible to us that essentialist modes of thinking, where a sense of what is 'natural' and fundamental, are overlooked, under-problematised and unchallenged.

Being caught up in binds of embedded social notions of normative masculine and feminine embodiment rendered me blind to the myriad of possibilities of gender as points on a continuum in which identifications may be "fluid, transitory, fragmented, episodic" (Pallotta-Chiarolli 2010, 30) and not encumbered by imperatives to conform to constraints of learned gender alignments (Taylor and Richardson 2005). In order to advance this proposition and broaden personal and social notions of what is choreographically possible, aesthetic and acceptable embodiment for all persons, regardless of biological sex or sexual orientation, there is a need to destabilise and challenge existing gendered hierarchical norms and taboos regarding the embodiment of gender.

For positive social change to occur in education, popular culture, performance arts and the everyday, it is vital that all persons, including those who are not oppressed, come to an understanding and recognition of how ideologies and discourses of worlds and disciplines into which we are inducted influence us. If not, then existing inequities that marginalise those who are not inclined to conform to common and limited socially prescribed norms of behaviour will simply continue. Through educating individuals to self-reflexively deconstruct and question perceptions and practices that to all intents and purposes feel natural, we may be able to expose and overcome existing inequities that continue to dominate. If unaddressed, then our own inequitable (and discriminatory) perspectives, blind spots, tastes and practices are likely to perpetuate and persist in the outlooks, orientations and behaviours of those who we raise and educate.

This chapter, couched in my own reflexivity regarding my own practices and blind spots to inequitable machinations that exist in the world of dance and choreography, is presented as a provocation to those inducted into other worlds in which inequitable ideologies and discourses are rendered invisible.

REFERENCES

Bourdieu, P. 1990. *The Logic of Practice*. Cambridge: Polity.
Buchbinder, D. 2004. "The Sign of the Dancing Men: Negotiations of Masculinity in Film Musicals." *Masculinities: Gender, Art and Popular Culture: Inaugural National Symposium on Art, Education and Popular Culture*. Accessed April 4, 2006. http://www.art-museum.unimelb.edu.au/events_transcripts.
Burt, R. 1995. *The Male Dancer: Bodies, Spectacle, Sexualities*. London: Routledge.
Burt, R. 2001. "Dissolving in Pleasure: The Threat of the Queer Male Dancing Body." In *Dancing Desires: Choreographing Sexualities on and off the Stage*, edited by J.C. Desmond. Madison: University of Wisconsin Press.
Butler, J. 1990. *Gender Trouble, Feminism and the Subversion of Identity*. London: Routledge.
Butler, J. 2004. *Undoing Gender*. New York: Routledge.
Cahill, H. 2010. "Re-Thinking the Fiction-Reality Boundary: Investigating the Use of Drama in HIV Prevention Projects in Vietnam." *Research in Drama Education: The Journal of Applied Theatre and Performance* 15 (2): 155–174.

Connell, R.W. 1995. *Masculinities*. Sydney: Allen and Unwin.

DePalma, R., and E. Atkinson. 2008. *Invisible Boundaries: Addressing Sexualities Equality in Children's Worlds*. Stoke-on-Trent: Trentham.

Dempster, E. 1988. "Let's Watch a Little How She Dances." In *Grafts: Feminist Cultural Criticism*, edited by S. Sheridan. London: Verso.

Ducat, S.J. 2004. *Wimp Factor: Gender Gaps, Holy Wars, and the Politics of Anxious Masculinity*. Boston: Beacon Press.

Dyer, R. 1997. *White*. London: Routledge.

Foster, S.L. 2001. "Closets Full of Dances: Modern Dance's Performance of Masculinity and Sexuality." In *Dancing Desires: Choreographing Sexualities on and off the Stage*, edited by J.C. Desmond. Madison: University of Wisconsin Press.

Foucault, M. 1977. *Discipline and Punish: The Birth of the Prison*. London: Peregrine.

Foulkes, J.L. 2001. "Dance Is for American Men: Ted Shawn and the Intersection of Gender, Sexuality and Nationalism in the 1930s." In *Dancing Desires: Choreographing Sexualities on and off the Stage*, edited by J.C. Desmond. Madison: University of Wisconsin Press.

Freire, P. 1990. *Pedagogy of the Oppressed*. New York: Continuum.

Fruehling Springwood, C., and C.R. King. 2001. "Unsettling Engagements: On the Ends of Rapport in Critical Ethnography." *Qualitative Inquiry* 7 (4): 403–417.

Fuchs, S. 2001. *Against Essentialism: A Theory of Culture and Society*. Cambridge, MA: Harvard University Press.

Gard, M. 2001. "Dancing around the 'Problem' of Boys and Dance." *Discourse: Studies in the Cultural Politics of Education* 22 (2): 212–225.

Gard, M. 2003a. "Being Someone Else: Using Dance in Anti-Oppressive Teaching." *Educational Review* 55 (2): 211–223.

Gard, M. 2003b. "Moving and Belonging: Dance, Sport and Sexuality." *Sex Education* 3 (2): 105–118.

Gard, M. 2006. *Men Who Dance: Aesthetics, Athletics, & the Art of Masculinity*. New York: Peter Lang.

Gorely, T., R. Holroyd and D. Kirk. 2003. "Muscularity, the Habitus and the Social Construction of Gender: Towards a Gender-Related Physical Education." *British Journal of Sociology of Education* 24 (4): 429–448.

Grosz, E. 1994. *Volatile Bodies*. London: Allen and Unwin.

hooks, b. 1994. *Teaching to Transgress*. New York: Routledge.

hooks, b. 2001. "Men: Comrades in Struggle." In *Men's Lives*, edited by M.S. Kimmel, & M.A. Messner. Boston: Allyn and Bacon.

Kamler, B. 1993. "The Construction and Reconstruction of Gender in Classroom Discourse: Disciplining the Student Body." Paper presented at the National Council of Teachers of English (83rd annual convention), Pittsburgh.

Kamler, B., R. Maclean, J. Reid and A. Simpson. 1994. *"Shaping Up Nicely": The Formation of Schoolgirls and Schoolboys in the First Month of School*. A Report to the Gender Equity and Curriculum Reform Project of the Australian Department of Employment, Education and Training (DEET). Canberra: Australian Government Publishing Service.

Kehily, M. 2002. *Sexuality, Gender and Schooling: Shifting Agendas in Social Learning*. London: Routledge.

Lincoln, Y.S. 1995. "Emerging Criteria for Quality in Qualitative and Interpretive Research." *Qualitative Inquiry* 1 (3): 275–289.

Lingard, B., W. Martino and M. Mills. 2009. *Boys and Schooling: Beyond Structural Reform*. Basingstoke: Palgrave Macmillan.

Mauss, M. 1979. *Sociology and Psychology: Essays*. London Routledge.

McRobbie, A. 2009. *The Aftermath of Feminism*. Thousand Oaks, CA: Sage Publications.

Migdalek, J. 2009. "Masculine Moves: The Measure of a Man." *NJ Drama Australia Journal* 32 (1): 45–54.

Migdalek, J. 2012a. "Aesthetics of Gender Embodiment." *ADRI Working Papers* 2 (37). Accessed December 15, 2012. http://www.deakin.edu.au/research-services/forms/v/3672/wps-37w.pdf.

Migdalek, J. 2012b. *Embodied Choreography and Performance of Gender.* Melbourne: Deakin University. Accessed December 15, 2012. http://dro.deakin.edu.au/view/DU:30047367.

Ollis, D. 2008. *Sexualities and Gender in the Classroom: Changing Teacher Practice.* Cologne: Lambert.

Pallotta-Chiarolli, M. 2010. *Border Sexualities, Border Families in Schools.* Plymouth: Rowman and Littlefield.

Paechter, C. 2007. *Being Boys, Being Girls: Learning Masculinities and Femininities.* Berkshire: Open University Press.

Pease, B. 2010. *Undoing Privilege: Unlearned Advantage in a Divided World.* London: Zed Books.

Renold, E. 2005. *Girls, Boys and Junior Sexualities.* London: Routledge Falmer.

Risner, D. 2007. "Rehearsing Masculinity: Challenging the 'Boy Code' in Dance Education." *Research in Dance Education* 8 (2): 139–153.

Shilling, C. 2003. *The Body and Social Theory.* London: Sage Publications.

Szarycz, G.S. 2010. *Research Realities in the Social Sciences: Negotiating Fieldwork Dilemmas.* New York: Cambria Press.

Taylor, A., and C. Richardson. 2005. "Queering Home Corner." *Contemporary Issues in Early Childhood* 6 (2): 163–173.

Tierney, W.G. 1997. *Academic Outlaws: Queer Theory and Cultural Studies in the Academy.* Thousand Oaks, CA: Sage Publications.

Trinh, T. 1992. *Framer Framed.* New York: Routledge.

Turner, B. 1992. *Regulating Bodies: Essays in Medical Sociology.* London: Routledge.

Zeig, S. 1985. "The Actor as Activator: Deconstructing Gender through Gesture." *Women and Performance* 2 (2): 12–17.

4 Mothers and Sons
Transforming Gendered Subjectivities

Sarah Epstein

INTRODUCTION

This chapter tells a collective story of feminist mothers' maternal practice as a form of resistance to gender inequality and originates from my research exploring feminist mothers' experiences of raising sons. Semi-structured interviews were conducted with twenty self-identified feminist mothers of sons. A grounded theory analysis was applied to the data and emerging themes were structured and represented through a post-structural feminist lens. The assertions made in this chapter stem from a specific focus on a particular, localised group. The interviewees are predominantly higher-degree graduates, middle-class and urbanised Australian women. The knowledge produced is authoritative only from and within this specified locale, but this does not mean the knowledge is ahistorical and non-contextual. The interviewees and their lived experiences are impacted by, enact and interact continuously with wider social narratives about gender and about mothers and sons.

I argue that the mother as maternal subject enacts feminist maternal practice that is informed by the personal, but positioned within, the political and social context of changing gender relations. While in a wider gender context, the mother as a woman could be considered part of a disadvantaged group, as the parent, she is also in a privileged position. Additionally her class, heterosexuality and race maintain her privilege. From her position of advantage, she undertakes practices designed to address her experiences of disadvantage. Feminist maternal practice shapes this practice. The theoretical concept of "doing gender" (West and Zimmerman 1987, 2009) creates the potential for feminist mothers to reposition their sons' masculine subjectivities.

THE GENDERED SUBJECT

Gender is the point of difference between men and women. As a category of identity, it is the boundary line drawn between male and female (Risman and Myers 1997) and is determined by what are seen as masculine and feminine expressions of biological difference (Mansfield 2000). Human beings are thus organised around the difference between men and women (Beasley 1999) and the idea that gender is an expression of an interior substance.

Post-structural accounts of gender mark a break from an essentialised and interior gendered being. Instead, the gendered subject is constituted through its location within the gender binary. That is, there is no identity behind the social process that renders the gendered subject legible (Butler 2006).

Masculine subjectivities are therefore constitutive; they are an ongoing invention that interacts with gender discourse. This interaction is not predictable, linear or consistent. As a gendered subject he is ongoingly constituted in the moment and by past constitutive actions (Butler 1992). This is a formative process where he is always being positioned in relation to the social context. The masculine subject acts on these social conditions at the same time as he is determined by these conditions (Foucault 1998; Fenstermaker and West 2002). The social context circulates gendered discourse, and this constrains language and ideas, making certain things available or unavailable. Understanding this concept helps develop ideas for working towards changed gender relations. Later in this chapter, I will present some examples where feminist mothers make alternative discourses available for the masculine subject to interact with and constitute alternative masculine subjectivities.

THE MATERNAL SUBJECT

Feminist maternal practice sits within a broader post-structural feminist framework and is a tactical response to the constraints imposed by motherhood as an institution. This institution essentialises and positions women within a structurally oppressive, static location (Firestone 1979).

Feminist maternal practice attempts to deregulate maternity and position both motherhood and the mother as culturally relative (Jeremiah 2006; Everingham 1994). The 'mother' is constituted through the 'motherhood' discourse. Consequently, motherhood is no longer taken as fixed or biologically driven but conceptualised as 'mothering' that is a set of ideas and practices that change across time and context (Jeremiah 2006).

Feminist maternal practice uses post-structural ideas about power as relational. With the maternal subject as mutable, multiple and constituted through discourse, mothering has been wrested from a structural location where it is constituted by external forces of power. Post-structural feminist ideas about power allow the concept of maternal practice to form a part of, be responsive to and inform relations of power.

Consequently, feminist researchers and theorists have been able to explore how feminist mothers engage with feminist values in their interactions with their children (Green 2004; Horwitz 2004). The maternal subject emerges by engaging in maternal practice, and we become mothers by enacting mothering (Chandler 1998).

The dominant discourse about the pre-social mother who exists prior to culture is contested because mothering positions women as external to the individual. Because mothering involves the taking up of maternal practice, this imbues the maternal subject as active, interactive and a part of an exchange (Jeremiah 2006). The concept of maternal subjectivity is important because feminist maternal practice with boys that transforms gender relations does not work unless there is a conceptual consideration for maternal agency.

Feminist mothers have clear ideas about what kind of masculine subjectivities are needed to resist gender inequity. They use alternative sources of recognition to develop new forms of masculinities. In order to better explore how this might be done, it is helpful to identify the conceptual frameworks about gender that feminist maternal practice is interacting with.

DOING GENDER

Doing gender may be unavoidable (Butler 2006) because the subject exists, always, in relation to gender discourse. It is positioned by and within gender discourse. Generally, "one's sex category can be relevant, and one's performance as an incumbent of that category can be subjected to evaluation" (Fenstermaker and West 2002, 21).

West and Zimmerman (1987) argue that doing gender involves the construction of differences between men and women. These differences then reinforce the notion of the essential nature of gender. Gender is not an attribute; rather it is configured through an action, oriented according to the awareness of the individual's accountability—"that is, how they might look, and how they might be categorized" (136). Activity is rendered accountable in a process of interaction rather than by attributed positions of masculinity and femininity as "social properties of a system of relationship" (West and Zimmerman 2009, 114). The subject is "never not" engaged in activity where they are held accountable to their sex category.

When we 'do' gender, we are not always proving ourselves appropriate for our correlative sex category; rather we are engaging "in behaviour *at the risk* of *gender assessment*" (West and Zimmerman 1987, 136; original emphasis). West and Zimmerman (2009) argue that doing gender is capable of recognising and spring-boarding from the multiple, complex social, historical and political contexts within which it is always, simultaneously practiced. These contexts both constrain and/or make possible specific iterations (Fenstermaker and West 2002; Messner 2000; West and Zimmerman 2009).

Gender accountability played out through interaction is regulated through a normative system that is absolutely contextual and historically specific. West and Zimmerman (2009) argue that this system is as wholly responsive as it is constitutive. They argue that the practices enacted to account for gender are drawn from and held against normative standards established and practiced in the institutional social domain. Whilst drawing on gender difference to include class and race, they suggest that individuals do difference as a way of categorising and creating distinctions. These practices appear to reflect naturality, essentiality and normality. Once difference is constructed, it is used to measure the individual's social location and access to the various and multiple categories (West and Zimmerman 2009).

There has been concern that their theory demonstrated a lack of attention to drawing on gender accomplishment in learning how interactions can be a process of undoing gender (Risman 2008). Risman (2008) argues that this critique is located in accounts of gender as fixed. However, and I would concur, West and Zimmerman (2009) counter that undoing gender suggests the idea that gender can be done away with. Instead, they suggest that such interactions of undoing gender could be reworded as "a change in the normative conceptions to which members of particular sex categories are held accountable" (117).

Accountability sits at the core of gender, and relies on difference for measure. They stress "the oppressive character of gender rests not just on difference but the inferences from and the consequences of those differences". Inferences and consequences are imbued within interaction whilst being embedded in socio-cultural and historical context. So a change in context can "facilitate inferential shifts in the terms of gender accountability and weaken its utility as a ground for men's hegemony". Gender cannot be undone; rather it can be redone (West and Zimmerman 2009, 117).

DOING GENDER AND THE MOTHER AND SON

Theories of intersectionality employ the idea that knowledge is situated (Davis 2008) and is a theoretical access point towards an understanding of "power differentials and normativities" (Lykke 2010, 51), shaped by feminist maternal practice with sons. Thus, intersectionality can demonstrate the machinations of resistance. Lykke (2010) suggests intersectionality can demonstrate how resistance to normativities is enacted through "signification of categorizations and normative identity markers" (51). The idea of intersectionality meshes with the interactional construction of gendered subjectivities of West and Zimmerman (1987).

Despite being constrained by gender discourse, the mother can engage (within these limits) in "ongoing meaning-making processes" (Lykke 2010, 74). Thus she adopts subject positions and invites her son to do the same where they are elaborated on and transformed. From her position as feminist woman and mother, her intersectional location critically engages with discourses about masculinity as it relates to her and her son. While theoretically, as woman and mother, she is vulnerable and subordinate, her feminism is a source of entitlement and empowerment (Green 2004; Horwitz 2004). She utilises her position as mother to enact change. Her sense of entitlement is used in part to construct masculine subjectivity. This act contests patriarchal narratives about the relationship of mother to son by interfering in her son's masculinisation process. Concurrently, she rejects the grounds of essentialised gender by considering multiple, alternative possibilities for masculinity practices.

Children's gender does not unfold or emerge; it is enacted by repeatedly performing relationships in multiple contexts. Gender discourse is constructed in these relationships and the subject is positioned around this discourse. The invitations for a young boy to account for his gender are located in multiple situations and contexts across which he is invited to account for his gendered behaviour differently. Each interaction informs another whilst being influenced by power structures and relationships.

I argue that the social and cultural climate of the feminist mother and son relationship is an important context where boys' masculine subjectivities are constituted. Gender is performed on an interactional level between mother and son via a process of negotiation, where activity occurs that is accountable to gendered norms. This is similar to the interaction between girls and boys in the school classroom or in the playground. In all locations, interaction is determined by the context of the relationship. The interactional activity draws on, co-opts and is co-opted by cultural symbolism of gender discourse.

The feminist mother and son relationship has particular cultural conditions where language, imagery and meanings can be oppositional to dominant culture. Feminist mothers work to "unsettle dominant meanings" (Threadgold and Cranny-Francis 1990, 23), and they activate and enforce different accountability standards.

Here, the mother is both agent and witness (Messner 2000), and it is in the interpretive action where she is a critical agent (Everingham 1994). By responding to the agency of her child in a particular socio-cultural setting, she actively constructs cultural meanings and forms of subjectivity within that milieu (Everingham 1994). Importantly, she *deliberately* activates cultural meaning to certain situations.

In order to redo gender and change gendered subjectivities, West and Zimmerman (2009) suggest that this "involves both changes in persons' orientation to these norms and changes in social relations that reflexively support changes in orientation" (118). In this way one can explore the intersection between categories of difference (men and women) and their relation to the cultural ideology of masculinity. Feminist maternal practice might alter this interaction's outcome.

FEMINIST MATERNAL PRACTICE WITH SONS

Normative Masculinity

A patriarchal narrative has historically circumscribed the relationship between mothers and sons (O'Reilly 2001). Within this narrative, attention has focused on gender difference (Smith 1996), the importance of the mother privileging the father's role in her son's developing masculinity (Biddulph 1998; Bly 1992) and of "maternal displacement and denial" (O'Reilly 2001, 94). Boys need to renounce their identification with their mothers in order to become men. The mother must retreat from her son, facilitating the break (Biddulph 1998). It is vital that he does not identify with her (Bly 1992) if he is to emerge a man.

These exhortations reflect hegemonic masculinity practices that construct a hierarchy of behaviour that men are implicated in and measured against (Beasley 1999; Connell 2005). The higher up the hierarchy, the less 'feminine' a man must look. Normative masculinity practices produce and sustain male domination by acting as ongoing measures of all males. Feminist and pro-feminist masculinities scholars have argued that masculinity practices have harmed men because they confine emotions, affect relationships and impose a conformity that limits their social consciousness and vision of multiple masculinities (Gardiner 2002).

I argue that masculinity itself cannot be seen as the problem; otherwise on what basis do we as feminist mothers form our bonds with our sons? This is the imperative at the core of feminist maternal practice with sons. Contemporary theorising about the social construction of gender can resolve this potential impasse by enabling a critical distance to develop between our sons and masculinity as an ideology, socially and institutionally entrenched in relations of power and enacted through a set of practices by boys and men (Gardiner 2002).

Both my own experience and analysis of research data show that feminist mothers do separate the boy from the discourse by providing a critical interrogation that identifies the mechanisms of power that maintain normative masculinity. Gardiner (2002) proposes that feminism cannot fully account for social and gender relations without understanding that this shapes men too. Because feminist mothers of sons are witness to and agents in the construction of masculinities, we are in a particular position to understand this and to intervene.

In the raising of sons, there are occasions where feminist mothers do not adhere to the patriarchal script; rather they hold normative masculinity practices accountable, identifying entry points to alter the constitution of their sons' masculinities. Above all, feminist mothers of sons do this because they believe that normative masculinity practices position our sons' masculine subjectivities in ways that limit our sons' opportunities and perpetuate gender inequity.

I turn now to a closer examination of how feminist mothers construct a supportive interactional context, facilitating a change in boys' orientation to normative masculinity practices. Non-normative standards are established and privileged; dominant discourse is contested; and masculine subjectivities relative to women can be constituted in ways that do not resemble male power and privilege.

Destabilising Dominant Discourse

> Feminism informs everything. (Gloria)

The feminist mothers interviewed for this project foreground their maternal practice in feminism. Feminism is the lens, strategy and values system through which they enact their maternal practice. The feminist paradigm provides context and form for the moral attitudes mothers enact with their children (Everingham 1994).

> My feminism is the way that I analyse the world and is constant and conscious and so I am constantly checking how I am dealing with them, what kind of people they are, what kind of discussions we have. (Kate)

Gloria draws on a feminist discourse, activating it. She becomes an agent of discursive activity (Horwitz 2004). Her destabilising of the dominant discourse about masculinity is deliberate:

> I just want to make sure that those concepts of what masculinity is, out there in the greater community, are challenged.

Iris attempts to displace the totalising effect of dominant discourse by introducing an alternative discourse:

> I am trying to give them as much opportunity, whereby in spite of all the other pressures on them, there are small opportunities to experience other options.

Nina identifies that the subordination of women does not just occur within political or economic structures. She refuses to collude with the grand narrative about gender:

> When he brings home, "Girls don't do this" and "Girls don't do that", it is more about challenging that.

Eleanor, in direct conversation with her sons, enacts alternative discourse. She openly challenges prevailing messages and makes visible the contradictions and gaps of the dominant discourse:

> I will say there is no such thing as boys' activities or girls' activities. We are socialised and acculturated into believing these things. And I can explain that in child-friendly language and I have. We do talk about these things and have always. You know "there is no such thing as boys' clothes and girls' clothes and there is no such thing as boys' colours and girls' colours".

Kate contests dominant discourse in multiple contexts where her son's gendered subjectivity is constituted:

> A little boy said in front of my son, "You can't be the dad coz you are a girl". They were three and I said, "Do you pretend to be superman?" And he said, "Sure". I said, "Well if you can pretend to be superman, she can pretend to be a dad".

Dominant gender discourse that positions men and women and boys and girls within restricted categories are interrogated:

> And I never say things like boys can't do this or girls can't do that. If my sons or actually my oldest son who can talk, if he does say things like that I really try to correct him . . . They obviously know that they are girls or boys but not to attach any significance to being a boy or a girl. (Leah)

Leah introduces doubt to requalify subjugated knowledge making women's experiences visible:

> One time he said, "Women don't build houses". And I said, "Well my mum built her own house'" So I got out photos of mum laying bricks and stuff and said, "See women build houses".

Anna consistently explores and names gender stereotypes that intersect with the private localised domain, thus identifying where ideologies of hegemonic masculinity are active:

> So I suppose it's a question of he's going to see that male domination he's going to come across that . . . and understand it in ways that I would like them to . . . little examples like the ads on TV when it's brought up we'll always discuss it, or if I read a story that's got funny gender roles in it, we'll talk about it. (Anna)

Catherine actively includes homosexuality (a distinctively non-normative masculine ideal) as a viable and valid sexual orientation and option for her sons:

> I've tried having more deep and meaningful discussions about their sexuality. I have said to them . . . whoever you are to become, whatever your preferences in the world are for what you want to do, who you want to be with, whatever, that's okay so long as we still love each other and we can still talk about it. And they've gone sure, yeah [*laughter*].

There is deliberate intent behind having these conversations, as Nina explains:

We were in Sydney . . . I said to [my son], you know I used to live in Sydney and where do you think you will like to live, in Sydney or in Melbourne or a different city? And he said, "I want to live with X [his friend]", he said, "a man and a man together". And I said, "Oh that is lovely, darling". So for me . . . I want to give him positive, you know, to allow him. I don't want to say, "Oh that is not what boys do". Or, you know, even question him or give him any idea that something like that might not be acceptable or may only be acceptable in a particular context.

While mothers are relied on to transmit dominant values and endorse hierarchical arrangements of contemporary Western society, feminist mothers cannot be relied on to do this accurately. Feminist maternal practice with sons can construct non-normative value systems, creating a more complex environment in which our sons' masculinities are constituted.

Repositioning Masculine Subjectivities

As mentioned earlier, masculine subjectivities interact with the social context and are always being positioned in relation to discourses about gender. Leah invites her son to engage in practices traditionally ascribed to girls and femininity. She realises that the subject acts on social conditions as well as being constituted by them:

He has always had dolls from a young age. We always had dolls around . . . so yeah that nurturing is still okay, that showing emotion is okay, that you don't have to go out and kick the footy to be a boy, that you can do other things.

By doing this, feminist mothers provide "different possibilities of interacting and positioning" (Staunces 2003, 104) thereby the subject is capable of being repositioned.

Leah goes on to facilitate a process where her son repositions himself, again by introducing an alternative discourse:

I will try and say things like, oh, you know, for a while there he was saying "boys don't like girls; I hate girls". And I said, "What does that mean? Does that mean you hate me? Your auntie? Does that mean you hate your grandmother?" And I named every female friend he had, you know. And he had to think about it and he goes, "Oh no, I don't hate girls".

Men and women are two groups who are relationally constructed and constituted within power-laden discourses of subordination and dominance (Lykke 2010). The gender binary is not neutral; it is hierarchical and it configures the masculine subject in relation to his distance to and rejection of femininity. Masculine subjectivity is constituted in relation to a femininity that does not share the same status. Feminist mothers are concerned that this results in their sons' masculinity being constituted with intentional disregard to their relationship to femininity, as Simran describes:

> It's not even how they get along; that is one aspect, but also to make meaning of themselves in relation to the other. You know, make meaning of themselves so it's not independent of the other because it is interrelated.

Kate attempts to trouble the relativity of the gender binary by developing her sons' awareness of others and the impact of their actions:

> Well, one of the things that is important to me is that they are considerate, that they think before they act and that they think about how they, their actions impinge on others.

Simran addresses this when she talks about recognising anger as a valid emotion but working with her son in developing appropriate ways of expressing this. Thus she hopes to develop his relational self, in part reflecting her concern to undermine male privilege:

> You know, so we worked out ways that he would talk angry and, yeah, maybe he could slam a door because I reckon we have to show angry and I am really loud when I am angry and how can we do that, but how can it be safe? How can it be safe and protected and that we are aware of others in that space?

Feminist mothers of sons have problematised male privilege. In so doing they make conscious decisions to invite their sons to take up non-normative masculinity practices in an effort to undermine male privilege. As Helen describes:

> I guess things that are important to me are that I will try and explain to [my sons] that you don't push people around, and I mean these are very preschool kind of issues. I guess when he gets older they will obviously be more complex ideas. But at the moment you don't push people around, you share, you take it in turns. So these are things that probably a lot of parents would be aware of, but to me it also seems connected to feminism. The idea that you don't let little boys think that they can rule the roost and push little girls around. And not thinking that you are in charge of things and you can rule the roost because you are a boy.

In Helen's description above, she articulates the connection between the standards she expects her son to meet and the way that this will work to mitigate male entitlement. In redefining masculinity, feminist mothers hold their sons accountable to masculinity practices that are in direct opposition to the norm. In the above description, Helen is concerned with undermining male entitlement by expecting him to take turns, share and acknowledge others around him. She does acknowledge that sharing and taking turns can be linked to general parenting practice. However, feminist mothers have identified that gender matters and gender is always being constructed.

Feminist maternal practice works to constitute boys' masculine subjectivities in specific regard to a relationship to women but in different ways than the norm.

> So you know, "Where's my footy jumper?" and I would say, "Oh I don't know". So consciously saying I don't know where your footy jumper is, so you are teaching your kids that women have to have that independence from them, whereas the boys you want them to go their own way but you also wanted them to know that their partners have to go their way as well. (Doreen)

Doreen's description reflects feminist discourses that problematise male privilege and entitlement. Drawing on these ideas, she is clear that she wants her son to both develop a capacity to attend to his own needs and to do so with an understanding that he cannot expect his mother (a woman) to do this for him.

Conversation that draws our sons' attention to gendered practices is an ongoing practice that feminist mothers identify as part of their everyday interaction with their sons. Simran recognises that gendered activity is enacted and re-enacted. Over time her son has begun to take up the role of noticing gendered practices. She starts her example below by describing a recent trip she and her family made to India:

> We were wandering around the streets of Jaipur and [my son] got really shirty at one stage . . . and he is going, "Mum, they are all just looking at you". And I said, "Yes, the men do . . . and it is a gendered response. They look at me because I am a woman . . . and it was gendered and it was sexual" . . . And then we had this lovely conversation about how he could make sense of it. And it was important for him . . . and that he noticed and that an eleven-year-old boy says why are they looking at you, and why are they looking at your breasts? I think he is able to do it because I keep going with it so there is always that retelling of it so I will tell people and I will tell people in front of him and I ask, "What do you think about it? Do you remember that happened?" And so he reflects along with what happened and I do that a lot otherwise things get taken for granted and gender only equals women and is static and there is no reflection or capacity to engage with it.

Teachable moments for feminist mothers of sons are about drawing attention to the gendered meaning that is continually constructed in the social world. They work to draw their sons' attention to this and at the same time take up their sons' noticing of these practices. They describe being open to engaging their sons in conversation as a practice that builds awareness of both male power and privilege but also the way that their social world is continuously informed by gender relations. By articulating the meanings and importance of certain gendered practices to their sons, they are engaging in a core component of doing gender (Fenstermaker and West 2002). The mother constitutes herself and her sons when she identifies discourse that positions both of them. When there is conversation that makes meaning of discourse and enacts alternative discourse, subjectivity is constituted (Davies 1989).

Privileging Non-Normative Practice

As mentioned above, part of the process of hegemonic masculinity is the constitution of our sons' masculine subjectivities in opposition to feminine subjectivities. This is also how the process of hegemonic masculinity conceptualises normative masculinity practices that create gender hierarchies between and amongst men (Connell 2005). Specifically, normative masculinity practices are identifiable through their observable difference to normative femininity practices. However, feminist maternal practice with sons establishes a different contextual environment for the performance of gender. Within this context, boys are not required to behave in ways that resemble normative masculinity. Within the feminist mother and son relation, non-normative behaviours are privileged:

> I think for [my son] being a boy, it is important that he cries. (Bonny)

And when their sons do enact non-normative masculinity behaviours, they are both validated and normalised as Nina describes:

> We let him cry and cuddle him and that sort of thing.

The transformation of gendered subjectivity is predicated on doing gender in ways that are aligned to the contextual norms even if the norms are not standard. And this context needs to be responsive to and supportive of the gendered activity. Feminist maternal practice with boys circulates discursive practices that do not resemble dominant discursive practices and evaluates the alternative as important and acceptable masculinity practice.

Non-normative masculinity practices are not only privileged; they are culturally imposed. When boys do gender in their interaction with their feminist mother, they are required to do gender differently. This is a form of hierarchical accountability where the son is answerable to and evaluated by his mother. Rose's description below is an example of the cultural conditions feminist mothers place on their sons' masculinity practices.

> Well basically, if anybody gets hurt at all, everything stops until the hurt person is seen to all right. If there needs to be an adjustment to the way that the wrestling is happening, like do we need to move a table or should the chair be pushed back further . . . and, yeah, be mindful of your surroundings and if someone is in pain, never ignore it, always stop and see to it, make sure you take care of each other, yeah.

Rose's sons are expected to engage in care-taking practices with each other, attending to pain, hurt and sadness. They are expected to pay attention to the way their bodies move within and around their space and adjust their behaviour accordingly. Importantly, these practices are to be enacted in relation to each other. These ideas are about more than care: they arise from particular values, goals and discourse. Rose establishes standards of behaviour in accordance with non-normative masculinity practices. These behaviours do not reflect or reproduce dominant discourse about gender difference.

CONCLUSION

Feminist mothers of sons' maternal practice can be described as doing gender with their sons. When we do gender, we are adjusting or correcting our behaviour according to standards and measures that are seen to best fit our sex category. These standards and measures are circulated through and in social situations and interaction.

The concept of doing gender argues that accountability is the core component of gender and that the transformation of gendered subjectivities requires the subject recognising the norms that they are being held accountable to and a social context that validates, encourages and supports the subjects' change in orientation to the norms.

Analysis of the interviews shows that the feminist mother and son relationship is a social situation with particular cultural conditions which place expectations and set standards of gendered behaviour. These conditions are responsive to these standards being played out.

In this culture, language, imagery and meanings are articulated that are oppositional to dominant culture. In this way feminist mothers work to disrupt dominant meanings. The mother activates and enforces accountability; thus she is both agent and witness. It is the interpretive action where she is a critical agent. When she responds to the agency of her child in a particular socio-cultural setting, then she is actively constructing cultural meanings and forms of subjectivity.

Feminists theorising social change in gender relations suggest that it is possible for social movements such as feminism to provide the ideology and impetus to question and transform existing arrangements (O'Reilly 2008). Feminist theory and practice have worked hard to address institutional change through restructuring of child-care, maternity and paternity leave, abortion rights and legislative change regarding violence against women (Everingham 1994). Fenstermaker and West (2002) argue that at the institutional level, legislative and policy changes have and may continue to "weaken the accountability of conduct to sex category, thereby affording the possibility of more widespread loosening of accountability in general" (21). I would suggest that, through feminist maternal practice with sons, the everyday mothering context is an extension of, and critical location for, social change. And I argue it is possible, at this domestic and familial interactional level, that feminist maternal practice has and continues to work toward contesting accountability to sex category by inviting our sons to take up non-normative masculine subject positions.

REFERENCES

Beasley, C. 1999. *What Is Feminism?: An Introduction to Feminist Theory*. St. Leonards, NSW: Allen and Unwin.

Biddulph, S. 1998. *Raising Boys: Why Boys Are Different and How to Help Them Become Happy and Well-Balanced Men*. London: Thorsons.

Bly, R. 1992. *Iron John: A Book about Men*. 1st Vintage Books ed. New York: Vintage Books.

Butler, J. 1992. "Contingent Foundations: Feminism and the Question of 'Postmodernism.'" In *Feminists Theorize The Political*, edited by J. Butler and J.W. Scott. New York: Routledge.

Butler, J. 2006. *Gender Trouble: Feminism and the Subversion of Identity, 3rd Edition*. *Thinking Gender*. New York: Routledge.

Chandler, M. 1998. "Emancipated Subjectivities and the Subjugation of Mothering Practices." In *Redefining Motherhood: Changing Identities and Patterns*, edited by S. Abbey and A. O'Reilly. Ontario: Second Story.

Connell, R.W. 2005. *Masculinities*. 2nd ed. Crows Nest NSW: Allen and Unwin.

Davies, B. 1989. *Frogs and Snails and Feminist Tails: Preschool Children and Gender*. North Sydney: Allen and Unwin.

Davis, K. 2008. "Intersectionality as Buzzword: A Sociology of Science Perspective on What Makes a Feminist Theory Successful." *Feminist Theory* 9 (1): 67–85.

Everingham, C. 1994. *Motherhood and Modernity: An Investigation into the Rational Dimension of Mothering*. St. Leonards, NSW: Allen and Unwin.

Fenstermaker, S., and C. West. 2002. *Doing Gender, Doing Difference: Inequality, Power, and Institutional Change*. New York: Routledge.

Firestone, S. 1979. *The Dialectic of Sex*. London: Women's Press.

Foucault, M. 1998. *The History of Sexuality, Vol. 1: The Will to Knowledge*. London: Penguin Books.

Gardiner, J.K. 2002. "Theorizing Age and Gender: Bly's Boys, Feminism, and Maturity Masculinity." In *Masculinity Studies and Feminist Theory: New Directions*, edited by J.K. Gardiner. New York: Columbia University Press.

Green, F. 2004. "Feminist Mothers: Successfully Negotiating the Tensions Between Motherhood as 'Institution' and 'Experience.'" In *Mother Outlaws: Theories and Practices of Empowered Mothering*, edited by A. O'Reilly. Toronto: Women's Press.

Horwitz, E. 2004. "Resistance as a Site of Empowerment: The Journey away from Maternal Sacrifice." In *Mother Outlaws: Theories and Practices of Empowered Mothering*, edited by A. O'Reilly. Toronto: Women's Press.

Jeremiah, E. 2006. "Motherhood to Mothering and Beyond: Maternity in Recent Feminist Thought." *Journal of the Association for Research on Mothering* 8 (1/2): 21–33.

Lykke, N. 2010. *Feminist Studies: A Guide to Intersectional Theory, Methodology and Writing*. New York: Routledge.

Mansfield, N. 2000. *Subjectivity: Theories of the Self from Freud to Haraway*. Crows Nest NSW: Allen and Unwin.

Messner, M.A. 2000. "Barbie Girls versus Sea Monsters: Children Constructing Gender." *Gender and Society* 14 (6): 765–784.

O'Reilly, A. 2001. *Mothers & Sons: Feminism, Masculinity, and the Struggle to Raise Our Sons*. New York: Routledge.

O'Reilly, A. 2008. *Feminist Mothering*. New York: State University of New York Press.

Risman, B.J. 2008. "From Doing to Undoing: Gender as We Know It." *Gender and Society* 23:81–84.

Risman, B.J., and K. Myers. 1997. "As the Twig Is Bent: Children Reared in Feminist Households." *Qualitative Sociology* 20 (2): 229–252.

Smith, B. 1996. *Mothers and Sons: The Truth about Mother–Son Relationships*. Sydney: Allen and Unwin.

Staunces, D. 2003. "Where Have All the Subjects Gone? Bringing Together the Concepts of Intersectionality and Subjectification." *NORA: Nordic Journal of Women's Studies* 11 (2): 101.

Threadgold, T., and A. Cranny-Francis. 1990. *Feminine, Masculine and Representation*. Sydney: Allen and Unwin.

West, C., and D.H. Zimmerman. 1987. "Doing Gender." *Gender and Society* 1 (2): 125–151.

West, C., and D.H. Zimmerman. 2009. "Accounting for Doing Gender." *Gender and Society* 23 (1): 112–122.

Part II

Recognising Resistant Sexualities

5 Conceptualising Disabled Sexual Subjectivity

Russell Shuttleworth

INTRODUCTION

The concept of the human subject suffered some damaging blows to its authority toward the end of the twentieth century. Following on from structuralism, post-structuralism in a de-centring move discredited the subject as a limiting and nefarious product of the Enlightenment. The Western subject was characterised as insular, closed off from the other and encased in a prison of insoluble but unstable binaries and hierarchies. Among post-modern efforts to theorise against the restrictions of the subject have been to dissolve it into desire, relationality or connectivity. Images of hybrids and cyborgs have also been championed as transgressive of a range of binaries, including subject–object and control–lack of control. For some critical disability studies scholars in the new millennium sympathetic to post-modern perspectives, these ideas and images fit with the fact that disability often requires prostheses or other technological aids, as well as personal assistants. Thus, a social and/or technological relationality or connectivity is increasingly being theorised in terms of disability (Gibson 2006; Shildrick 2009, 2012; Fritsch 2010; Goodley and Lawthom 2012). Moving beyond the modernist binaries also fits with those efforts to reimagine the restrictive dualisms that have structured the various socio-political models of, for example, individual versus social, social versus medical, impairment versus disability. Then, too, for some of these scholars, disability has become something of a key figure of human identity or embodiment, with all its inherent vulnerability and fragility (Davis 2003; Turner 2006; Shildrick 2009). In this chapter, I do not wish to discredit this conceptual narrative, what Shildrick (2009, 2012) characterises as a "post-conventional" approach to disability. In many ways, post perspectives offer significant insight into the constitution of disability in the twenty-first century. However, in the final analysis I want to provide a vision of disability that retains what I believe is a critical space for an agentic subjectivity, one that can work in productive tandem with a diversity of differently embodied disabled people together to transform the negative understanding of disability that permeates Western societies.

In opting for what might appear on the surface to be a less radical approach to the 'problem' of disability, I draw from the conceptual framework of Cornelius Castoriadis, a social theorist of a decidedly more modernist bent but with a twist on the usual Enlightenment pre-eminence of reason. Castoriadis demoted reason beneath the imagination as the most distinguishing feature of human being, which had wide-ranging implications for his theorisation of psyche and society. He nevertheless clearly saw the closure and determinism that continually worked against this primary imagination. Castoriadis's most trenchant criticisms on this front were aimed at the determinism inherent in the functionalist, Marxist and structuralist approaches within the human sciences during the first two-thirds of the twentieth century (Castoriadis 1987; Klooger 2009; Adams 2011), and he similarly saw the implications of post-modern and post-structural approaches in the latter part of the century as an abdication of responsibility and conceding critical imagination to conformism—a reflection of the conformism that he saw occurring within the West as a whole (Castoriadis 1997b). As he put it, "All this talk of the death of man and the end of the subject has never been anything other than a pseudo-theoretical cover for an evasion of responsibility—on the part of the psychoanalyst, the thinker, the citizen" (1989, 5).

Castoriadis's promotion of the imagination as that which precedes any rationality or symbolism should in part be read against perspectives mentioned above that attempt to divest human subjectivity (read rational subject) of not simply executive function but also any operative value whatsoever; that is, those de-centring approaches which have been pressed into action recently within critical disability studies, as they have previously in feminism, race theory, queer theory and gender studies. While I cannot abide by Castoriadis's wholesale dismissal of these 'post' perspectives in which he elaborates on their weaknesses and does not concede that they may have either elucidatory or strategic usefulness, I nevertheless ally myself with his belief that a critical space for the autonomous subject working in dynamic tension with the quest for political autonomy needs to be maintained in theories of psyche and society. Elucidation of this process can provide insight into how individual agents and collectivities work toward and often effect socio-cultural transformation. The subject matter for this exploration of individual and collective agency is the current carving out a space for sexual subjectivity by disabled people. Disabled people can harbour both ordinary and extraordinary sexual hopes and desires, and, depending on their corporeal differences, may express themselves in innovative ways. Claiming a sexual subjectivity derived from not only their 'apparent' differences, but also their similarities with 'non-disabled' people, disabled people are in the process of transforming understanding of their sexuality. I begin this elucidation by describing a recent event in the popular culture that some disabled people and their allies, myself included, initially felt as a 'shock'.

DISABLED PEOPLE'S 'REAL SEX' LIVES?

The key event was proclaimed in a news story that circulated disability listservs and which appeared in *USA Today* in late November 2012. The following is a brief excerpt:

> The pursuit of sex is certainly not a new subject in Hollywood. But when the characters are disabled, as seen in a host of award-caliber movies this fall, then it denotes a remarkable shift. This natural drive looms large and unmistakable in the disabled subjects' minds in movies ranging from *The Sessions, Rust and Bone . . . The Intouchables* and even with the polio-survivor Franklin Delano Roosevelt in *Hyde Park on Hudson*. (Alexander 2012)

Implicit in the news story is an apparent media turn to focusing on disabled people's sexual lives. As Carter-Long put it later in the story, "we haven't seen sexuality in terms of disability displayed like this before" (Alexander 2012). Previously, representation of disabled sex in the mainstream media was minimal and highly stereotyped, and even those depictions that glimpsed the occasional moment of convergence with disabled people's actual concerns eventually succumbed to the well-worn images. Carter-Long also refers to the possibility that the audience may have grown tired of the same old representation of disability. Which begs the question, does the audience now crave the depiction of disabled people's 'real' sex lives? And does the making of these mainstream films that deal with the issue of sexuality and disability in more 'realistic' and less stereotypical ways actually represent the beginnings of a shift in the Western social imaginary or just a Hollywood fad that will quickly fold?

As a longtime personal assistant and sexual advocate for disabled people, as well as a researcher on sexuality and disability, I have been close to their struggle for sexual rights during much of the past twenty years. There has been a steady growth during this time of disabled people's resistance to hegemonic restrictions on their sexual lives and the claiming of their sexual subjectivity. In fact, several antecedent signs, albeit not causal, nevertheless assist in contextualising this 'breakthrough' in the mainstream media, which may signify the beginning of a cultural shift. For their part, the disability rights and the sexuality rights movements, along with academic writings in feminism, race theory and queer theory, have revealed the oppressions and silencing of a range of minority voices. Harlan Hahn's work in the 1980s on sexuality and disability (1981, 1988), which culminated in his article, "Can Disability Be Beautiful?" (1988), must be acknowledged as seminal in the emergence of disability as inclusive of desirability. Disabled scholars and researchers and sundry programs and conferences that contributed to this effort during the late 1980s through the 1990s include Barbara Waxman, Anne Finger, Corbett O'Toole, Carol Gill, Tom Shakespeare,

Kath Gillespie-Sells and Dominic Davies, the University of California, San Francisco's short-lived Sexuality and Disability Program, Mitch Tepper's SexualHealth.com and several sexuality and disability conferences in San Francisco at the turn of the millennium.

More recently, television shows such as *Cast Offs* in the UK on Channel 4 have provided a much more realistic vision of disabled people's lives, including their sexuality. More specific to sexuality are showcases such as Sins Invalid, which presents a diversity of disabled artists who perform their sexuality on stage (via short drama pieces, skits, poetry, film, etc.) to an audience. The artists' explicit intent in these performances is to transform the cultural understanding of what constitutes a desiring and desirable body. Of course, sporadic references to sexuality and disability themes have been part and parcel of disability performance art in general, but Sins Invalid revels in transgressive eroticism. Then again, the infamous performance artist Frank Moore has been performing erotically and nude for over thirty years, usually including the audience participating in and the filming of these performances (see his videos on Vimeo). If we look at the global context, the proliferation of local and transnational media representation of the sexual lives of disabled people and importantly less stereotypical sexual images certainly counters the long-standing cultural perception of their asexuality.

In an analysis of research I conducted in the mid-to-late 1990s, in which I had extensively interviewed fourteen men on their search for sexual intimacy, I argued that the majority of disabled men I interviewed moved back and forth from incorporation of hegemonic notions of desire and desirability to resistance to these ideas (and sometimes both occurring within the same situation), which became manifest in both their understanding and their practices. However, several men had developed an ethical aesthetics of the self, forged in their resistance to hegemonic notions of desire and desirability, in line with Foucault's rendering of this notion late in his career (Shuttleworth 2000, 2002). That is, employing both old and new Western practices of self-management and care, they were able to carve out an ethical relation to the adverse contexts of disability and desirability that they traversed. The three men who managed to carve out these practices of the self were highly successful lovers. At the time, since I was theorising these latter men's sense of sexual self through a Foucauldian lens, I implicitly restricted my view of resistance within the circle of power of his account of the subject.

Yet, as Tovar-Restrepo (2012) argues more recently, Foucault did not possess the conceptual tools to adequately theorise the process of the generation of different subjectivities adequately:

> Foucault through his lifetime work, had theorized the subject as entirely constructed through social practices without developing a solid theory of individual subjectification, which made him unable to conceive

emancipation coherently. . . . In his later development Foucault worked with a notion of the subject that implied dimensions and aspects for which he had no ultimate explanation. . . . To talk about a process that would free the individual from social constraints to become more autonomous, required theoretical tools that Foucault never elaborated. (107)

Therefore, as useful as Foucault's thinking is for his understanding of the implicit restrictions of normativity, to adequately theorise a more nuanced understanding of the formation of diverse subjectivities, individual and collective resistance and the larger goal of social transformation, other conceptual frameworks are necessary.

THEORISING THE SEXUAL LIVES OF DISABLED PEOPLE

The landscape in sexuality and disability theorising has moved well beyond the mid-1990s when *The Sexual Politics of Disability* was released (Shakespeare, Gillespie-Sells and Davies 1996). Shakespeare et al.'s research in the United Kingdom was conceived and implemented primarily within the parameters of the British social model and provided disabled people with a much needed voice to talk about the many barriers they face to their sexual participation but nevertheless also about their resistance to sexual oppression and taking up the banner of sexual rights. In my radicalisation of the notion of access beyond its traditional meaning in disability studies (Shuttleworth 2000, 2007; Grossman et al 2013), I attempted to incorporate an understanding of how the structural, symbolic, social and interrelational all worked in conjunction to construct barriers for disabled people in their sexual lives, which ostensibly constructed them as asexual. I perceived that the connections between the myriad socio-political structures and cultural meanings interwove to create the myth of disabled peoples' asexuality and with which they existentially contended with on an everyday level in trying to access sexual well-being. I also believed it socially responsible and necessary to show how some disabled people, despite the adverse context of disability and desirability they faced, managed to create for themselves through the employment of various conventional and unconventional strategies, significant sexual lives, while others simply resigned themselves to a life with less sexual intimacy. Hence my employment of the notion of resistance and Foucault's practices of the self (Shuttleworth 2000, 2002).

Recent theorisation has taken the intersection of sexuality and disability into uncharted terrain. Tremain (2000) and Sherry (2004) were early pioneers in the effort to introduce queer theory into the conceptual mix. Also notable is Wilkerson's (2002) work, which employs the concept of cultural erotophobia, an irrational reaction to eroticism which suggests a shamefulness associated with sex, to highlight some of the sexual harms that are perpetrated on disabled people, as well as other marginalised others. McRuer and Wilkerson's (2003) important group of essays, "Desiring Disability: Queer Theory Meets Disability Studies", is also noteworthy in setting the scene for the introduction of queer approaches in sexuality and disability.

The most ambitious and conceptually rich understanding of sexuality and disability presented recently has been that of Margrit Shildrick (2009), who also employs queer theory to good effect in her work. In a theoretical tour de force, Shildrick develops her understanding by employing a range of theories, including those of Foucault, Butler, Derrida and Lacan, which she characterises as a "post-conventional" approach. Shildrick argues against modernist binaries and their constitution of what counts as an embodied subject; she perceives the autonomous subject as threatened by the corporeal instability that, albeit universally present, is most exemplified by disabled people's functional differences. This anxiety becomes most acute in the vulnerability of sexual encounters and thus is crucial in the aversion non-disabled people have toward disabled people as sexual partners. More specifically, Shildrick theorises that the child's suppression of a fragmented self in order to achieve "a normatively embodied subject", which occurs in Lacan's mirror stage, can re-emerge as a corporeal anxiety toward and repudiation of bodily difference, and "always recalls the self's incompletely repressed experience of infantile disorganisation" (2009, 90). Continuing along these lines, Shildrick finally abandons her previous employment of Lacan because his conception of subjectivity and desire is constituted by lack. She instead turns to Deleuze's understanding of productive desire:

> In place of prohibition, repression and disavowal, Deleuzian desire is expansive, fluid, connective, grounding sexuality itself as highly plastic and as no longer reliant on the terms of any binary oppositions such as those of male/female, active/passive or human/animal. And because the emphasis shifts from the integrity of the whole organism to focus instead on the material and momentary event of the coming together and disparate parts, bodies need no longer be thought of as either whole or broken, able-bodied or disabled, but simply in a process of becoming through the unmapped circulation of desire. (2009, 134–135)

Shildrick conceptualises socio-sexual transformation via Deleuze's vision of productive desire and his radicalisation of connectivity. She perceives Deleuze's understanding as fitting more with the explicit interconnections that disabled embodiment often requires, most visibly via the use of prostheses and the assistance from others in, for example, personal care routines. Again, it is not that disabled people are unique in their experience of interconnectivity, but that it is usually obscured for 'normative' others because of its threat to their 'sovereignty' as autonomous subjects. Thus, despite interrogating the dynamics involved in disabled people's sexual stigmatisation, in part Shildrick's larger Deleuzian inspired project is to show how the modernist sexual subject is a major stumbling block toward perceiving a "subjectivity [that] only emerges through the erotics of connection" (2009, 14).

Other post-conventional scholars who focus on sexuality and disability while perhaps not drawing as explicit a boundary as Shildrick does between post theories and modernist theories of the subject nevertheless tend to dismiss the latter (Gibson 2006; Shildrick 2009, 2012; Fritsch 2010; Goodley and Lawthom 2012). Thus, it is understandable given this blanket eschewing of the modernist subject that post approaches ignore Castoriadis's innovative elucidation of the mutually affecting projects of autonomous subjectivity and political autonomy (see below). Tellingly, Shildrick herself cannot wholly do without the notion of the subject in her work, as she talks about "subject effects" as still being involved in the fluid relationality and connectivity she posits. But the question should nevertheless be asked, what would the function of these subject effects be? And additionally, mightn't it be possible that there are understandings of sexuality and disability, no less innovative than the positing of productive desire, that have yet to be fully drawn out which are not strictly post-conventional?

Implicit in my last question is a point of divergence that is occurring between two different approaches taking form in CDS. One strand dichotomises approaches between 'modernist' and 'post-conventional' approaches and implicitly perceives the latter as the only theories that matter. This strand of theorising appears to take the socially relevant notion of post-modernity at face value without critically reflecting on its divisive function as a convenient fiction to obscure a complex socio-cultural continuum and advocates an either-or position (you are with us post-conventionalist theorists who are on the cutting edge of theorisation of disability or against us in your simplistic theorising with outmoded concepts of modernity). The other 'seemingly' less radical strand cannot adhere to this dichotomisation of theories that the former implies is necessary (Meekosha and Shuttleworth 2009; Shuttleworth and Meekosha 2012; Meekosha, Shuttleworth and Soldatic 2013; Soldatic, forthcoming). Rather than view the processes that form "'the illusory' subject" as those that must be abandoned for those that promote relationality and a fluid connectivity, the second strand doesn't necessarily perceive them as in opposition. As a proponent of this second strand, I myself follow Castoriadis in believing that the maintenance of a critical space for autonomous subjectivity and the striving for political autonomy is crucial to assist both individuals and social movements in transforming social relations and in this case disabled people's socio-sexual relations.

THE PSYCHE AND SOCIETY IN CASTORIADIS

In Castoriadis's theory the individual psyche as radical imagination and society as social imaginary are two poles that are mutually inherent and generative, and not totally derived from or determinant of each other. As Castoriadis puts it, they "lean on" each other and remain in creative tension. Castoriadis anchors an understanding of the psyche, what is originally the "psychical monad," in his notion of the "radical imagination" as imaginative flux, that is, as the continual creation of forms. Castoriadis conceives the living being or body to have a corporeal imagination that responds to the "shocks" it receives from the external world. In human beings, however, this bodily imagination has been appended by an "incessant flux that is at once representational, intentional, and affective", an imagination that in short is now defunctionalised (Castoriadis 1997a, 178). This imaginative flux in fact cannot be distinguished from the psyche, which undercuts both Freudian and Lacanian forms of psychoanalysis. McNay (2000) makes this point succinctly, "Understood as a process of originary phantasmatization, the radical imagination pre-exists and presides over every organization of the drives, even the most primitive ones" (136). In terms of Lacanian psychoanalysis, his assumption of a specular structure to the imaginary, which is reduced to a misrecognition of a fragmented self as autonomous, cannot provide any explanation why the child is "first impelled to identify, invest, and recognize itself in the mirror or from the gaze of the other" (McNay 2000, 137).

Although Castoriadis discusses weaker senses of the subject within psychical reality throughout his writings, he also employed a stronger sense of subjectivity. In this account, the subject cannot be naively considered natural by any stretch of the imagination. For Castoriadis, subjectivity in this stronger sense can never be assumed: it "is virtual in every human being, but it is certainly not a fated process" (1989, 37). Here, Castoriadis conceives of subjectivity as a project that strives for critical distance between the processes that shape and form the psychical being and the social individual; that is, a project that aims for an autonomy in which the conditions of its closure and thus determination are continually put into question. "It is a matter of not being slave to the Unconscious, that is to say, it is a matter of being capable of stopping oneself from speaking out or acting out, while being conscious of the drives and of the desires that push one in that direction. It is this sort of subjectivity that can be autonomous and it is this kind of relation that is autonomy" (Castoriadis 1997a, 190). While the radical imagination assures that the individual can never fully close themselves off from the process of creative change—the strict iterability of thought or deed is in fact an impossibility—it is the autonomous subject, aware of its socially derived and psychic impulses and that it can affect its relations to them, that is best able to not only transform itself, but in whom lies the best possibility for socio-cultural critique and transformation.

For Castoriadis, the psyche becomes individual when it undergoes a process of socialisation. The psychical monad cannot survive without relinquishing its omnipotence and becoming socialised into the world of others. Far from responding to a lack, this process provides the psyche and radical imagination, with access to the social imaginary significations of its society:

> whose instauration and incredible coherence (the differentiated and articulated homology of its parts as well as their synergy) goes unimaginably beyond everything that "one or many individuals" could ever produce. These significations owe their actual (social-historical) existence to the fact that they are instituted. They are not reducible to transubstantiation of psychical drives: sublimation is the psychical side of the process whose social side is the fabrication of the individual. (Castoriadis 1991a, 62)

The social imaginary thus encompasses the symbolic, the ideological and the mythical with these codes "interwoven, and . . . characterized by an oscillation between the tendencies to impose order and to self-alteration" (McNay 2000, 144). Castoriadis's understanding of society, of what he terms the social-historical, is that social action always contains an instituting and creative moment but that there is always a strong pull toward perceiving what has already previously been instituted as autonomous, determined and beyond the ability to change. However, some change no matter how gradual occurs in all societies due to this oscillation.

Similar to his reserving a space for the autonomous subject, Castoriadis also perceives a political space where a society's laws and determinisms in general can be continually challenged and open to critique. Castoriadis's political project has the aim of creating an autonomous society. He argues that traditionally societies have had a heteronomous relation with their institutions; that is, they attribute final authority to an aspect external to that society, e.g. God, science. Thus, the deterministic imposition of order is fully externalised. However, the political aim should be an awareness of that fact that only society can posit its institutions, and thus can revoke and change them through direct democratic process. Further, Castoriadis perceives the primary aim of these institutions to be "the creation of autonomous individuals" (1997a, 190). On the political level, autonomy is an ethically normative goal that does not posit how or what a society should do, just that a critical reflectiveness remain open and can feed into manifesting autonomous subjects.

Both the autonomous subject and political autonomy, however, do not mean a project of autonomy aimed at the creation of sovereign individuals, closed in upon themselves, with strict self-interests and opposed to relations with the other. In fact, Castoriadis's notion of autonomy is inherently relational, which is in line with those feminists who have argued against the extremism of some critiques of this concept (Mackenzie and Stoljar 2000). As Castoriadis (1987) emphasises, "if autonomy is the relation in which others are always present as the otherness and as the self-ness of the subject, then autonomy can be conceived of, even in philosophical terms, only as a social problem and as a social relation" (108). As McNay observes, for Castoriadis:

> Autonomy involves . . . the establishment of another relation between the discourse of the Other and the subject's discourse, a relation of activity-passivity where the subject critically reflects upon the relation between the self and the imaginary relations in which she is situated. The content of the self neither belongs to the self nor the other; rather there is a 'produced and productive union' of the self and other. . . . As a relation in which the other is always present, autonomy cannot be conceptualised as a moment of pure subjectivity; rather it leads to a broader notion of sociality and politics. (2000, 152–153)

In maintaining a relational aspect to the autonomous subject and as an essential feature in the project of political autonomy, Castoriadis effectively issues a challenge to post-conventional critiques of autonomy. That these perspectives have conveniently ignored feminist conceptualisations of relational autonomy (Mackenzie and Stoljar 2000), as well as Castoriadis's elucidation, appears to point toward the setting up of a static, closed-off, autonomous straw man who cannot stand up to the seductive vision of an orgy of fluid connectivities. Contrary to post-conventional critiques, Castoriadis's theoretical frame makes it possible to work with the notion of the subject instead of abandoning it as bereft and not relevant for 'late modernity'. A critical but relational subject can move between moments of critical reflection and decision making and interpersonal and embodied connections and relations of self–other. Castoriadis's understanding enables us to theorise social transformation as autonomous individuals and social movements striving towards and carving out an autonomous society together.

DISABLED SEXUAL SUBJECTIVITY

In the psyche's embryonic ego development, there may well be dynamics that initially incline it to imagine the other as threatening to its 'illusory' cohesion (not only in Western societies but perhaps in some form across cultures), but there is no justification for the point of view that the subject cannot subsequently imagine a positive relationality and critically counter an original imagining of the repudiation of difference. The strong relations, interconnections and bonds of friendship that I have witnessed between disabled and non-disabled people within the disability rights movement in the past thirty years, as well as many sexual relationships between disabled and non-disabled people of diverse sexualities, including several of my own relationships with disabled women, would seem proof of the possibility of the recuperation of difference in sexual intimacy. That these relationships are often atypical in their appearances and can include personal assistants, wheelchairs, leg-bags and prostheses may indeed make visible an inherent corporeal instability and point to the significance of interdependence, relationality and connectivity as less hierarchical ways of imagining embodied process. However, any initial connections made between persons either in fleeting or full-blown sexual relationships nevertheless necessitate bringing into play distinctions and agentic choices around such interpersonal aspects as familiarity, compatibility and attraction. Intimate and sexual relations are especially forged in the hit and miss of the current search for a "pure relationship" (Giddens 1992). That 'impairments' and 'functioning' did not figure much into partner choices may indicate that they were critically re-imagined by autonomous subjects as markers of desirability for those involved.

Whilst interesting and perhaps useful to enable individual disabled men and women to apprehend the range of ways and ethical positions by which other disabled people contend with their sexual stigmatisation and the strategies they employ to access sexual well-being, Foucault's notions of practices of the self and also his understanding of resistance are nevertheless inadequate to fully apprehend the dynamics at play in the constitution of a non-negatively perceived sexual subjectivity. To be sure, resistance can never stand exterior to power in that it is initially a response to power and both derive from the same context. However, this does not mean there can be no creative emergence stemming from a particular resistant act and that new socio-cultural forms are prohibited. Foucault's later problematic about how there could be a "transformation of power regimes through the promotion of new forms of subjectivity" (Tovar-Restrepo 2012, 121), which, it is generally accepted, he failed to adequately theorise, is productively opened up by Castoriadis's innovative approach. It is thus the inability to imagine an agentic subject, either individual or social, during the process of resistance that actually limits our creative vision. In Castoriadis's terms, the social-historical as instituted-instituting, determinism and creation, form a non-synthetic dynamic. Thus, there is always a moment of creation and undetermined remainder within any social activity, including resistance. Therefore, any act of resistance by either an individual or a social movement can potentially alter the already instituted terms, and across time invariably does so. In this regard Castoriadis especially highlights the transformative power of new social movements such as the women's movement and the environmental movement (e.g. Castoriadis 1981, 1991b).

Perceived through a Castoriadian lens, the resisting and challenging of hegemonic norms of desire and desirability that is occurring amongst disabled people shows autonomous individuals (performers, writers, researchers, filmmakers) and social collectivities such as Sins Invalid in San Francisco, and the Sexuality and Disability Alliance in Melbourne, a group whose members include young disabled people, critically working in tandem for a positive change in the perception of their sexuality. Commitment to an imaginative vision for socio-sexual change is a requisite and demands working against the determinism inherent within instituted society by continually siding with the instituting and creative moment. For example, the latter group above is engaged in drafting policy guidelines for sexual facilitation in Victoria, which entails research with a range of disabled people, much discussion with all constituents and countering normative resistance encountered along the way (Shuttleworth, forthcoming). Indeed, while the media move towards less stereotypical representation of disabled people's sexual lives likely bodes well for a positive change in perception, disabled sexuality will no doubt continue to threaten a naïve normative sexuality (including both heteronormativity and bodily normativity) and encounter resistance in multiple ways for some time yet. Nevertheless, it will be disabled people, their lovers and allies whose positive presentation of disabled sexuality, dedication to their imaginative and collective vision and on-the-ground work that will offer the most trenchant critique of that norm and which may eventually effect changes to sexual subjectivity and sociosexual relations in general.1

CONCLUSION

For those critical disability studies scholars who follow a strictly post-conventional approach and view the modernist subject as that illusory structure which presents a barrier to recognition of disabled people's difference as other than 'other', to facilitate disabled people's sexual subjectivity would seem a ludicrous aim. The innovative understanding of sexuality and disability that these scholars are developing is a testament to imaginative thinking. Yet, their positing of an all-or-nothing approach to socio-sexual transformation (e.g. modernist versus post-modernist, stable identities versus fluid identities, egocentric subject versus relationality and connectivity) is narrowly construed. Attempts to be more varied in one's conceptual approach, providing multiple perspectives, which may not immediately fit within a strictly non-binary or hierarchically transcendent schema are not considered or summarily dismissed. However, markers between temporal periods, whether they be historical markers or implicitly meant to indicate the self-referential 'progress' of a certain theoretical approach are convenient, although not entirely without evidence, fictions and cannot convey the complexity of experiences and interpretations that are occurring on the ground. In fact, the employment of hybrid theoretical frameworks incorporating various perspectives both 'conventional' and 'post-conventional' may provide a more experiential understanding (how many of our participants still employ modernist binaries in their understanding?) and orientative map toward a gradual but nevertheless creative socio-sexual transformation than the idealism of strict 'post-conventional' approaches. Indeed, a world in which the subject and its divisive defences to difference are dissolved and in which the differences of disabled people, unencumbered by negative attributions, are viewed as positive exemplars fits neatly with the transcendence of binaries, the transgressive image of hybrids and Deleuze's theorisation of desire as expansive, fluid and connective. But the critical and autonomous subject as Castoriadis renders her is a necessary prerequisite to posit this future panacea.

NOTES

1. The conceptualisation of disabled sexual subjectively in this chapter has unfortunately not engaged with the issue of intellectual disability. Future work might explore the difficult issue of how to nurture a sense of sexual critique and relational autonomy with this population both individually and collectively.

REFERENCES

Adams, S. 2011. *Castoriadis's Ontology: Being and Creation*. New York: Fordham University Press.

Alexander, B. 2012. "Hollywood Wakes Up to Disability and Sexuality." *USA Today*, November 24. http://www.usatoday.com/story/life/movies/2012/11/24/disabled-sex- movies/1654411/. Accessed 10 December, 2012.

Castoriadis, C. 1981. "From Ecology to Autonomy." *Thesis Eleven* 3:8–22.

Castoriadis, C. 1987. *The Imaginary Institution of Society*. Translated by K. Blamey. Cambridge, MA: MIT Press.

Castoriadis, C. 1989. "The State of the Subject Today." *Thesis Eleven* 24:5–43.

Castoriadis, C. 1991a. "Individual, Society, Rationality, History." In *Philosophy, Politics, Autonomy: Essays in Political Autonomy*, edited by D.A. Curtis. New York: Oxford University Press.

Castoriadis, C. 1991b. "Reflections on 'Rationality' and 'Development': Presentation and Response to Critics." In *Philosophy, Politics, Autonomy: Essays in Political Autonomy*, edited by D.A. Curtis. New York: Oxford University Press.

Castoriadis, C. 1997a. "From the Monad to Autonomy." In *World in Fragments: Writings on Politics, Society, Psychoanalysis and the Imagination*, edited and translated by D.A. Curtis. Stanford, CA: Stanford University Press.

Castoriadis, C. 1997b. "The Retreat from Autonomy: Postmodernism as Generalized Conformism." In *World in Fragments: Writings on Politics, Society, Psychoanalysis and the Imagination*, edited and translated by D.A. Curtis. Stanford, CA: Stanford University Press.

Davis, L. 2003. *Bending over Backwards: Essays on Disability and the Body*. New York: New York University Press.

Fritsch, K. 2010. "Intimate Assemblages: Disability, Intercorporeality, and the Labour of Attendant Care." *Critical Disability Discourse* 2. http://pi.library.yorku.ca/ojs/index.php/cdd/article/viewFile/23854/28098. Accessed 17 December, 2012.

Gibson, B. 2006. "Disability, Connectivity and Transgressing the Autonomous Body." *Journal of Medical Humanities* 27:187–196.

Giddens, A. 1992. *The Transformation of Intimacy: Sexuality, Love and Eroticism in Modern Societies*. Stanford, CA: Stanford University Press.

Goodley, D., and R. Lawthom. 2012. "Disability, Deleuze and Sex." In *Deleuze and Sex*, edited by F. Beckman. Edinburgh: Edinburgh University Press.

Grossman, B., Shuttleworth, R., and Philip Prinz. 2003. "Locating Sexuality in Disability Experience, A Report from Disability Studies: Theory, Policy, and Practice, The Inaugural Conference of the Disability Studies Association. *Sexuality Research and Social Policy* 1:91–96.

Hahn, H. 1981. "The Social Component of Sexuality and Disability." *Sexuality and Disability* 4:220–233.

Hahn, H. 1988. "Can Disability Be Beautiful?" *Social Policy* 18:26–32.

Klooger, J. 2009. *Castoriadis, Psyche, Society, Autonomy.* Leiden: Brill.

Mackenzie, C., and N. Stoljar. 2000. "Introduction: Autonomy refigured." In *Relational Autonomy: Feminist Perspectives on Autonomy, Agency, and the Social Self,* edited by C. Mackenzie and N. Stoljar. New York: Oxford University Press.

McNay, L. 2000. *Gender and Agency: Reconsidering the Subject in Feminist and Social Theory.* Cambridge: Polity.

McRuer, R., and A. Wilkerson, eds. 2003. "Desiring Disability: Queer Theory Meets Disability Studies." A special issue of *GLQ: A Journal of Lesbian and Gay Studies* 9 (1/2).

Meekosha, H., and R. Shuttleworth. 2009. "What's So Critical about Critical Disability Studies?" *Australian Journal of Human Rights* 15 (1): 47–75.

Meekosha, H., Shuttleworth, R., and K. Soldatic. 2013. "Disability and Critical Sociology: Expanding the Boundaries of Critical Social Inquiry." *Critical Sociology* 39:319–323.

Shakespeare, T., K. Gillespie-Sells and D. Davies 1996. *The Sexual Politics of Disability: Untold Desires.* New York: Cassell.

Sherry, M. 2004. "Overlaps and Contradictions between Queer Theory and Disability Studies." *Disability and Society* 19:769–783.

Shildrick, M. 2009. *Dangerous Discourses of Disability, Subjectivity and Sexuality.* New York: Palgrave Macmillan.

Shildrick, M. 2012. "Critical Disability Studies: Rethinking the Conventions for the Age of Postmodernity." In *Routledge Handbook of Disability Studies,* edited by N. Watson, C. Thomas and A. Roulstone. New York: Routledge.

Shuttleworth, R. 2000. "The Pursuit of Sexual Intimacy for Men with Cerebral Palsy." Unpublished dissertation, University of California, San Francisco and Berkeley.

Shuttleworth, R. 2002. "Defusing the Adverse Context of Disability and Desirability as a Practice of the Self for Men with Cerebral Palsy." In *Disability and Postmodernity,* edited by M. Corker and T. Shakespeare. London: Continuum.

Shuttleworth, R. 2007. "Disability and Sexuality: Toward a Constructionist Approach to Access and Inclusion of Disabled People in the Sexual Rights Movement." *Sexual Inequalities and Social Justice,* edited by N. Teunis and G. Herdt. Berkeley: University of California Press.

Shuttleworth, R., and H. Meekosha. 2012. "The Sociological Imaginary and Disability Enquiry in Late Modernity." *Critical Sociology.* doi:10.1177/0896920511435709.

Shuttleworth, R. Forthcoming "The Sexuality and Disability Alliance: Occupying Disabled People's Sexual Lives." In *Occupying Disability: Identity, Community and Justice,* edited by P. Block, N. Pollard and D. Kasnitz. New York: Springer.

Soldatic, K. Forthcoming. "Transnational Justice: Disability Praxis and the Politics of Impairment." *Disability & Society.*

Tovar-Restrepo, M. 2012. *Castoriadis, Foucault, and Autonomy: New Approaches to Subjectivity, Society and Social Change.* London: Continuum.

Turner, B. 2006. *Vulnerability and Human Rights.* University Park: Pennsylvania State University Press.

Tremain, S. 2000. "Queering Disabled Sexuality Studies." *Sexuality and Disability* 18 (4): 291–299.

Wilkerson, A. 2002. "Disability, Sex Radicalism, and Political Agency." *NWSA Journal* 14 (3): 33–57.

6 "New Rules, No Rules, Old Rules or Our Rules"

Women Designing Mixed-Orientation Relationships with Bisexual Men

Maria Pallotta-Chiarolli

INTRODUCTION

> If you're not being hurt and if you're not being coerced, then it is actually possible to design a relationship with a bisexual man. (Monica, 31, 15 years)

This chapter draws from an Australian semi-structured interview project with seventy-eight culturally, sexually and geographically diverse women, aged nineteen to sixty-five, who were in monogamous, open and polyamorous marital and de facto relationships with bisexual men, abbreviated as MOREs (mixed-orientation relationships).[1]

To date, health service providers, as well as the neoliberal 'self-help' genre, are misrecognising MOREs by defining them only as 'straight/gay marriages', and denying or denigrating them in such terms as exemplified below:

> I never dignify them by calling them something chic like mixed orientation marriages. . . . Straight/gay marriages are . . . distorted at best. . . . If anything, call them what I call them, mismarriages, meaning a mistaken marriage. (Kaye 2008, 115)

The interviews were undertaken by either myself or Sara Lubowitz, coordinator of the Women with Bisexual Partners Project at the AIDS Council of New South Wales (Lubowitz 1995, 1997). Initial discussions of the project were published in Pallotta-Chiarolli and Lubowitz (2003) and Pallotta-Chiarolli (2010). The larger project (Pallotta-Chiarolli, forthcoming) will provide more detailed analyses and insights into the research methods, participants' demographic data, the themes and issues that recognise the border existences, boundary demarcations, devastating oppressions, exhilarating affirmations and innovative negotiations of the women and their partners as they relinquish destructive relationships, or 'design', maintain and/or regain healthy sexual, emotional and social relationships. These journeys also entailed navigating a route through sometimes converging, sometimes conflicting external codes, such as those of straight peer groups, gay communities, ethnic and religious communities whereby "their heterosexuality is now an 'issue'—not a privilege" (Buxton 2011, 542; for pioneering work on MOREs, see also Buxton 1991, 2001, 2006; Gochros 1989; Whitney1990).

For the purposes of this chapter, I will provide an overview of the shifting subjectivities, agency and resistance of those women and their male partners who stated that, without coercion or repression, they undertook processes of 'designing' their long-term MOREs. As Heath writes, relationships involving bisexual people are either "excluded from the research or the people involved in those relationships treated as if they hold an identity they have not chosen and might not accept" (2010, 119). Thus, rather than constructing women in relationships with bisexual men solely as passive and ignorant "wounded identities" always at risk, an "ethics of pleasure" requires that "a crucial counter-narrative" is made available that recognises the pleasure, agency and power many women experience in these relationships (Rasmussen 2004, 456).

This chapter is a space for women in MOREs to present the "different rules" they and their partners have designed. I provide women's names or their chosen pseudonyms, ages and the lengths of their relationships to provide some context. In some interviews, the male partners were present or later read the transcripts, as requested by the women.

> My partner and I had quite a conversation around "new rules or no rules" and what that might mean. . . . People have assumptions that if there's a bisexual relationship, then there's no rules at all, when in fact maybe it's about different rules. (Jude, 33, 4 months)

"THERE'S A VARIETY OF WAYS OF LIVING AND YOU'RE ALLOWED TO PICK": WOMEN DISCUSS 'THE RULES'

In the rest of this chapter, I will explore what every woman stated as being an essential component of consensually and creatively entering or being in a relationship with a bisexual man: designing, negotiating and maintaining some "ground rules" and "boundaries". Heckert (2005, 196) calls these relationships "nomadic exclusivities" wherein participants "create space to discuss, define and refine their boundaries, which are always open to change." "Nomadic autonomy" is very empowering as it entails self-organisation and self-realisation "through co-operation and self-management (i.e., power-to) rather than domination and representation (i.e., power-over)" (Heckert 2005, 243; see also Heaphy, Donovan and Weeks 2004; Rust 1996).

Verna: Mark and I discuss absolutely everything . . . until we can get to a final thing in which everybody is happy with what's happening.

Mark: If something starts to interfere with the primary relationship, it
         has to be nipped in the bud. . . . and that is probably our main
         golden rule; nothing can affect our marriage. (Verna, 43, 24
         years)

There appear to be three overall groups of 'rules' within which specific
'designs' are created:

1. 'Old Rules': Monogamy is considered the only workable or desirable
   rule, and a partner's inability to adhere to monogamy would mean
   the end of the relationship.
2. 'New Rules': A range of negotiations and design-specifications establish non-monogamous boundaries and operational strategies.
3. 'Our Rules or His and Her Rules': Decisions are made regarding to
   what extent the rules will be equitable to both, or there are separate
   regulations for each partner.

I will also discuss how these 'rules' are not necessarily permanently fixed
but often require revisiting, redesigning and renovation based on temporal,
spatial and other contextual shifts, as well as being a consequence of or
leading to shifting subjectivities. Thus, a fourth theme to emerge is the
shifting and ongoing nature of the negotiating and boundary-maintenance
processes. For example, Peterson refers to the "Fidelity Factor" as a "continuum similar to the Kinsey Scale, with total monogamy at one end and an
open marriage for both spouses at the other. In between these extremes lie
several options" (2001, 196) which can be traversed and tried.

"I'M JUST NOT PREPARED TO SHARE": DESIGNING MONOGAMOUS RELATIONSHIPS

For some women, monogamy was the relationship design of choice. What is
significant here is that monogamy was not an externally ascribed presump-
tion and automatically performed. Women were clear that they had had
the opportunity to think agentically, or what Wosick-Correa (2010) calls
"agentic fidelity", about what they wanted from a relationship:

I have had the opportunity to think about what I want out of a relationship, and it is very much for me a one-on-one thing and I couldn't
consider anything else. (Sue, 38, 19 years)

Many women who chose monogamy also discussed how they believed
they would become open to the idea of non-monogamy as the relationship developed over the long-term. Katie provided examples of the types
of discussions she and her partner have when they revisit the monogamy

status of the relationship, even constructing a "script" and questions to use if either of them should wish to redesign the relationship into a form of non-monogamy:

> We check in with each other probably once every six months, you know, are you still comfortable with staying monogamous? Is there anyone you've met in the past six months that you'd like to explore a further relationship with? We have kind of scripted a conversation we'd have if we did meet someone . . . and we have a line that goes, "That conversation we always said we'd have, I want to have it". (Katie, 25, 8 years)

Indeed, for some women, the external ascriptive definition of monogamy was also open to deconstruction and reconstruction into specificities, such as what I call "gendered monogamy" whereby a bisexual partner could only have sex with other men:

Verna: I don't see it [her partner having male partners] as an invasion of our marriage. It's an extension of what we have.
Mark: If I was seeing another girl it would be different, totally.
Verna: Yes. I mean, it's still a monogamous relationship in my view. (Verna, 43, 24 years)

Another variation was what I call "shared-partner monogamy", where women stated their relationship was monogamous if they were sexual together with another male, or had agreed on certain forms of non-monogamous pleasure for both herself and her partner that they defined as "faithful":

> A threesome with a guy who my boyfriend is very fond of [is monogamous for us]. (Sylvia, 47, 12 years)

> My partner is faithful to me and I am faithful to him . . . and if he wants to watch me with another man, he will sit in the same room and watch, but I will never cheat on him. (Tammy, 30, 2 years)

"KNOW THE GUIDELINES AND WHERE TO SET THE GOAL-POSTS": DESIGNING NON-MONOGAMOUS RELATIONSHIPS

> We just kept bringing up the worst possible scenarios just to be able to talk it through and know where the guidelines are and where to set the goal-posts. (Christine, 38, 3 years)

Most women in consensual non-monogamous relationships had negotiated a wide range of boundaries, guidelines and rules, usually involving lengthy and detailed discussions and scripting of possible scenarios (Anapol 1997; Easton and Liszt 1997; McLean 2004). Other women did not delineate detailed boundaries but constructed a framing code of communication, "trust and truth", that would be used to address any issues and shifting circumstances as they arose:

> I didn't really have expectations necessarily of monogamy, and as long as there was also room for me to have a relationship with him. But, no, there were no boundaries . . . because no matter what happens, if there's a trust and a truth that does come out in the very beginning, then you have some strength on either side to deal with whatever comes up. (Nicola, 47, 24 years)

The following are the kinds of 'rules' negotiated in MOREs.

The Genders of External Partners

This was a very common issue and the most common consensus was the 'same-sex rule'—only being allowed to have external partners of the same gender:

> He decides what to do with the men and I decide what to do with the women. (Alda, 26, 1.5 years)

Other women talked about the differences between sex with a woman and sex with a man, thereby perceiving the 'same-sex rule' as removing any threat or competition:

> I said to him: "If you ever have sex with another woman our marriage will be over straight away" . . . It's like I can't compete with a man, like I don't have what he's got and there is just nothing to compare, whereas another woman you do feel like there is a bit more competition. (Maryse, 47, 19 years)

Thus, there appeared to be, on one hand, a socially recognised and endorsed acceptance and adherence to a gendernormative binary construction of male and female sexualities. On the other hand, this binary was strategically used by the women to assert their primacy, uniqueness and 'territory' as the sole female partner in the relationship:

> He's told me how he's felt after having sex with a man, completely different to being with a woman. Men are very aggressive, hard and fast, and women are much softer. There's just really no competition. However, if he showed an interest in a woman, I would get very upset. An invasion of my territory sexually. (Rachel, 38, 10 years)

> I could put on a strap-on and pretend to be the guy, but it wouldn't be the same as being a real-life penis. (Sherry, 42, 11 years)

There were some women who allowed their partners to have other women as sexual partners, particularly if this was as a shared partner:

> It was a strange thing at first [another woman] . . . but now I'm fine . . . I thought, do I really want this lifestyle and this freedom of the lifestyle, and I did. (Simone, 54, 5.5 years)

Sexual Health Negotiations

Every woman listed STIs/HIV as a primary concern requiring clear rules and honest communication.

> Always has to be safe, and he doesn't have anal sex. . . . even using a condom, if they go anal sex, they can still break and there's that risk factor. (Lee, 34, 20 years)

> If we do get to bed together with another guy, the two of us will not use condoms with each other, but anyone having sex with us will. (Naomi, 40, 9 years)

"Emotion Management"

The degree of emotional attachment, or what I call "emotion management", with outside partners was also a strong point of negotiation. While some women preferred their partners to settle into a "closed loop" of partners (Barbara, 44, 26 years) or have a polyfidelitous relationship with one other partner as this would minimise the health risks of random sexual encounters and establish emotional stability and continuity, other women wanted their partners to experience sexual connections with many partners but not establish intimate loving relationships, which they saw as exclusively for the two of them.

For those women whose partners were just embarking on exploring their bisexuality, it was agreed that this question of 'love or sex' in the future would remain unresolved but open to honest communication along every step of the way:

> We started to have rules about how he was going to go out and play. Did he need a male to love; did he need a male just for sex? He was only just coming to terms with the fact, that "hey, I'm bisexual, I like guys", so it was really hard for him because he'd grown up thinking he was straight . . . and he didn't know whether he was going to really want to go any further or just look at some pictures. . . . So when we started

talking about the open relationship we had to develop rules. (Helen, 38, 12 years)

"Energy Management"

Another area of discussion was the pragmatics of the everyday, what I call "energy management", such as time management, parenting, home duties, work/career demands, economic/financial resourcing, as well as the sexual energy and rosters required to be intimate with more than one partner. Many women were very clear that any energy given to sexual or other activities with outside partners was not to sap away energy required in the primary relationship:

> Obviously there's all these time issues. He's got quite a demanding job and the kids adore him and he adores them and their activities and we sort of haven't been in this house that long and there's things to be done and we both garden, and all of that. (Barbara, 44, 26 years)

Another code was to not engage in any outside activities with other partners if they were experiencing problems within the primary relationship:

> We make sure we are emotionally up to handling outside relationships. At times of stress we simply take time out from our same-sex relationships to focus on each other and whatever the problem is. (Shelley, 27, 10 years)

Some women designed systems of time compartmentalisation whereby their partners had their temporal, sexual and emotional "gay time" (Julia, 44, 7 years) and the rest of the time was for the female partner, children and home. Other women wanted geographical compartmentalisation, such as no outside sexual relationships in the town where they lived. This was particularly pertinent for women who lived in rural or remote townships:

> He travels out of town a lot, which provides opportunities, because it's a small town, while we're here, we're a unit; we're a couple. He treats me respectfully. He supports me. That's what I want, and what he does when he's away, as long as it's safe, I don't care. I don't see it at all as a threat to our relationship. . . . [but] I'm not having my home and my child and my job interfered with. . . . I'd rather keep the two in separate boxes. (Julia, 44, 7 years)

From DADT to TMI

Many couples spoke of constructing agreements regarding how much detail about outside relationships would be discussed. While a few women preferred the DADT (Don't Ask, Don't Tell) rule, most women wanted to know something about their partner's other relationships and sexual activities without overstepping a comfortable boundary into TMI (Too Much Information):

> We've done enough group sex, I know roughly what things Gennaro likes, so that's no great mystery to me, which I like . . . I don't suppose we talk about every tiny little detail, but we do talk about how it feels generally, the really good points, the really bad points but maybe not the exact minutiae of it cos that could be a little harsh on the other person. (Liz, 24, 3.5 years)

Sometimes, women needed to know sufficient detail in order to feel secure and reassured about their own relationship: "I don't want to know details really, but I do want to know our relationship's on track" (Barbara, 44, 26 years). Other women wanted to know and have a say in what sexual practices their partners were engaging in outside the relationship:

> Once I realised that he hadn't partaken in anal sex, something clicked then . . . I said, well, I'd like that boundary to remain. I had to feel that there's a little bit of him that is still mine—not that I use that particular part—but it was representative. (Karen, 46, 26 years)

For other women, being informed before a partner had a sexual relationship with someone else allowed for "emotional preparation" (Sabina, 26, 4 years) and any discussions that needed to be had.

Some of the older women stated that they wanted "no secrets" as their partners' sexual activities had decreased with age and therefore they were happy to listen to whatever activities might occur:

> There's no secrets; I want to hear all about it. . . . But he doesn't go out that much now, or he'll go into town and then he'll drive home . . . I said, "Well, who did you meet?" and then he'll tell me, "Oh, I met this nice person, so we had tea together." . . . Honesty, openness, trust, and our own time. (Brenda, 62, 40 years)

Other women would shift in how much detail they wanted, and expected their partners to be responsive to the level of detail they required at various times:

> You don't give more detail than the other person wants to hear. And, even in a relationship as open as ours, there are times I don't feel like the details. I'm not in a self-confident enough state that I want to know how gorgeous this other person was or whatever. And he respects that. And, there are other times when I'm in a fun mood and I'm like, "Oh, yes, so, what was he like? What happened? And, then what?" It might

even titillate me. . . . He took me a couple of times to the public toilets because I said, "What's this all about? Show me what happens?" It was interesting watching. (Julia, 44, 7 years)

The 'Sacred Bed' rule

Many couples set agreements on where sex with outside partners could occur. Many women did not allow their partners to have sex in their shared bed, being very clear about keeping their bed as "sacred space" with only their "sex energy" in it (Sabina, 26, 4 years):

> But we have another room . . . with all of our crap in it, but it also has a bed in there so that if we do have another lover we go into that. (Sabina, 26, 4 years)

For some women, the sacred bed extended to the whole home:

> This is the family home, okay. I have children. You want to fuck somebody, go to their place or go to the park, or wherever it is. But, you're not doing it here. It's our sanctuary. (Suze, 36, 1.5 years)

Informing the Other Man's Partner

Some women designed the code that their partners could not become involved in a relationship which involved the other men cheating on their other female or male partners, particularly if they had been placed in positions where they found themselves becoming complicit or accomplices in the cheating:

> I don't want to be cheated on, and I wouldn't do it to another one. That's one of my ground rules. That's it, end of story, and he's happy with that, because we did do it once with a married guy and it was a shambles. . . . I would hate to be the other woman, so I won't do it to anybody else. (Lee, 34, 20 years)

Separate or Shared Partners

Some women negotiated a relationship wherein any outside partners would be shared with their partners rather than either or both of them having separate partners:

> It's always with me, in a small group situation or usually just a threesome, with certain parameters with that person: they have to be a bit bright and actually have a conversation and be a little bit interesting as well, there has to be some connection. (Simone, 54, 5.5 years)

Others wanted the encounters to be between the men and not include them, while a third group were happy to negotiate either way depending on the circumstances and contexts:

> Strategies for doing things if we are both looking for a couple, for example, what sort of couple are we interested in, what are our upper limits and lower limits for certain types of things to do with sex and to do with socialising as well. . . . and then there is also a bit of debrief thing to sort out if we were happy about things. . . . the next day we will often sit around and munch on some food and have chat about it, "You know that was really good" or "That didn't seem to work" or "I felt really bizarre". (Liz, 24, 3.5 years)

Rules for Socialising Together

Couples would negotiate behaviours and protocols for when they were out socialising together. For many, it was important to set the parameters beforehand.

> If we were going some place together, we would sometimes negotiate well, okay, we're here together, we're going home together, or maybe not, that sort of stuff. (Corinna, 49, 3 years)

How to Handle Mistakes and 'Cheating'

Some women stated that the possibility of rule violation required acknowledgment, which then required designing strategies to address this. Indeed, the rules for breaking the rules in polyamory and other forms of non-monogamy seem "less regulatory and more participatory, encouraging an overall commitment to oneself, current partners and potential partners rather than restricting certain sexual and/or nonsexual interactions" (Wosick-Correa 2010, 55).

> My feeling is that if someone gets in certain situations, they just happen, and I'd rather not have to feel, "Oh, my God, you've ruined our relationship by having sex with this person and I will never see you again". (Corinna, 49, 3 years)

Some women, however, were adamant that there was no allowance for cheating or rule violation as the whole point of designing workable boundaries for non-monogamy was to avoid this scenario:

> I've told him, ever catch him going behind my back and he can say goodbye to his balls, they'll be hanging from the rearview mirror. [*laughing*] . . . I probably wouldn't go to that extent, but his bags would be packed

before he got home. Especially when we're open about it; there's no need for him to go behind my back. (Lee, 34, 20 years)

The Female Partner Having 'Veto' Power

Some women spoke about having "veto power", the final say in whatever occurred in their non-monogamous relationships:

> Anytime that I'm not comfortable with anything between us, then I'll just say. I know I have complete freedom to say, or with a look or a word anything can stop or start. (Simone, 54, 5.5 years)

In some relationships it was agreed that the woman would meet all potential partners before any relationship was established, and had "veto power" if they believed the other man "wasn't right"

Verna: If I have met a guy that Mark had been looking at and I said, "I don't like him, I don't think he's got it all together" or "he's hiding from his wife", it wouldn't be on.

Mark: I've got to get approval.

Verna: Not that I've got him under the thumb or anything but it's just an equal relationship.

Mark: I know what's right and wrong and if Verna has been so wonderful she gives me the freedom to go away and have a little bit of fun, I respect that so I've got to abide by the rules and I'm quite happy to do so . . . They must meet my family, they must meet my wife, and they're pretty basic things. (Verna, 43, 24 years)

Resisting Relationship Myths

Many women, particularly those in polyamorous relationships, believed in the need to completely rewrite the 'rule book' about relationships and intimacy and debunk many of the social myths that prevailed in the mainstream rather than just reconfigure them for specific issues (Anapol 1997; Davidson 2002; Barker and Langdridge 2010). This kind of rule rewriting occurred within ongoing processes of conversations/recognitions and actions/reconstructions:

> You're doing a project together and the project is constructing this life that is going to work for both of you in all its aspects and have both fulfilling your potential. . . . So I think it's important to get the word out into the world that it's possible, because I didn't even know this level of communication was possible. . . . Just totally giving up all of the past, wipe the slate, no expectations . . . and there's nothing to control; there's only something to create. Like, we're constantly bringing something into

existence that didn't exist and we can only do that together. As soon as one of us stops, there is no creation. (Jacinta, 34, 15 years)

For some women, it was important to not only rewrite the rules for their partners, but for themselves as well, leaving behind heteropatriarchal and monogamist systems and rules in order to completely redesign and redefine what relationship and home could mean:

I feel very lucky as I've had the opportunity to live two parallel lives for the last nine years with two men, one my heterosexual husband of fourteen years and the other my bisexual husband of nine years. Negotiation, cooperation and trust that I love them both make the relationships work. The benefits the men gain is freedom from the traditional rules full-time wives might impose on men. Both are very independent men who have strong feminist principles. My straight partner chooses to be monogamous with me and my bisexual partner has male partners, but it's up to them in the end. My homes are with my partners where they live, where my clothes, toothbrushes, books reside. Home is also my suitcase in which I permanently keep things like hair-dryer, a bag of underwear. . . . It's like I'm a modern turtle carrying my home with me. . . . But in becoming polyamorous and poly-home like this, I've had to leave behind home as a place of social approval, or else I would've had to leave behind my bisexual partner in order to stay in that traditional thing of one home, one husband. (Naomi, 40, 9 years)

"THERE ISN'T A POWER IMBALANCE": THE IMPORTANCE OF EQUITY

We decided on similar rules about how he would play, how I would play. (Helen, 38, 12 years)

The discussions in the sections above have already shown the prevalence of issues such as equity, balance, power and agency in women's negotiations with bisexual male partners, and the awareness that there would be ramifications when there are situations of imbalance and inequity. Apart from sexual equity, what I call "activity equity" was also considered important to establish, or not feeling as if one partner is having fun while the other partner is left "sitting at home":

It's a great pleasure to feel that our relationship is equal in that way, that there isn't a power imbalance. . . . I am happy for Gennaro to go out with a guy and have a good evening, come home or stay the night, or whatever. But I have to kind of have some plans as well cos I don't want it to feel like I am sitting at home doing nothing and I would like it to be in the reverse situation as well, for example, when I am seeing someone I don't want Gennaro to feel I am randomly going out and ignoring him. (Liz, 24, 3.5 years)

It was also important for many women that the male partner strive for equity between NRE (New Relationship Energy) and LTRE (Long-Term Relationship Energy) in the amount of attention and affection shown to new partners and long-term women partners.

It's really, really important to maintain balance. . . . I think the woman needs to have her needs fulfilled first, before he goes outside the marriage. . . . I've noticed that he becomes gushy over the other new person. I must admit it's that adolescent, that new feeling . . . and if I'm getting what I need within our relationship I won't begrudge that at all. (Helen, 38, 12 years)

"IT JUST CHANGES AND SHIFTS AND FLOATS AROUND": ONGOING RE-MAPPINGS

I guess I've always been the kind of person who, if it's two o'clock in the morning and there's no visible traffic, I will go through the red light. So, there's rules for a reason and you work out what the reason is, and then the rule is flexible. . . . You just do what everyone's comfortable with and then it just changes and shifts and floats around. (Jacinta, 34, 15 years)

Many women discussed the need for recognition that negotiations would shift according to individual, relational, external and other contexts and circumstances, thereby requiring rule renegotiations and re-evaluations. Their discussions concur with Davidson (2002), who presents how agreements often proceed through stages of self-assessment, communication, negotiation and experimentation, with subsequent ongoing application or reconfiguration.

Talking and establishing ground rules just sounds so military, but then again, I am flexible insofar as I think if he changes or if I change that we can discuss and not let it become a problem. . . . I mean, it's not like I'm holding the upper hand or anything, because we came into this together on equal ground. (Suze, 36, 1.5 years)

Some of the older-aged couples who had been together for decades explained that flexibility and responding to shifting needs gets easier over the years as individuals strive to fulfil any unfulfilled desires "before it's too late". They had also arrived at a place and time in their relationships where they no longer felt the need to set any rigid rules, nor undertake any surveillance; the hard work had been done, and they had such faith in each other and deep love for each other that they would be able to resolve and adjust to whatever the future held.

Paul: Even though I'm old, I've suddenly found the man I want to live with.

Alice: In fact, I encouraged Paul to try living with him. "You deserve to try it, Paul, after all these years. Don't die without taking that opportunity. I'll still be here. Plus you know I can take care of myself." (Alice, 65, 40 years)

Some women who had been together with their partners since they were adolescents spoke of how this allowed them to design their relationship as they went along:

> I really do think that one of the upsides of being together since we were so young is that we've basically made it [their relationship] up as we went along. We had ideas about how this sort of thing works, but not from direct experience, and that's evidenced now by the fact that I'm the full-time worker and he's the full-time carer of the children . . . we're always realistic and . . . take it day to day. I'm in love with him and we're still together, and he's in love with me and we really like our kids so that's how things are at present. . . . I've always just assumed that one of us may have sex with someone else; you can't be together since you're so young, and getting to our old age and that won't happen, or we might do it in our old age [*laughing*]. (Monica, 31, 15 years)

Having the relationship withstand the tests of time also meant previously sacred rules, such as "the sacred bed" rule, could be waived:

> I came to realise later it's only a bed, for heaven's sake; the sheets can be taken off and washed. And the same with the house. Shouldn't your husband or your partner feel comfortable to do things in your house, the same as you? These things I had to come to my own conclusions because society again doesn't teach us this. . . . You've got to have all those guidelines because society puts you in a box. You then put your own relationship in another box, and it has changed significantly over the years. (Helen, 38, 12 years)

"WE ENJOY OUR LIFE TOGETHER": THE RESULTS OF RECONSTRUCTION AND DESIGNING

> We are very happy . . . and we enjoy our life together. We are both very open about his attraction to men and I enjoy many gibes at his expense! (Karen, 46, 26 years)

This Australian research supports the findings of existing research that partners who design successful MOREs share a number of characteristics:

open communication, primary commitment to the marriage . . . rewriting marriage "rules", love, honesty, the wife's autonomy and acceptance, the husband's compromise, and personal capacities of empathy and flexibility. (Buxton 2001, 163)

Internal recognition and "day-to-day interactions through which to modify parameters of their marriage" (Buxton 2001, 183) were also significant traits that counteracted external community and societal misrecognition. As Whitney writes: "they are the reluctant pioneers of a different family form" (1990, 114). And "in making their choices these couples have agreed to live with an on-going reformation" of their relationships, thereby influencing the broader reformation of societal ascriptions, understandings and recognitions of various relationship forms and options (1990, 136; see also Gochros 1989). It is fitting that I end this chapter with the words of a research participant in Buxton's pioneering research:

Our relationship has internal validity regardless of outside standards . . . It took a while for us to write this script for ourselves. (1991, 231–234)

NOTES

1. The following definition of bisexuality was used: "Bisexual persons are sexually, emotionally, and erotically attracted to both men and women, usually in varying degrees that may fluctuate over time; and may or may not have sex with partners of both genders, in the same time period or over time; and self-identify as bisexual" (Buxton 2006, 109–110).

REFERENCES

Anapol, D. 1997. *Polyamory: The New Love without Limits*. San Rafael, CA: IntiNet Resource Center.

Barker, M., and D. Langdridge, eds. 2010. *Understanding Non-Monogamies*. London: Routledge.

Buxton, A.P. 1991. *The Other Side of the Closet: The Coming-Out Crisis for Straight Spouses*. Santa Monica, CA: IBS Press.

Buxton, A.P. 2001. "Writing Our Own Script: How Bisexual Men and Their Heterosexual Wives Maintain Their Marriages after Disclosure." In *Bisexuality in the Lives of Men: Facts and Fiction*, edited by B. Beemyn and E. Steinman. New York: Harrington Park Press.

Buxton, A.P. 2006. "Counseling Heterosexual Spouses of Bisexual Men and Women and Bisexual-Heterosexual Couples: Affirmative Approaches." *Journal of Bisexuality* 6 (1–2): 106–135.

Buxton, A.P. 2011. "Reflections on Bisexuality through the Prism of Mixed-Orientation Marriages." *Journal of Bisexuality* 11 (4): 525–544.

Davidson, J. 2002. "Working with Polyamorous Clients in the Clinical Setting." *Electronic Journal of Human Sexuality* 5, April 16. www.ehjs.org. Accessed 23rd July, 2013.

106 *Maria Pallotta-Chiarolli*

Easton, D., and C.A. Liszt. 1997. *The Ethical Slut*. San Francisco: Greenery Press.

Gochros, J.S. 1989. *When Husbands Come Out of the Closet*. New York: Haworth Press.

Heaphy, B., C. Donovan and J. Weeks. 2004. "A Different Affair?: Openness and Nonmonogamy in Same-Sex Relationships." In *The State of Affairs: Explorations in Infidelity and Commitment*, edited by G. Allan, J. Duncombe, K. Harrison and D. Marsden. Mahwah, NJ: Lawrence Erlbaum Associates.

Heath, M.A. 2010. "Who's Afraid of Bisexuality?" *Gay and Lesbian Issues and Psychology Review* 6 (3): 118–121.

Heckert, J. 2005. "Resisting Orientation: On the Complexities of Desire and the Limits of Identity Politics." Sociology PhD. University of Edinburgh. Accessed November 5, 2009. http://sexualorientation.info/thesis/index.html.

Kaye, B. 2008. *Bonnie Kaye's Straight Talk. A Collection of Her Best Newsletters about Gay Husbands*. British Columbia, Canada: CCB Publishing.

Lubowitz, S. 1995. *The Wife, the Husband, His Boyfriend . . . Her Story*. Canberra: AIDS/Communicable Diseases Branch of the Commonwealth Department of Human Services and Health.

Lubowitz, S. 1997. *Three in a Marriage: Video and Booklet Training Package for Health Care Workers*. Sydney: AIDS Council of NSW.

McLean, K. 2004. "Negotiating (Non)Monogamy: Bisexuality and Intimate Relationships." In *Current Research on Bisexuality*, edited by R. Fox. New York: Harrington Park Press.

Pallotta-Chiarolli, M. 2010. *Border Sexualities, Border Families in Schools*. New York: Rowman and Littlefield.

Pallotta-Chiarolli, M. Forthcoming. *"Outside Belonging": Women in Relationships with Bisexual Men*. New York: Lexington Books.

Pallotta-Chiarolli, M. and S. Lubowitz. 2003. "Outside Belonging: Multi-Sexual Relationships as Border Existence." In *Women and Bisexuality: A Global Perspective*, edited by S. Anderlini-D'Onofrio. New York: Haworth Press.

Peterson, L.W. 2001. "The Married Man On-Line." *Journal of Bisexuality* 1 (2/3): 191–209.

Rasmussen, M.L. 2004. "Wounded Identities, Sex and Pleasure: 'Doing It' at School. NOT!" *Discourse: Studies in the Cultural Politics of Education* 25 (4): 445–458.

Rust, P.C. 1996. "Monogamy and Polyamory: Relationship Issues for Bisexuals." In *Bisexuality: The Psychology and Politics of an Invisible Minority*, edited by B.A. Firestein. Thousand Oaks, CA: Sage Publications.

Whitney, C. 1990. *Uncommon Lives: Gay Men and Straight Women*. New York: Plume.

Wosick-Correa, K. 2010. "Agreements, Rules, and Agentic Fidelity in Polyamorous Relationships." *Psychology and Sexuality* 1 (1): 44–61.

Part III

Validating Racialised Subjectivities

7 Crossing Borders as Mestizas and Coyotes

Recognising Older Somali Women's Shifting Subjectivities in Australia

Georgia Birch

We shall not cease from exploration
And the end of all our exploring
Will be to arrive where we started
And know the place for the first time.

(Eliot 2010, 22)

In 2009 I set off on a research journey to explore the influences on participation in physical activity amongst a group of older Somali women living
in Melbourne, Australia. Over a three-year period, qualitative data were
gathered through conversations, observations, journaling, photography
and art undertaken within a weekly health group established for older
Somali women at a local community service. The research revealed that
older Somali women are not meeting the National Physical Activity Recommendations for Older Australians and Western concepts of activity are
not transferable or relevant to their lives (Sims et al. 2006). Most participants were active in Somalia, where physical activity was entwined in daily
gender, maternal and cultural roles. In Australia, the women lead a seden-
tary lifestyle, where physical activity is constrained by factors such as lack
of money, time and a private space to exercise; tiredness and illness; racial
abuse and Islamophobia; limited transport and formal exercise facilities;
and community and dominant cultural perceptions of older Somali women
participating in exercise.

The reader should be aware that I started this journey believing that
I would easily measure, analyse and evaluate the influences on physical
activity for older Somali women. I came to the research with my own
Western experiences and understandings of physical activity and how it is
measured. However, I soon discovered that understanding the context of
the participants required me to look at things differently, including how
physical activity is perceived, measured and valued in diverse ways according to the women's subjectivities. I also had to look at myself differently
and understand how I have been influenced by my context. The Somali
women participating in this research also went on a journey, exploring

how their exercise behaviours were interwoven with the dominant culture's understandings of physical activity. Thus, this chapter will explore two intertwined journeys of a white, middle-aged, middle-class researcher and a group of older Somali women from a refugee background. It will consider how they all meet and mesh on the borders of old and new, dominant and marginalised, knowledge and process, and the subsequent shifts in their multiple and multiplying subjectivities. Their journeys will continue as they face ongoing challenges for as some shifts in subjectivities occur, other situations arise that need to be negotiated. For the purposes of this chapter, I will focus on how the women perceive and understand the personal, social and racial meanings of their lives within a dominant culture and how they create a new space in which to exist. I will also highlight how I, as the researcher, shifted my own subjectivity about where and how I sit within, between and amongst the dominant culture and the Somali culture.

Some photographs are included in this chapter; however, as the Islamic religion does not allow photographic images unless for essential paperwork, most of the participants only allowed images to be taken of their hands and feet.

The theme of crossing borders—physical, cultural and psychological—arose often from the research data and throughout the research process and researcher–participant relationships. To explore this theme, I drew on two powerful frameworks: Gloria Anzaldua's (1987) borderlands theoretical framework and Valadez and Elsbree's (2005) coyote methodological framework. Anzaldua's framework considers how people navigate and live between cultures and in what Homi K. Bhabha calls "the third space" (1994, 209). Anzaldua (1987) uses the term "mestizas" to refer to women who are in this third space and are crossing borders, aware of their interweaving identities within and between two cultures. The image of Hawo (Figure 7.1) reflects a mestiza consciousness; her hijab and runners depict a point of arrival as the women explored and experienced the realities of being older Somali Muslim women living in Australia and having to negotiate shifting understandings of health and healthy behaviours. The following words from Hawo represent where she began, when she saw people running on a treadmill in a local gymnasium.

> We never learn these things that you do. I thought you were crazy; I can't believe why you just do, running on those road machines why? What are they doing that for, not even running from anything? (Hawo, participant)

Valadez and Elsbree's (2005) coyote framework explores how researchers work with marginalised communities. Fadumo, my research informant, and I became coyotes, guiding others through different worlds, changing and shifting our subjectivities to cross borders and understand the context of each other's lives. In Valadez and Elsbree's (2005, 176) framework, the coyote has four characteristics: first, *en secreto*, developing trust and understanding

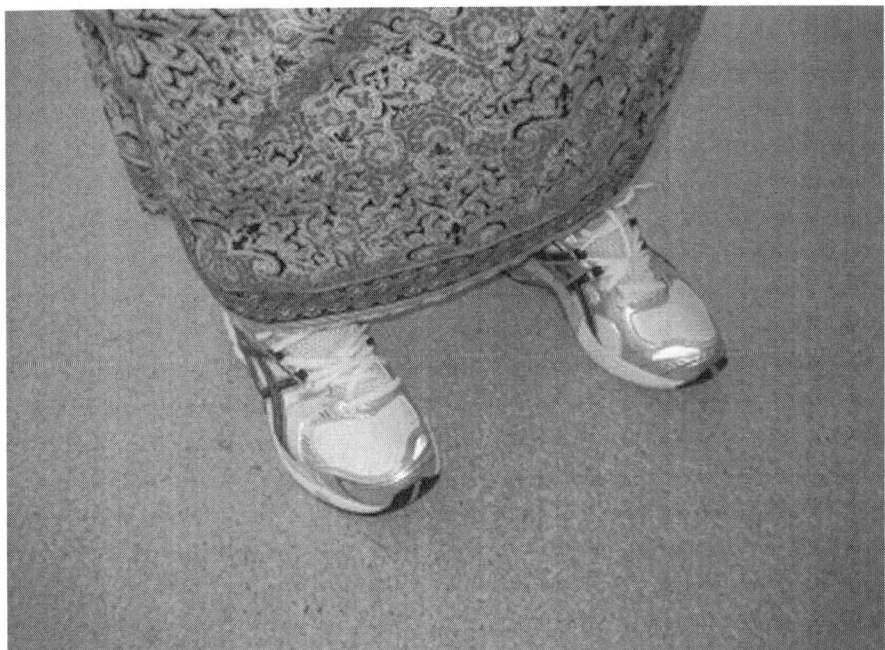

Figure 7.1   Hawo.

the participants' border positionings so that they trusted us to hear their perspectives; second, *los codigos*, as coyote researchers we understood the codes of their community and the wider Western society values, systems and institutions, and helped guide the participants between life on the margins and the dominant culture; third, *la facultad*, we were able to read situations quickly and understand the realities that the participants were living; finally, we expressed a "sincere *compromiso* commitment" to the women to have a voice and reach a destination that will benefit them.

To set the context for the reader, I will briefly describe the physical world that the participants and I live in. While we share the same suburbs, we are separated by streets and class and wealth. The Flemington Housing Estate that the women live in (Figure 7.2) would rank as the fifth most disadvantaged area in Melbourne; however, because of its locality in a wealthier suburb the ranking moves to the eighteenth most disadvantaged (Moonee Valley City Council 2010). The diversity in this municipality can result in the needs of disadvantaged residents being overlooked because the focus is on the postcode rather than on pockets that are substantially disadvantaged. Figures 7.2 and 7.3 compare streets within the municipality of Moonee Valley. One shows Flemington Housing Estate, and the other picture, taken less than two kilometres away, is one of the most affluent streets in Melbourne and similar to the street in which I live.

Figure 7.2   Flemington Housing Estate.

Figure 7.3   Moonee Ponds.

THE RESEARCHERS AS BORDER CROSSERS

I came to the project having established a relationship with Fadumo through an earlier volunteer program; this relationship developed into a firm friendship that continues today. I was aware from the outset of the project that I am located within a privileged white position and that my privilege is normalised (Pease 2010). This "particular construction of the human" defends a "Western, patriarchal and colonialist world view" (Pease 2010, 13). My field notes reflect these positions and while they are not deliberately patronising or colonial, they represent who I am and where I have come from and may also, unconsciously, reflect colonialist and patronising views. Figure 7.4 is an example of me trying to leave those colonial views with my shoes at the front door of a Somali woman's home. My white, athletic Western shoes are in stark contrast to the dark, practical shoes of Somali women. I took off those shoes to step across what Anzaldua (1987) describes as a physical and psychological border to be a part of their world. An awareness of who I was and where I entered as a white, middle-class woman began at the women's front doors. While I cannot step in and out of my colonial views by stepping into and out of a Somali woman's house, Figure 7.4 reflects my awareness of my colonial mind-set. It was also here that the Somali women left the dominant culture behind to enter the comfort zone of being Somali, feeling safe and being themselves.

Figure 7.4   The shoes and crossing over into Somali life.

Even the position of my shoes is revealing; they are on the edge, reflecting my border-dwelling positionality, my attempts to cross over and understand those in the Somali culture by inhabiting the margin of that culture.

To effectively challenge privilege from within, Pease (2010) argues that we must "accept our oppressor status . . . before you can become an ally to the liberation of others" (173). I tried to do this by acknowledging this privilege and the benefits that come with it. In some ways I became a 'traitor' to the dominant group, rejecting the ideals and values that it holds and at a cost to my relationships, where those in 'my group' felt I had left them and irresponsibly 'moved away' to be 'with others'. Developing this traitorous character must include being a "world traveller" (Bailey 1998, 38). In the process of travelling, "our identities fall apart" and we get a glimpse of how we are seen "through the eyes of whom we have been taught to perceive arrogantly" (Bailey 1998, 40). In many ways I was in neither place, what Somali women call "kooyto": nowhere but on the borders of everywhere. Those in the dominant group felt I 'had become one of those', as reflected in the response of family and friends when I had my hands hennaed.

> My friends have asked, "so when is the hijab coming" or "why don't you get a real tattoo that says LOVE or HATE across each knuckle". It is always the same as family await me to arrive at a dinner with a hijab on or when I rejected the notion of traditional religious celebrations such as Christmas or Easter, it's always been "she is becoming one of those, a Muslim". Ahhh this border life. (Field notes, 2011)

I was experiencing a view of the dominant culture from the Somali women's standpoint. Bailey (1998) suggests that people who occupy the edge, as I did, have a way of seeing that is "off-center" and that they "destabilise their insider status by challenging and resisting the usual assumptions held by most white people" (32). While I gained the women's trust, I lost the trust of my own culture. Anzaldua (1987) put this best when she described her identity in the United States as a Mexican woman: "I have so internalized the borderland conflict that sometimes I feel like one cancels out the other and we are zero, nothing, no one" (85). My shifting subjectivities challenged my positionality as a researcher but also as a white woman understanding what it was like living on the border.

Fadumo, my informant, was the link between me and the participants, the wider Somali community and the stakeholders. Over the four years of the project, Fadumo and I developed a close personal friendship. Kleinman and Copp (1993) highlight that good relationships with informants are not only about our feelings of competence in getting along with others or our exceptional skills of establishing rapport, but rather about what we are offering that makes us attractive and useful to them. Engaging Fadumo in the research provided her with new ways of thinking, feeling and relating to the research. It allowed her a greater understanding of the community and promoted her commitment to social change.

> Fadumo discusses the frustrations of getting the women to the group. She said today "it is extremely hard to break this kind of thinking because praying and religion is all they care about, but we must keep going, we need these projects to make change, we need this Georgia, we really need this". (Field notes, 2010)

Fadumo's determination in resisting and challenging the misconceptions about the Somali community from the dominant Western wider society and about older Somali women from within the community progressed throughout the research. Although her commitment never wavered, there was a downside for Fadumo as the project caused clashes with community members, conflicts around who represented the community and competition turf issues between the Community Health Service stakeholder and the Somali groups. As a skilled coyote, Fadumo was developing trust and protecting the participants while trying to maintain trust within the Somali community. She 'smuggled' participants within and around the stakeholder, negotiating and protecting them. As a result, Fadumo was placed in a position of losing trust from those who respected her most, her community.

> Fadumo was very upset today about Isha complaining about her to other community members. Fadumo is trying to recruit participants but this is proving difficult as Isha is establishing her own community organisation and wants women to go to that and not ours. When these insults establish themselves within the community it not only affects the individual but their entire family, so now Fadumo's relatives are part of the clash which extends to all hours of the day and to all celebrations. The project has infiltrated her life beyond anything I imagine and, in this case, not in a good way. (Field notes, 2010)

It was part of my ethical coyote duty to protect Fadumo from harm while remaining culturally sensitive to community clashes. The Community Health Service provided counselling and mediation to Fadumo and Isha to develop ways of operating. However, the Western concept of mediation was a difficult process as conflict within the Somali community runs deep within clans and this clash was to continue beyond one or two mediation sessions. It seemed that the conflict had to 'run its course' as this is how disagreements are settled within the Somali community, with discussions, stories and group conversations. Fadumo became more skilled at these roles, shifting her thinking as a researcher and navigating her role as a Somali community member.

The bond between Fadumo and I influenced how the data were collected. Our combined knowledge enhanced our understanding of the issues and the timing and placement of questions. Both of us came to the project with 'cultural baggage', but we were able to cross cultural borders to guide and inform the methodology. This term 'cultural baggage' was chosen after a discussion.

Georgia: I think 'cultural baggage' is a term we could use that describes what we carry with us wherever we go and it influences what we listen to, what we record, and how the study flows.
Fadumo: This is a good word but I will have a very bad back as my baggage will be much bigger than yours Georgia [*laughing*]. (Field notes, 2010)

Fadumo's comment made me realise that perhaps she felt what Anzaldua describes as "chaos" in living in between overlapping and layered cultural spaces (Betancor 2000, 238). As a highly respected member of the Somali community and a Community Health Service employee, she wanted to make sure that the participants could trust her and that she could provide guidance. She straddled the border of Somali and Australian cultures, sensitive to both yet wrapped closely in the "husks of her culture" (Anzaldua 1987, 103). Figure 7.5 represents this crossroads of cultures, Fadumo's hands hennaed with Somali symbols and her nails matching her hijab or dress. She had two phones, one for work and one for her personal life. To each

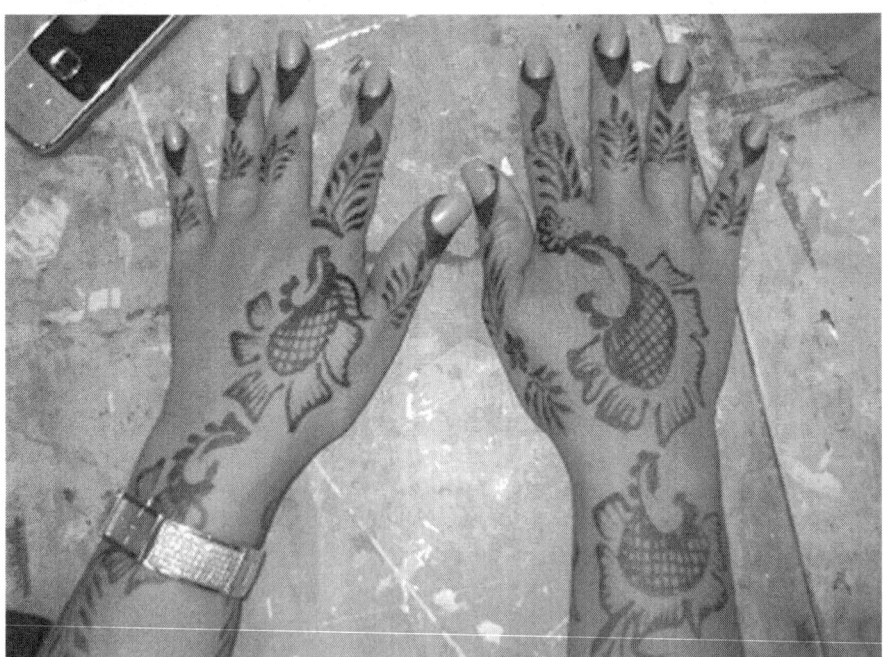

Figure 7.5   Fadumo and her hennaed hands told a story every week.

she spoke either Somali or English or the language of the "forked tongue" (Anzaldua 1987, 77). The phones were slipped into her hijab and she could run two different conversations and languages at once. After months in the field, Fadumo would speak to me in Somali, forgetting I was 'not one of them' and I would say "English, Fadumo, remember I need English".

When Fadumo and I met it was usually at her house due to her child care commitments or in a neutral place such as a café. Finally, with much reluctance, Fadumo visited my house, and so I experienced someone crossing a border to visit me. When she entered my home, she took her shoes off but was surprised that I did not. I explained that it was not necessary, which she found strange because for her being "at home" is being "free" to walk in bare feet. I asked her what she thought of my house and to my shock she replied, "It is the first white house I have ever been in".

> I asked Fadumo to describe what she thought of my house. She was hesitant because she did not want to offend me. I explained that I had crossed her border and written about that, so she could do the same to me. She said my house was quite sterile and separate as everyone had their own rooms, they were not altogether. She asked why there was no specific cultural room to take guests into for 'tea'. She said "it is very clean but everyone is separate doing their own things, not coming together as we do". In her world communal family life is so central and yet she did not feel this in my home. (Field notes, 2011)

It is expected that a white researcher can enter a non-white person's home and analyse it, so it was thought-provoking to hear the response when the border is crossed the other way.

"A REAL SHIFT IN MY SUBJECTIVITY": WHEN PREVIOUSLY KNOWN WESTERN FRAMEWORKS BECOME ALIEN

There were a few pivotal moments in my research that highlighted my shifting subjectivities. Spradley (1979, 10) says that "ethnography is a culture studying a culture" and I had been in the field for over eighteen months when I noticed that I was living inside a reality that reflected the women's daily lives. I began to fit into Somali gatherings without feeling as if my whiteness was an issue. One particular visit provided the turning point, a shift in my subjectivity about where I was placed.

> Today Fadumo and I visited Miriam's house because her daughter had had a baby and she was looking after her and the baby for the first 40 days. When we arrived the maternal child health nurse was there with five other older Somali women. I was welcomed warmly and easily slipped into the cultural rituals of visiting. But I soon noticed the maternal child health nurse, who was white and middle class like

myself, looked out of place. She was trying to get the young woman to read material on recommended baby's sleeping arrangements. I knew this was never going to happen because Miriam's daughter is not very fluent in English and the nurse was looking at me wondering how I was fitting into this picture so easily. I realised that I had become so immersed in how things were done in Somali women's culture that I could clearly see how inappropriate this particular service was for this setting. To me it seemed so simple yet I felt so far away from where this nurse was I wondered how I never noticed that this process of immersion had happened. (Field notes, 2010)

This experience made me realise how separate the dominant culture is from the Somali community, yet eighteen months before I was just as separate as this maternal child health nurse. Descriptive ethnographic work by Western researchers presents information that is formed around well-established, orthodox Western views of society. The nurse followed a traditional format of questions, ticking off answers; however, the information she was giving did not reflect the young woman's understanding. Just being in the room and knowing more about Somali culture, I could see how this situation should have been handled.

I thought to myself how would I have related this material now that I have been with these women for some time? Involving the older women in the room would have been crucial as they have each had about 5–10 children and know a lot about how to care for a baby. When I was trying to explain some of the written material Miriam said "I know all this I have had six children myself". This child was going to be raised by many, not by just the mother but grandmothers, aunties, cousins and friends and not to include them was a mistake, an insult that traditional ways were not part of the written white material. (Field notes, 2010)

This experience reflected my learning on the borderlands and the women's ability to see the dominant culture from the "third space" (Bhabha 1994, 209). They resisted and challenged the misconceptions that this maternal health nurse had of them as mothers and carers of children. When I was amongst this borderland behaviour, I could see the women's resilience and agency in negotiating Western frameworks.

"I HAVE STARTED TO THINK TO GET OUT OF THE HOUSE": THE NEW MESTIZA'S SHIFTING HEALTH BEHAVIOURS

As highlighted in Figure 7.1, Hawo described running as "crazy", understanding exercise to be connected with home duties or work rather than "for no reason". In Somalia a person who walked around without a purpose was considered mentally unstable. During the project, the women began to shift their understanding of health. They began walking around the Flemington Housing Estate within their own small groups, recognising that they needed to think differently about exercise. They created a new space where traditional identity and physical activity were combining with the dominant culture. There was a progressive change in their subjectivities around themselves as walkers in a new culture.

> Since I started coming here, I have started to think to get out of the house in the afternoons and then walk and walk and when I get tired I sit down a little bit and then walk, until I come back home. It's nice. (Hawo)

The runners shown on Hawo in Figure 7.1 were the product of discussions I had with my connections within the white world; they were donated from a company that heard about this project. This was part of the coyote behaviour I had adopted. I felt that providing the runners was a way of giving back to the women after they had discussed the difficulty of walking long distances in open-toed shoes.

> We wear these shoes because they are easy to slip on and off when we enter a Somali family house but we know they cannot be used for walking long distances. In Somalia we walked in either bare feet or open shoes because of the heat, but we don't need to do that here. Now, because we are old we can slip over, it's not good, we need to learn better ways. (Aziza)

Once the women were fitted in their new runners, they wore them every week to the group and even at other times when they arranged to meet to walk and shop. Many of the women who started exercising weekly would tell me how much they had done and the benefits they felt. Fadumo told them she had seen them walking together.

> I saw you all walking on the weekend going around the estate and your shoes, you all were wearing the shoes. You looked like you were enjoying yourselves. Georgia and I are very proud of you for this.

The women replied, "We have been enjoying ourselves, and nobody thought that we were crazy".

The women's behaviour reflected a change in their subjectivity as a result of the research project. Walking challenged their familiar ways. They were able to dismantle the traditional white mind-set about what physical activity means and dismantle traditional Somali ways in order to reconstruct a mestiza sense of who they are and how physical activity fits on the borderlands of being Somali in an Australian context (Hernandez-Wolfe 2011). This is visually represented by the traditional dress and modern runners in Figure 7.1. Most older, ethnic women recognise the usefulness of exercise and express a desire to participate but have difficulty initiating this, therefore requiring coyote health workers/researchers to support them to find strategies around participating in exercise that fits within their identity: "she realises she has to fit in to be accepted, recognised and allowed access to opportunities" (Hernandez-Wolfe 2011, 299).

"IS THIS WHAT RACISM FEELS LIKE?": EXPERIENCING RACISM TOGETHER

My experience throughout the research strengthened my commitment to address the racism faced by the Muslim community in Melbourne. My small but first taste of feeling isolated was at one of my first communal gatherings at a participant's house.

> I have just had this moment when I realise that I was the only one out of the group of 20 women who was white. Is this what racism feels like? I know I am part of the dominant group so my experience of difference is not the same as the Somali women, however I feel vulnerable, exposed, out of place, wanting to suddenly get away. Women are staring and asking "why is she here?". I look different, my clothes are different, my blonde hair, my 'Australian-ness' stands out, the smell of incense overwhelms me. Is this how these women feel getting on a tram, shopping, going to the bank, trying to learn English? (Field notes, 2009)

These everyday experiences of isolation and segregation are reminders to Muslim Australians that they do not belong. Unlike them, I can walk out the door and escape to my world of belonging in a white Australia. Their spaces, however, become "landscapes of social exclusion because they define who belongs and who does not. They are targeted for being who they are, where they are and where they don't belong" (Noble and Poynting 2010, 496).

On one occasion towards the end of my project, the women and I were faced with racism on a personal, interwoven level when Fadumo and I took the participants on an excursion to the Mount Macedon heritage site picnic area called Hanging Rock (a Parks Victoria recreation site approximately fifty kilometres north of Melbourne). This experience tested my commitment to addressing racism and proved to me how connected I was to the women. We had enjoyed a picnic and decided to end the day with a coffee in the local café.

My field notes from that day tell the story:

> When we got to the café it was like we had crossed a border and the women and I had entered another country. Surely this was not the Australia I thought I lived in? There were only a few people in the café and we ordered coffees. I soon realised we were being treated differently and

Figure 7.6   Walking to the café for coffee.

that the waitress did not like us being there. When the coffees arrived, we were asked to pay again and I insisted that we had already paid when we ordered. One of the coffees was ordered as a skinny latte and the waitress insisted that this would cost extra. I was lost for words. I hadn't thought this was a race issue but the women had already identified that this was happening and tried to be compliant.

I asked what seemed to be the problem and the waitress said there wasn't one, so I asked for some of the coffees to be take-away. She returned fuming, throwing the coffee on the tables with lids spilling and the coffees spilt across my lap. I then noticed the participants' subdued reaction and knew it was because of who they were. I was fuming because I felt like I was one of them, I represented them, I, we are all Australians and I was so ashamed and embarrassed that this had happened.

I let this go and asked the women to come to the gift shop attached to the café. We were looking at and smelling various soaps and creams and two women went to the counter to purchase some items when all of a sudden the owner started yelling, snatching the products from the women, throwing their money back at them and telling them to leave. I asked calmly what the problem seemed to be, thinking maybe there had been a misunderstanding in language and she openly said "These are good products that need to be treated properly" and that we were opening the bottles. I knew this was not true and that she just wanted us out of the shop. The women said "ok" and walked out of the store. I was fuming and said that nobody was being disrespectful of the products and that it was me who was telling the women to smell and sample them. She said "No you are all opening the products" and told me to get out with "the rest of them". I told her she was being a racist and disrespectful to other Australians who had come to this country under humanitarian circumstances. She flicked her hand and said "I am not a racist, I just don't want to serve you".

I was ashamed to be Australian, to see this in reality, and angry that I was part of this Australia. And I now knew what it was like to receive this treatment. It was like crossing over and then going back again, being one of them but also not. The amazing thing was that the women were calming me down saying "Don't worry, this happens all the time, you just have to move on". Where and how did they learn to cope with this? My researcher whiteness was beaming as I don't think I have ever really experienced such blatant discrimination and disrespect. I have been angry for days over the injustice and ashamed that in Australia this is happening to these women all the time. (Field notes, 2010)

Pease (2010, 112) states that "most white people have very little awareness about their own racial identity". It is easier for white people to see themselves as individuals rather than racialised people because they look at their characteristics first rather than the colour of their skin. My whiteness gives me unearned privileges of being treated with respect as a consumer; but in the café at Hanging Rock I felt discrimination against me because of my association with the women. My role had become blurred: I was accepted as one of them but was still aware of my whiteness and my role in the dominant society. Valadez and Elsbree (2005) refer to this as a psychological border that represents "a conceptual boundary that we have socially constructed" (173). My role was to connect these women into the community in a culturally sensitive way and this experience of discrimination reinforced my "sincere *compromiso* commitment" and strengthen my resolve to address this behaviour in my dominant culture (Valadez and Elsbree 2005, 176).

As a coyote I was determined to make sure these women had a voice and could travel a path that would benefit them. The coyote belongs in neither world but navigates its way along with others to establish paths that are safe, beneficial and understanding. Inasmuch as I have been welcomed into Somali culture, I can never really be part of it because I can never really know what it is 'to be Somali'. Fadumo discusses how I fit in.

We will always need and love you, whatever problems we have I know we can come to you and you always have an answer for us no matter how busy you are. You are always trying to help us; we don't have people like you and that is why we struggle in this country. We need strong voices; our language lets us down and this is what we need. (Fadumo)

"THE FULLNESS OF EXPLORATION": SHARING NEW MESTIZA REALITIES

Figure 7.7 reflects my understanding that every experience is integrated with all the others, so the "fullness of exploration means a return, with a better understanding, to the point where you started" (Eliot 2004, 466). I, like Hawo and Allawia, have walked the estate and I have begun a new journey of understanding myself as a researcher and as a white Australian woman. In the photograph, Hawo and Allawia are wearing their runners and their traditional Somali dress, having shifted and navigated between and within traditional and new health behaviours. When this photograph was taken, towards the end of the project, the women asked me to wait until they reached a point where they were not identifiable. As they walked ahead, Hawo commented: "This is nice for us; this is where we fit in".

Figure 7.7 also reflects Anzaldua's (1987) borderland. The older Somali women straddle both the physical border of the estate and the psychological border between Somali culture and the dominant culture; they have created a new culture, a new way of navigating and negotiating themselves between the two.

> And if going home is denied me then I will have to stand and claim my space, making a new culture—*una cultura mestiza*—with my own lumber, my own bricks and mortar and my own feminist architecture. (Anzaldua 1987, 44)

Figure 7.7   Hawo and Allawia walk the borders of the estate.

Every day the women walk out of one culture and into another; in doing so they have created a new way of thinking and surviving, "a new mestiza consciousness" (Anzaldua 1987, 99). They have learnt to juggle cultures and subconsciously adjust their inner selves to create an energy that sometimes causes intense pain and anxiety. Their space is also a place of creativity, of agency and resistance, where new mestiza energy is created.

> And suddenly I feel everything rushing to a center, a nucleus. All the lost pieces of myself come flying from the deserts and the mountains and valleys, magnetized toward the center. *Completa.* (Anzaldua 1987, 73)

In the following, Hawo reminded me that Somali women are able to develop powerful strategies to live on the border, to navigate physical activity within their own framework, one that works for them.

> First when I came to this country my son came long time ago and he says to me come out of the house mummy walk like Chinese womans, they doing, they doing something. I say am I crazy what I am just walking with no purpose why don't you leave me alone. Now I am getting used to it all here, I just realise we need that so I am coming now I am sitting here and trying to do some. (Hawo)

As I move within the suburbs of Ascot Vale and Flemington, which I share with the older women and where I see them walking, I hold a new respect and understanding for their skills at living amongst, negotiating and navigating, the whites. These women have interwoven and changed their subjectivities within a dominant culture around health and walking; they have developed new ways of living. This research has been a reflection of my changed subjectivity as a researcher, having crossed borders as a coyote, developing new research relationships and becoming more mocha than white, a blended mix of milk white and chocolate, a border colour perhaps.

REFERENCES

Anzaldua, G. 1987. *Borderlands/La Frontera: The New Mestiza.* San Francisco: Aunt Lute Books.

Bailey, A. 1998. "Locating Traitorous Identities: Toward a View of Privilege-Cognizant White Character." *Hypatia* 13 (3): 27–42.

Betancor, M.H. 2000. "Writing: A Way of Life." In *Gloria E. Anzaldúa: Interviews/Entrevistas*, edited by A. Keating. New York: Routledge.

Bhabha, H. 1994. *The Location of Culture.* London: Routledge.

Eliot, T.S. 2010. "East Coker (1940); Burnt Norton (1941); The Dry Salvages (1941); Little Gidding (1942); Four Quartets (1943)." In *The Contemporary Reviews*, edited by J.S. Brooker. New York: Cambridge University Press.

Hernández-Wolfe, P. 2011. "Decolonization and 'Mental' Health: A Mestiza's Journey in the Borderlands." *Women & Therapy* 34 (3): 293–306.

Kleinman, S., and M. Copp. 1993. "Emotions and Fieldwork." *Qualitative Research Methods Series* 28: 1–62.

Moonee Valley City Council. 2010. *Community Well-Being Strategy 2008–2012*. Melbourne: MVCC Community Partnerships Department.

Noble, G., and S. Poynting. 2010. "White Lines: The Intercultural Politics of Everyday Movement in Social Spaces." *Journal of Intercultural Studies* 31 (5): 489–505.

Pease, B. 2010. *Undoing Privilege: Unearned Advantage in a Divided World*. London: Zed Books.

Sims, J., K. Hill, S. Hunt, B. Haralambous, A. Brown, L. Engel, N. Huang, N. Kerse and M. Ory. 2006. *National Physical Activity Recommendations for Older Australians: Discussion Document*. Canberra: Australian Government Department of Health and Ageing.

Spradley, J. 1979. *The Ethnographic Interview*. New York: Holt, Reinhart and Winston.

Valadez, G., and A. Elsbree. 2005. "Queer Coyotes: Transforming Education to be More Accepting, Affirming, and Supportive of Queer Individuals." *Journal of Latinos and Education* 4 (3): 171–92.

8   Performative Subjects
Migrants and Their House-Building Practices

Mirjana Lozanovska

INTRODUCTION

The aim of this chapter is to investigate the relationship between agency and subjectivity of migrants in relation to their everyday practices of house-building in the immigrant-receiving countries. It argues that there is a productive relationship between human subjectivity and building practices, and more specifically that the migrant's participation in their own house adaptation, extension and building assists in extending their subjectivity into the broader cultural and social system. Migrant houses in Australia are cultural products that present intriguing images of sameness and difference, invariably perceived negatively as representations of un-Australian ideas and aesthetics. This contradiction between the positive efforts to be productive and to belong through house-building and the negativity of the reception of the house as product creates a field in which both assimilation and resistance occur.

This chapter will consider these issues through Judith Butler's theory of performative subjectivity (Butler 1993, 101–129).[1] Butler has emphasised that performativity refers less to the idea of a single act or enactment as a theatrical and major event, and more to the reiterative everyday practices that enable or disenable normative subjectivity. Butler's detailing of the production and yet exclusion of identities focuses on gender and sexuality but her argument can be brought to bear on any strong binary structure, including the host–guest binary structure that serves to reproduce ongoing exclusions in the ways that nations are imagined, naturalised and normalised (Butler 2004, 204–231). In this chapter, Butler's theory will be translated and reappropriated onto a spatial and cultural context using the migrant house as the object of investigation. It claims culture, race and ethnicity are performative practices, like sexuality. It will consider the migrant's actions in the production of the migrant house via three points extrapolated from Butler's theory. Firstly, if practices related to houses and house-building are central to the regulatory production of normativity, how and what are the exclusionary frameworks that operate to divide between migrant and non-migrant house-building practices? Secondly, can migrant house-building practices as temporal process introduce a pathway for migrant subjectivity? And, thirdly, Butler's question of which bodies matter frames the argument between skilled bodies and unskilled migrants.

This chapter will draw from extensive typological and visual documentation of migrant houses in several areas of Melbourne, Australia— the inner-city suburb, Northcote, and other northern suburbs (Thornbury, Preston, Epping) that were destinations for southern European migrants (Lozanovska 2009; Winkler 2009; Gantala 2009). This broad approach is elaborated by two in-depth projects—the first explored brick-veneer houses constructed by migrants constituting a migrant enclave in North-cote (henceforth called the Northcote Enclave). Seven houses of immigrants from southern Europe, predominantly Italy and Greece, who migrated during the 1950s and 1960s, were examined in 2009 (Lozanovska 2009; Gantala 2009). The second project, carried out in 2001, complemented the above by examining alterations to three existing housing typologies—a timber worker's cottage, a Federation-style bungalow detached house and a newly built brick veneer. These were inhabited, adapted and owned by elderly first-generation Macedonian migrants who have lived in their houses for thirty years or more.

Northcote study of existing housing typologies:

Figure 8.1 House Turquoise is a Victorian worker's cottage.

Figure 8.2 House Bitola is a Federation weatherboard.

Figure 8.3 House Aegean is a 1960s brick-veneer house. Each house is adapted by the migrant household inhabiting it.

The methods used included in-depth interviews with the migrant dwellers of the houses, photographic and architectural documentation of the house and recollections of the house in the original homeland. The chapter is in two sections. The first section sets up a historical background of migration in Australia and the theoretical framework of subjectivity and migration through Butler's theory of performativity. This provides the ground for the discussion of the house-building practices of migrants in the second section.

HISTORICAL AND NATIONAL NARRATIVES OF MIGRATION

Studies on modern Australia have stated that in the most fundamental sense it is the product of immigration, a point cleverly reiterated by a controversial Immigration minister (Castles et al. 1998; Ruddock 1997). The paradox of Australia's relationship to migration was that it produced one of the world's most ethnically diverse countries by advocating the superiority of British culture (Castles et al. 1988, 50). The inflow of people (from Europe, America and Asia) into Australia attracted by the Australian gold rush brought the population to three million by 1900 (Hawkins 1974, 23). By 1947, the non-European population (other than Aborigines) was measured by the Census as 0.25 percent of the total, a result of the exclusionary White Australia Policy implemented in 1901. Australia had become one of the 'whitest' countries in the world outside north-western Europe (Jupp 2002, 9). The government had set a paradoxical trajectory of Australia's history by transforming the nation from a potentially plural society to an exclusionist, homogenous and racist Anglo-Celtic society (Murphy 1993).

The turning point of the Second World War found the government developing a huge immigration campaign (Jupp 1991, 71). By the 1950s, the desirable sources—primarily the United Kingdom and the "blue-eyed and fair skinned" Nordic nations—diminished; southern Europe, while least racially desirable, became the major source of immigrants (Kunek 1993, 93). Melbourne was a major Australian gateway for thousands of immigrants from Italy, Greece and later Yugoslavia each year (Burnley 2001; Department of Immigration and Citizenship 2007).[2] Representations of such post-war migrants were of unskilled, uncultivated and undesirable people that were meant to fill the arduous and unsafe jobs unwanted by the host-citizens of the nation (Burnley 2001; Murphy 1993). Studies have elaborated on the continuing concentration of post-war non-English migrants in lowly status employment, boosting the development of the Australian manufacturing industry (Storer 1981; Lack and Templeton 1995).

Large-scale labour migrations were generated by short-term market interests and nation building, rather than a desire to create multi-ethnic societies (Castles et al. 1988). Different ways to manage the impact of this influx of diverse peoples is evident in the immigration policies, which can be summarised as follows: 1947–1964 'Assimilation'—assimilation programs included the adoption of the English language, English values and lifestyle and advice not to behave in a way which would attract attention (Castles 2001, 93; Jupp 2002, 19). From 1964 to 1972 the policy known as 'Integration' responded to the realities that many migrants did not speak English when they arrived, worked in factories or construction sites and lived in like-cultural communities. In 1973 'Multiculturalism' was introduced, and for a short time, ethnic minorities were supported in the preservation of their cultural identities (Jupp 1996, 5).

Nations wanting growth participate in the fantasmatic dimension of an infinite and relentless capitalism (Cope, Castles and Kalantzis 1991; Sayad 2004).[3] Migrants were considered labouring bodies in the economic equation; and in Butler's terms, their needs, traditions, desires, lives were not eligible for recognition. Additionally, their skills and capacities were not acknowledged. Migrants were paid markedly lower salaries but incurred higher rents or mortgage repayments, endured hardship and had little support (Storer 1981, 4; Lack and Templeton 1995). In this context the emergence of the migrant house is a strange and powerful paradox. The migrant house is the house occupied, adopted, extended or built by migrants, and it is a knot in the narrative that the migrant is lowly, unskilled and does not belong because it illustrates dignified existence, skill and domesticity. In contrast to the complex analysis of migration, there is a stark omission of both interest in and analysis about migration and housing (Price and Martin 1976; Junankar et al. 1993; Lozanovska 2011).

THEORETICAL FRAMEWORK: SUBJECTIVITY AND MIGRATION

Butler (1993) argues that reiterative practices are integral to a discourse on power. Normativity is a temporal process of the production of these practices as part of the regulatory forces within the power structures of society. "Performative subjectivity" refers to a forcible reiteration of the norms that are mobilised by the law through labour and the repetition of the actions that effect the materialisation of that norm. Normativity is thus consolidated through the reiterative practices. This aspect of Butler's theory establishes the theoretical framework for the analysis of assimilation in relation to the house-building practices of migrants. Assimilation into Australian society is par excellence the ownership and construction of a house, and it is this regulatory apparatus of power that the migrant participates in. The migrant reproduces the 'house' (materialisation of citizenship, order, domesticity) as integral to the norm of Australian society. Butler speaks of the "assimilating passion by which an ego first emerges," and this is illustrated in the excitable attitude of migrants towards their houses and therefore towards assimilation (Butler 1993, xxii).

An emphasis on "precarity" in Butler's theory considers the differential allocation of who is recognisable within the symbolic and actual law as citizen (Butler 2009). All subjects are already acted upon prior to performative practice, but some have a more precarious, marginalised, lawless position from which to act and from which to perform agency. Some subjects are eligible for recognition, while others are less so or not at all. Considering this exclusionary matrix, the house built by migrants is appropriated within the normative apparatus and yet excluded from the laws constituting the norm. The excluded is within the very logic of the cultural and national symbolic. In other words, the migrant house is a house, but it is not recognised as an Australian house.

However, the "paradox of subjectivation" refers to the resistance to norms enabled by such norms, emphasising agency as immanent and not an opposition to power. Butler's theory of "citation" enables an analysis of the way the migrant house is very similar to the normative Australian house. But performativity may also be considered as "citational politics" whereby a temporal process brings attention to the gaps and fissures that exceed the norm and make resignification possible (Butler 1993, 28).[4] This chapter discusses the following question: what do inhabiting, occupying, adapting, or building a house mean if a migrant with different social and cultural references carries out those actions? Butler (1993) has argued that a human body only qualifies as a body that matters according to a constructed domain of cultural intelligibility, giving rise to questions about the performance of skills and capacity against a norm related to the migrant as unskilled. Citation becomes a critical resource in the struggle to become a subject, especially within a politicisation of the norm in which the migrant is a priori not a host-citizen and therefore not allocated subject status.

CULTURAL CONFRONTATION

Australian cities have been historically planned according to pragmatic and expedient modes of settlement in which a gridded subdivision is superimposed over the topography of the land (Gleeson and Low 2001). The ubiquitous suburban block results in a strict matrix of single and detached house morphologies, producing a powerfully adhered to image of a normative Australian urbanisation (Butler 2004, 206). The ownership and construction of a house is a central indicator of an "Australian way of life" (Junankar et al. 1993, 7; Troy 2000, 724; Lewis 1999, 41). As a result Melbourne has developed into a vast suburban web, firstly developing concentrically along the lines of train and tram transportation, then in the post-war developing as sectors with low-rise, low-density suburbs of brick-veneer housing. More recent fringe regions have their own distinct urban centres due to the distance from the Melbourne CBD (Central Business District). The style of the early housing established a dominant British origin that mixed with an

Australian myth of the 'Aussie battler' and dominated the culture of the suburbs (Ang 1999, 194; Castles et al. 1988, 8; Gleeson and Low 2001, 55). A political limit of the apparatus of assimilation and its exclusionary matrix about what counts as Australian can be seen in the representation of the migrant house.

Many of the households have narrated their migration as a process involving adversity. In the early period of arrival, male migrants were in rental accommodations, sharing one room with several other individual male migrants in other people's houses, where often "if you go out, you came back like a cat (you had to be quiet). The Australians wanted it quiet" (Lozanovska 2009; Gantala 2009, 21; Storer 1981; Lack and Templeton 1995, 97). Female migrants were accommodated with other migrant families, vulnerable to the patriarchal hierarchies. The policy promoted assimilation, but the reality of the migrant's entry into society was by way of becoming invisible, squeezing into the tiny crevices of existence.

House and land acquisition by migrants has presented a problem to immigrant receiving societies that have imagined a national unity through hegemony and homogeneity (Butler 2009, vi). Many migrants built their own homes in the context of the severe housing shortage after World War II (Lewis 1999; Davison, Dingle and O'Hanlon 1995). The house makes claim to land, capital and cultural and national space, and for the migrant is pivotal in the trajectory of settlement and assimilation, promoting fields of belonging and rights to citizenship. The houses of southern European migrants made the most visible prominent impression on the architectural and urban environment in Melbourne. Their houses presented a confronting image to a public that had held a lowly perception of migrants. Enacting the desires that belong to a normative subject has exposed the unspoken limit of the assimilation equation and that the migrant's place has never been settled within a national host–guest imaginary (Vulker 1986; Lozanovska 2011). In other words the migrant house claims a right, but operations of exclusion rewrite this "performative act" in the negative: both that the migrant does not have this right, and that the house is not 'Australian'. The migrant house performs a social function of the 'norm' within Australian society and yet announces the limits of assimilation, illustrating what Butler has defined as "a phantasmatic field that constitutes the very terrain of cultural intelligibility" (1993,15).

In addition to the space of the suburban block, The Northcote enclave evolved after the local convent subdivided the southern section of its land-holdings in 1962. The planning pattern deployed the court or cul-de-sac. Each block was sold separately but on the same day in 1965, and five of the houses have remained with the original purchasing families. This urban form of courts has contributed to the formation of the social structure of the neighbourhood: "if you can imagine the street at its height, there was a lot of children (playing on the street), making a lot of noise. [A former neighbour] would come out in his pyjamas and yell at everyone"

Figure 8.4 Northcote enclave migrant houses illustrating the cul-de-sac urban pattern and the topography of the site.

(Lozanovska 2009; Gantala 2009, 25). In contrast to the isolation and lack of community characteristic of the suburbs, this intermediary space was transformed by the inhabitants' social interactivity, producing a cultural enclave. Importantly, the neighbourhood evolved from a capacity to speak to one another in a common (non-English) language and familiarity of references to similar homelands.

THE PRODUCTION OF THE MIGRANT HOUSE

In the 1960s, Northcote would not have reflected the history and cultural background of the migrant households that had begun to settle there, but it has since developed a hybrid urban and architectural appearance (Lemon 1983; Castles et al. 1988; Murphy 1993). The adaptation of existing house typologies and the construction of new migrant houses have produced an environment that alleviated the earlier experiences of acute alienation (Lozanovska 1997, 101–129). While the migrant houses in the Northcote

Enclave represent the characteristics of typical migrant houses built in the 1960s, their close proximity has produced a neighbourhood context. The house is both a pragmatic and fictional construction, and involves memories, desires and fantasy (Gardiner 1975; Rybczinski 1987). The aspiring migrant makes a crucial decision—to build a house. The households in the Northcote enclave expressed strongly that the decision was for procuring land on which to build a house and imagined their houses expressing their identities and transforming the land, similar to the architect's desire to work on a blank white page. Further, they organised the realisation of that idea into a built house. Like others, the dream of household Trieste was for a modern, enduring, dignified brick house, horrified by the small timber houses (Lack and Templeton 1995, 103). She looked at books and magazines for inspiration, resulting in the modernising systems of a pantry and built-in wardrobes, rare amongst her friends at the time.

House-building was carried out by the household with the assistance of a network of migrant members of like homelands. Men carried out much of the construction work, and the women and children contributed and maintained an environment that was nurturing and productive (Lozanovska 2009; Gantala 2009). Many first-generation southern European migrants have deployed their skills—carpentry, plumbing, painting, concreting and joinery work—calling on particular expertise (Church 2005). These practices have been described as communal festivities (Sagazio 2004, 73–92). Less researched are the skills of sewing and crafting that were employed in the fabrication of the interior of the house, including making curtains, sofa covers and seat cushions. Household Abruzzo's late husband was a skilled concreter from the Abruzzo region in Italy. The high-quality finish of the concrete in the garage and basement was done by sprinkling a layer of 'dust' (cement) and working it to attain a smooth and polished finish to the surface. A social network of immigrants from like homelands was developed alongside the processes of assimilation. This might be considered

Figure 8.5 House Nono illustrating the attention to building construction and detailing that produces an image of the migrant house.

a 'homeland-cultural' parallel Australia through which the migrant could both be informed and disseminate information on several significant factors: where there is work, how you can find accommodation, how you can buy a house and who has the necessary building skills to assist with the construction of the new house (Lozanovska 2009; Gantala 2009, 26–30).

Terrazzo or a pebble mix was evident in all the houses in the Northcote enclave as the preferred paving of the exterior of the house, including the terraces. Lewis (2009) has argued terrazzo had already been established through British connections, challenging the widely held belief that the terrazzo technique was imported and developed by Italian immigrants. He concedes that the Italian immigrants 'took naturally to the trade' and made it their own. Lewis does not consider it possible the Italian immigrants were not aware of those (obscure) examples and developed a successful trade in terrazzo construction. These skills remained invisible in the migrants' 'unskilled' jobs but appeared in the reiterative practices of house-building, contrasting the narratives of migrants as lowly, passive, peasants, and as uncultivated, disorganised communities.

The suburban block is privately owned and spacious and has allowed for a proliferation of private worlds. This has generated interiors and house-worlds or enclaves of cultural expression within the broader suburban context. In this way, migrant houses, appropriating the suburban house and occupying the ubiquitous quarter-acre block, have inscribed spaces for the practices of different traditions, languages and rituals. Photographs, paintings or prints displayed on the walls of the interior referred to the village but did not necessarily depict a real place. These were 'citations' of an imagined or real homeland of the emigrant household. They were often placed at the entry or the circulation pathways in the house, and the migrant household members passed these homeland citations in their daily activities and movements. Butler has emphasised the reiterative sense of performative subjectivity—the everyday passing of the homeland reference produces a literary palimpsest of invented or real memory inscribed onto the domestic space. It thereby associates and aligns the migrant house with these other homelands, and it is this repetition that contradicts the British origin of the post-war Australian house (Troy 2000; Lozanovska 2011).

The interior of House Turquoise appears formal through lack of use. Overlaid onto this formal order is a layer of privacy expressed by drawn curtains and blinds, making the front rooms darker than is necessary. The privacy seems to be about concealment; the interior is hidden deep within the enveloping layers of the house. Paraphernalia of objects and photographs of a life history veil the walls. It is difficult to explain the life stories as they do not fit or resonate in the normative Australian contexts; they are in Butler's terms not eligible for recognition. In contrast to the darker shades of privacy, the kitchen of House Turquoise is a naturally lit space. This was a lived space of everyday conversation during the preparation of a meal. The participant sat there in quiet contemplation.

Figure 8.6 House Aegean, like many migrant houses, has an elevated position, offering a view of the street and beyond, a characteristic that many participants commented about. The garden comprises plants and landscape design enabling a familiar setting for the migrant household, but distinguishing the migrant house.

The new houses were constructed to have an elevated position in relation to the street and many existing houses were selected for their elevated position. The participants commented positively on the raised topography of the area, and they had ideas that the house should express dignity. Critics of migrant houses have commented on this characteristic, arguing it was about the expression of status and wealth, a comment that does not consider the migrant's aesthetic or cultural preferences (Lozanovska 2011; Apperly, Irving and Reynolds1989). The elevated position produced a structure for surveillance such that the parents could look over the children playing in the street (Gantala 2009, 25). And it produced distant views over the terrain. The picturesque image of the convent to the north, a hybrid mixture of Italianate and Gothic revival architecture, and the exotic deciduous trees adorning its gardens are seen from the first-storey rear terrace of House Aegean. This view is a citation of somewhere else, an imaginary place in (southern) Europe, yet this aesthetic is integral to an Australian nineteenth-century eclectic style. It is an illustration of Butler's link between the copy and the original in the production of the norm: "the ostensible copy is not explained through reference to an origin, but the origin is understood to be as performative as the copy" (Butler 1993, 209).

Figure 8.7   Distant view from the rear terrace of House Aegean illustrating the layering between real landscape and imaginary place.

Literature on gardens has proposed that many migrant gardens are places in which creative labour is expended to symbolise connections to homeland and to Australia and creating a garden in the host country is an early stage of accepting the new country, making the unfamiliar familiar (Morgan, Rocha and Poynting 2005, 93). All the houses that were studied (except for the worker's cottage) had ornamental and edible gardens and maintained a range of fruit trees, vegetables and herbs (Lozanovska 2009). Large backyards and front yards are characteristic of all suburban houses; the difference is the detail and use (Chessell 2004, 2–6). The formation of the Anglo-Australian national identity, evoked as part of the colonisation process, involved garden cultivation of the land otherwise perceived as hostile (Holmes, Martin and Mirmohamadi 2008). Southern European immigrants, however, would use a different variety of plants and landscape aesthetic to fabricate and adorn the front gardens as revealed by the cacti and the white pebbles of some of the houses.[5] The migrants would cultivate vegetables, raise small livestock and prepare farm produce, as they had learnt to use agricultural methods in the villages that many came from. These practices differentiated migrants from aspiring Anglo-Australians, who had not engaged or were moving away from edible gardens, illustrating how the host–guest structure was inscribed onto home-making practices (Chessell 2004, 4).

The backyard of the migrant house enables migrants to re-create landscapes with familiar plants, restore smells and tastes and enable skill in gardening and cooking practices, as seen in the Northcote examples. Many had special cooking and food preparation facilities. Since coming

Figure 8.8   House Bitola 'summer kitchen' and backyard illustrating cultural expression and citation of other homelands

from a village in Italy, Household Abruzzo tends a vegetable garden, where she has lemon, mandarin and persimmon trees. Her husband, who passed away nineteen years ago, built a concrete barbeque still used for making tomato sauce; she also makes wine and salami, and all prepared foods are stored in the cellar. The migrant stories demonstrate that diverse everyday practices evident in gardens and backyards produce a sense of creativity and thereby exceed the subjected roles of the migrants in their lowly positions as unskilled labourers. This migrant suburban creativity negotiates and transforms symbols of Australia through reiterative "citation" practices referring to other homelands (Morgan, Rocha and Poynting 2005).

Like the other houses, and yet also exceptional, is the House Bitola, which comprises a бавча, a vibrant and large vegetable garden, mature trees, flowers, two dogs and an aviary.[6] The members of the Bitola household were urban dwellers before migrating to Australia. This other world is thus not imported from the homeland, but an enclave of a lively nature, produced within the diaspora framework of an immigrant house and, in this case, a Macedonian diaspora in Australia. In her ethnographic study on material culture of Turkish immigrants in Vienna, especially practices of home decoration, Şavas has argued that objects do not have traditional connections with prior pre-migration contexts or ethnic associations. Rather they have developed and are identified with the Turkish diaspora community in Vienna (Şavas 2010, 313–340). The house-worlds of the migrant construct a narrative that exceeds the trajectory of assimilation and cultural alienation, towards alleviation and cultural expression.

CONCLUSION: THE MIGRANT SUBJECTIVITY

Butler's theory of performative subjectivity has assisted in the analysis of the efforts migrants invest into the desire to belong. This chapter has argued that house-building is a reiterative practice in the process of the migrant assimilating towards the socio-ideological context. The house becomes a product that symbolises belonging: space has been appropriated and has laid a foundation for a 'proper and normative' inhabitation. This effort is generated by a necessity that impels the migrant to construct and to make, to order and clean, as a repetitive inscription of existentiality. Even so, this chapter has highlighted that while the migrants who build the houses are not illegal, the house is not eligible for recognition by the socio-ideological context of the immigrant nation.

In a seminal publication on the migrant, John Berger has stated:

> To be underdeveloped is not merely to be robbed or exploited: it is to be held in the grip of an artificial stasis. Underdevelopment not only kills:

Figure 8.9   House Turquoise as migrant house.

Figure 8.10   House Turquoise after a makeover into a heritage house.

its essential stagnation denies life and resembles death. The migrant wants to live. It is not poverty alone that forces him to emigrate. Through his own individual effort he tries to achieve the dynamism that is lacking in the situation into which he [*sic*] is born. (Berger and Mohr 1975, 32)

Migrants have chosen to live, but Butler's theory has assisted in analysing the processes of subjectivation that follow this choice. This includes how to qualify as a body that has access to the domain of cultural intelligibility (Sayad 2004). One tendency for the migrant is a preoccupation with and an endless process of attending to the house. The elderly resident who had acquired the worker's cottage, House Turquoise, has described the house as "чурук кука," a house that is bad (Lozanovska 2008). He talked about his difficulty, discomfort and lack of fit with the house. The elderly inhabitant was in his early nineties when the interviews were conducted, and for more than thirty years, had tried to make the house better with various colours and textures. The house was sold, transformed into a heritage aesthetic and resold at a much higher price. The regulatory apparatus erases differential practices and reabsorbs practices into a normative agenda.

Stories that migrants found the aesthetic appearance and organisation of existing typologies such as the terrace house unusual unfolded in the studies. Migrants have perceived the changes they made on the existing houses as improvements "before there were very bad houses, but the new Australians bought the houses and made them better" (Gantala 2009, 40; Redfern 2008). Contrasting the popular and academic criticism that migrants ruined the heritage of the existing houses, migrants identify how they have modernised the houses, making them brighter and cleaner (Lozanovska 2008; Allon 2008). The migrant's wish to assimilate is checked by the scope and limit of the norm: assimilation is not only the dissolving into the regulatory apparatus of power through reiterative practice, but becoming a part of defining the norm, and this includes "citations" that are related to the house but unrelated to the typology of the Australian house. In this sense, the proliferation and manifestation of migrant houses redefines the cultural norm of the house in Australia. Whether this evolves into a 'potentially productive crisis' depends on the interest and representation given to the empirical manifestation on the ground: there is no guarantee of recognition as an Australian house, even if there has been an emergence of the migrant house as a type.

Relations between the migrant and the house are invigorated through the repetitive nature of building, adapting, making and maintenance of the migrant house. Performative subjectivity as a reiterative practice is also temporal and a process. Everyday inhabitation and interaction with new physical conditions and new materialities produce an extension of the migrant's sense of being. The house as cultural product extends the migrant's agency into the social and cultural fields of the community, the neighbourhood and the accumulative production of the Australian city.

NOTES

1. These issues can be dealt with from various theoretical perspectives: Lozanovska (1997, 2004).
2. By 2006, 35 percent of the Melbourne metropolitan area's population was born overseas.
3. The progressive work by Jean Craig (alias Martin) is informative in this context.
4. An image that is evident in the houses of both studies is the mixture of Australian icons (Hills Hoist) and symbols of migrant space (outdoor kitchen and concrete cooking facilities).
5. This landscape makes evident the intuitive awareness of the dry climate, unacknowledged in the environmental discourse.
6. The Macedonian word бавча (Bavcha) refers specifically to a vegetable garden. The idea of edible landscape made popular with new environmental paradigms makes no reference to this history of the бавча.

REFERENCES

Allon, F. 2008. *Renovation Nation: Our Obsession with Home*. Sydney: UNSW Press.

Ang, I. 1999. "Racial/Spatial Anxiety: 'Asia' in the Psycho-Geography of Australian Whiteness." In *The Future of Australian Multiculturalism*, edited by G. Hage and R. Crouch. Sydney: Research Institute for Humanities and Social Sciences, University of Sydney.

Apperly, R., R. Irving and P. Reynolds. 1989. *A Pictorial Guide to Identifying Australian Architecture: Styles and Terms from 1788 to the Present*. North Ryde: Angus and Robertson Publishers.

Berger, J., and J. Mohr. 1975. *A Seventh Man: The Story of Migrant Worker in Europe*. Cambridge: Granta Books.

Burnley, I.H. 2001. *The Impact of Immigration on Australia: A Demographic Approach*. Melbourne: Oxford University Press.

Butler, J. 1993. *Bodies that Matter: On the Discursive Limits on "Sex."* New York: Routledge.

Butler, J. 2004. *Undoing Gender*. New York: Routledge.

Butler, J. 2009. "Performative Preclarity and Sexual Politics." *AIBR: Revista de Antropologia Iberoamericana* 4 (3): 321–336. Accessed September 28, 2012. http://www.aibr.org/antropologia/04v03/criticos/040301b.pdf.

Castles, S. 2001. "Globalization and Citizenship: An Australian Dilemma." *Patterns of Prejudice* 35 (1): 91–109.

Castles, S., W. Foster, R. Iredale and G. Withers. 1998. *Immigration and Australia: Myths and Realities*. St. Leonards: Allen and Unwin (in conjunction with Housing Industry Association).

Castles, S., M. Kalantzis, B. Cope and M. Morrissey. 1988. *Mistaken Identity: Multiculturalism and the Demise of Nationalism in Australia*. 2nd ed. Sydney: Pluto Press.

Cope, B., S. Castles and M. Kalantzis. 1991. *Immigration, Ethnic Conflicts and Social Cohesion*. Canberra: Australian Government Publishing Service.

Chessell, D. 2004. "The Italian-Australian Backyard: Italian's Sweetest Little Acre." *Italian Historical Society Journal* 12 (1): 2–6.

Church, J. 2005. *Per l'Australia: The Story of Italian Migration*. Carlton: Miegunyah Press.

Davison, G., T. Dingle and S. O'Hanlon. 1995. *The Cream Brick Frontier: Histories of Australian Suburbia*. Clayton: Monash Publications in History.

Department of Immigration and Citizenship. 2007. *Settlers Arrival 1995–96 to 2005–06—Australia States and Territories*. Australia: Commonwealth of Australia. Accessed September 15, 2011. http://www.immi.gov.au/media/publications/statistics/.

Gantala, M.V. 2009. "Migrant House of the 1960s: Transforming Australia's Brick Veneer House." Thesis for Master of Architecture Course, Deakin University.

Gardiner, S. 1975. *The Evolution of the House*. London: Constable.

Gleeson, B., and N. Low. 2001. *Australian Urban Planning: New Challenges, New Agendas*. St. Leonards: Allen and Unwin.

Hawkins, F. 1974. *Immigration Policy and Management in Selected Countries: A Study of Immigration Policy and Management and Their Implications for Population Growth in the United States, Australia and Israel*. Ottawa: Canadian Immigration and Population Study.

Holmes, K., S.K. Martin and K. Mirmohamadi. 2008. *Reading the Garden: The Settlement of Australia*. Carlton: Melbourne University Press.

Junankar, P.N., D. Pope, C. Kapuschinski, G. Ma and W. Mudd. 1993. *Recent Immigrants and Housing*. Canberra: Australian Government Publishing Service.

Jupp, J. 1991. *Immigration*. Sydney: Sydney University Press.

Jupp, J. 1996. *Understanding Australian Multiculturalism*. Canberra: Australian Government Publishing Service.

Jupp, J. 2002. *From White Australia to Woomera: The Story of Australian Immigration*. New York: Cambridge University Press.
Kunek, S. 1993. "Brides, Wives and Single Women: Gender and Immigration." *Lilith: A Feminist History Journal* 8:82–113.
Lack, J., and J. Templeton, eds. 1995. *Bold Experiment: A Documentary History of Australian Immigration since 1945*. Melbourne: Oxford University Press.
Lemon, A. 1983. *The Northcote Side of the River*. North Melbourne: City of Northcote (in conjunction with Hargreen Publishing Company).
Lewis, M. 1999. *Suburban Backlash*. Hawthorn: Blooming Books.
Lewis, M. 2009. *Australian Building: A Cultural Investigation*. Melbourne: University of Melbourne. Accessed July 23, 2009. http://www.mileslewis.net/australian-building.
Lozanovska, M. 1997. "Abjection and Architecture: The Migrant House in Multicultural Australia." In *Post-Colonial Spaces*, edited by G. Nalbantoglu and W.C. Thai. New York: Princeton University Press.
Lozanovska, M. 2004. "Emigration/Immigration: Maps Myths Origins." In *Drifting: Architecture and Migrancy*, edited by S. Cairns. London: Routledge.
Lozanovska, M. 2008. "Resisting Assimilation: The Mild Aesthetics and Wild Perception of the Migrant House." Paper presented at the History in Practice, 25th Annual Conference for SAHANZ, Geelong, Victoria.
Lozanovska, M. 2009. "Northcote Enclave Study." Unpublished fieldwork, Deakin University.
Lozanovska, M. 2011. "Aesthetic Anxieties: The Problem of Defining the Migrant House in Australia." Paper presented at the AASA Conference, Geelong, Victoria.
Morgan, G., C. Rocha and S. Poynting. 2005. "Grafting Cultures: Longing and Belonging in Immigrants' Gardens and Backyards in Fairfield." *Journal of Intercultural Studies* 26 (1–2): 93.
Murphy, B. 1993. *The Other Australia: Experiences of Migration*. Cambridge: Cambridge University Press (in association with the Ethnic Affairs Commission of NSW).
Price, C., and J. Martin. 1976. *Australian Immigration: A Bibliography and Digest 3, 1975 (1)*. Canberra: Australian National University.
Redfern, L. 2008. "Interview M. Lozanovska, The Old House." *Radio Eye*. Radio National, ABC, September 6, 14:00. Accessed March 15, 2013. http://www.abc.net.au/radionational/programs/radioeye/the-old-house—-stara-kua-architecture-immigration/3200606.
Ruddock, P. 1997. *Dispelling the Myths about Immigration*. Canberra: Department of Immigration and Multicultural Affairs.
Rybczinski, W. 1987. *Home: A Short History of an Idea*. New York: Penguin Books.
Sagazio, C. 2004. "A Lasting Impact: The Italians." In *Carlton: A History*, edited by P. Yule. Melbourne: Melbourne University Press.
Şavas, Ö. 2010. "The Collective Turkish Home in Vienna: Aesthetic Narratives of Migration and Belonging." *Home Cultures* 7 (3): 313–340.
Sayad, A. 2004. *The Suffering of the Immigrant*. Cambridge: Polity.
Storer, D. 1981. *Migrant Families in Australia: A Review of Some Social and Demographic Trends of Non-Anglo-Saxon Migrants 1947 to 1981*. Working Paper 3. Melbourne: Institute of Family Studies.
Troy, P., ed. 2000. *A History of European Housing in Australia*. Cambridge: Cambridge University Press.
Vulker, J. 1986. *Housing in Australia*. Gladesville: RAIA Educational Consultant, Jacaranda Press.
Winkler, S. 2009. "Cultural Place Identity: A Study in Melbourne's Western Suburbs." Master's thesis, Deakin University.

9 Indigenous Subjectivities
How Young Women Prisoners Subvert Domination Representations to Maintain Their Sense of Intrinsic Worth

Sophie Goldingay and Tania Mataki

INTRODUCTION

It is only since the industrial era (between 1700 and 1750) that prisons have been used as a primary means of punishment in Western society. Indigenous populations worldwide have used other systems of redress in response to offending against accepted laws and customs prior to their being colonised by European settlers. For New Zealand Maori prior to colonisation, justice revolved around the concept of Utu—which is closely related to reciprocity and mutual obligation and requires a process of compensation to a wronged party by an offender (Mead 2003). In New Zealand and around the world, the colonisation process has led to the dominance of an imposed settler process for justice, and hence, today few people of Euro-Western extraction would imagine any other response to crime than imprisonment, despite much evidence as to its ineffectiveness at reducing it (Foucault 1979).

Recent global renewal of retributive philosophy, sparked by media coverage of horrific crimes and subsequent lobbying by victims-rights groups, has further incited fear, disgust and hatred towards those who offend (Pratt and Clark 2005) and further entrenched the use of long prison sentences as a sanction for crime in New Zealand and overseas. Foucault has observed that discourses regarding prisoners in the public domain form an "anchor point to what actually happens in the institution" (1979, 222). Thus, the impact of these discursive formations outside the prison walls affects both the ways prisoners construct themselves and the way staff and other prisoners construct them. As will be seen in this chapter, prisoners are constructed as not worthy of respect or dignity. Women prisoners are even further vilified, as not only have they broken the law; in failing to uphold society's moral codes, they have transgressed what is considered acceptable female behaviour.

Drawing from data from a study conducted in New Zealand women's prisons between 2005 and 2008 with young women prisoners aged seventeen to nineteen years, and Maori tribal representatives who support them in prison, this chapter will consider the impact of imprisonment on the type of self-hood and identity possible for young women prisoners serving time in New Zealand prisons. It will do this by considering seminal and recent literature around prison processes, and then the discursive formations used by both prisoners and staff within the women's prison and those circulated by politicians, policymakers and the media. It will then explore the ways these young women resisted these limiting subjectivities through discourse, by drawing on Indigenous notions of what constitutes worth in a person. Thus the chapter is underpinned by post-structural assumptions of the fluidity and contingency of identity (Burr 2003) and the link between identity and material and subjective effects (Allan 2008).

DYNAMICS OF PRISON CULTURE AND TYPE OF SELF POSSIBLE WITHIN THE PRISON

Prisons have been described as 'total institutions', where there is limited opportunity for those outside to see what is happening within and for inmates to have contact with the outside. As such, prisoners experience total immersion (Paterline and Peterson 1999), where prisoners are likely to have limited opportunities to claim or maintain the identity they construct and have constructed by others in their lives outside prison walls. Earlier researchers observed that prisoners may be constructed by staff as "bitter, secretive and untrustworthy" (Goffman 1961, 18), and "must be bad, because prison is a place where bad men [*sic*] are locked away" (Klare 1960, 16). In addition, staff members may bring into the prison populist retributive sentiments which mirror the hatred incited by the media towards those who offend and which affect the ways staff members construct prisoners and their worth.

POWER RELATIONS, DIVIDING PRACTICES

Foucault developed an account of how power operates in institutionalised environments and observed that "prison is the only place where power is exercised in its naked state, in its most excessive form, and where it is justified as a moral force" (1977, 210). Thus, the use of power to repress prisoners is part of a normal routine for prison staff. Researchers have described prisons as 'authoritarian' (Royal Commission into Aboriginal Deaths in Custody 1998; Jennifer, Cowie and Ananiadou 2003), punitive, hierarchical, individualistic and impersonal (Royal Commission into Aboriginal Deaths in Custody 1998, para. 4). The dynamics of prison life have been studied throughout the years, and the Stanford Prison experiment carried out in 1971 found that staff mistreating prisoners had little to do with in-built personality or personal deficiency and more to do with where staff members are placed in the power dynamic between those in the role of prisoner and those in the role of custodians of them (Zimbardo, Maslach and Haney 1999). Such power dynamics have a significant impact on how prisoners negotiate their identity, because repressive power may lead to dividing practices which serve to "objectivize" (Foucault 1982, 208) those who are powerless and put them in a category that is less than, or inferior to, those not objectivised. They may be seen as subhuman, and words and actions toward them will be guided by this construction. Goffman posited that the ways prisoners are constructed are likely to make them "feel inferior, weak, blameworthy and guilty" (1961, 18).

CONSTRUCTIONS OF YOUNG WOMEN PRISONERS' IDENTITIES

Identity vectors can be used to conceptualise aspects of the self within which people are constituted and constitute themselves, with respect to prevailing discourses (Allan 2008). For young women prisoners, their sense of self is thus brought into being through multiple subjectivities in relation to the identity vectors of prisoners, women/girls, of being members of particular ethnic groups and of being young people. This next section of the chapter will consider these aspects of young women prisoners' identities and how they are constructed, with the view of considering the social and discursive climate that they live within. From here, the chapter will turn to ways they creatively use their agency to construct themselves and each other in positive ways, and resist positionings which are experienced as oppressive and limiting.

PRISONERS AS WOMEN

The ways women prisoners are constructed by prison staff and those outside prison walls have been shown to belittle and demean to an even greater extent than that experienced by male prisoners due to stereotypes circulated in the media. These stereotypes include that women prisoners are "expendable" and "evil" (Singer et al. 1995), thus even further de-valuing the self-hood and worth of women prisoners. Scholars have also observed that women's crime is perceived as even worse than men's as they have violated a code of femininity (see, for example, Bishop and Frazier, as cited in Jeffries 2001). Criminal activity is not associated with behaviour which is nurturing and caring, or with people who are physically weak and vulnerable, and these are qualities often associated with femininity (Allan 2008; Constantinople 2005). In addition, literature reflects a pervading view amongst prison staff (both custodial and allied health) that women prisoners are harder to work with (for example, Belknap, Holdinger and Dunn 1997; Gaarder, Rodriguez and Zatz 2004; Pollock 1984; Sim 2002), and "emotional, temperamental, complaining, moody, quarrelsome, demanding and changeable" (Pollock 1984, 85).

PRISONERS AS YOUNG WOMEN

Even when young people have not broken the law, they are still constructed as irresponsible (McCrone 2008) and a threat to community peace (Panelli, Nairn and McCormack 2002). Those young women who have broken the law have been particularly vilified by the New Zealand media by the use of animal imagery such as "barbie bitches" (Fairfax NZ News 2008), "queen bees" (Fairfax NZ News 2008) and "pitbull women" (McLeod 2006). The effect of such constructions is to dehumanise and further demean young women prisoners to the status of an animal. Such a construction is contrary to a dignified and humanised subject-self and is instead objectivised, inferior and of little worth.

RESISTANCE TO LIMITING CONSTRUCTIONS OF THE SELF

Nevertheless, while dominant discourses within the prison and outside prison walls may construct young women prisoners as subhuman, the women themselves enlisted counter discourses which resisted such positionings and limiting identities. This next section of the chapter will draw on data collected between 2006 and 2008 in New Zealand women's prisons from young prisoners, to consider how young women prisoners construct and negotiate their identities from the cultural resources available to them, or, in other words, how they employ "practices of the self" (Foucault 1997, 21). This will be supplemented by data collected through focus groups with Maori tribal representatives from the areas where women's prisons are located.

We would like to start this section by detailing some demographic information about the sample of twenty young women we spoke to during data collection, to help you as reader to get a sense of who they are, beyond their status of being young women prisoners. Our team consisted of the first author, Sophie Goldingay, then a doctoral student of predominantly Anglo-Celtic descent; Marcia Marriott, of Nga Puhi and Ngati Kahagnugnu descent; and the second author, Tania Mataki, of Kai Tahu, Ngati Mamoe and Whanau Apanui descent. Three young women were seventeen years of age, ten were eighteen and the remaining seven were nineteen years of age. There were twelve identifying as full Maori (60 percent), four (20 percent) as both Maori and from a Pacific nation (i.e. Tonga, Samoa, Niue), and one (5 percent) as Maori and Pakeha (New Zealand Anglo-Celtic). The remaining two included one who identified only as Pakeha, and one from an overseas country.

The complexity and difficulties faced in the lives of these young women became apparent from listening to the women and viewing their files. Thirteen of the twenty women had given permission for our research team to view their personal files, and from this we could see that two had been in foster care as children, six had served time in youth justice facilities, five had fathers who were gang members, four were victims of childhood sexual abuse or rape and five were reported to have mental health disabilities. Out of the thirteen files, we could see that twelve young women had convictions for a violent offence and twelve (not necessarily the same twelve) had a substance dependency issue prior to sentencing (Goldingay 2008). Three young women had engaged in sex work to support themselves and to obtain drugs; two before their fifteenth birthday. At the time of interviewing, three were pregnant and five already had a child, including one who had two children. Thus, these young women have been in positions of victims and aggressors, experiencing significant psychological and psychiatric difficulties, addiction and hardship. They were only just out of childhood, yet already mothers, responsible for the next generation.

It would be useful, therefore, to consider the wider context of these young women's lives and the fact that seventeen out of the twenty identify as either Maori or part Maori. Maori are the Indigenous peoples who were colonised by British settlers from the 1800s. Colonisation is a process of using power to impose a foreign culture onto native peoples, such as language, cultural practices, law, institutions and worldviews. In such a process the Indigenous worldviews and practices are made invisible and irrelevant, and the Indigenous population become marginalised and 'othered' (Foucault 1977). The impact of colonisation on the well-being of Indigenous peoples is well documented, especially the issue of high imprisonment rates amongst Indigenous populations (see, for example, Bishop 2005; Te Momo 2004; Hogg 2001; Huriwai et al. 2001; Tuhiwai-Smith 2005).

Nevertheless, like all participants in a power dynamic, the colonised peoples can and do adopt various strategies to resist unfavourable and negative positionings, and, as noted by Spivak (1988), the key site of change is in the language or discourses used by the colonisers and the colonised. In saying this, it is important to bear in mind the variety of ways Maori people will identify as Maori and the variety of identities and worldviews both within Maoridom and beyond in the New Zealand context. As will be seen later in the chapter, at various times, young women drew on various discourses relating to their Maoriness, which had the effect of resisting the dehumanising and demeaning discourses in circulation in the prison context. In order to contextualise some of the discursive formations used by young women prisoners, I will first discuss some key aspects of culture which I learnt from literature and from the tribal representatives with whom I consulted.

One key aspect of identity which I will explore in this chapter is how a young woman prisoner might position her sense of self along the individualist-collectivist continuum and how this might be a way of fashioning a sense of self with a greater number of possibilities than that on offer from limiting prison discourses. In Euro-Western culture, a person's sense of self is constructed by discourse in an individualist manner. For example, the self is talked about as if "defined in terms of its unique personal attributes, traits and characteristics" (Tassell, Flett and Gavala 2010, 139). The self is measured, defined and evaluated according to his or her achievements, and seen as entirely responsible for their situations. In addition, in an individualist culture, relationships with others are voluntary and exist primarily to meet one's needs (Harrington and Liu 2002). In such a framework, those who do not actively work to enhance the self are easily dismissed as lazy, irresponsible and not worthy of help and support.

Some Maori, however, may see their sense of self as intricately bound with the collective. Rather than define their worth by individual self-enhancing achievements, their sense of self (and self-worth) may spring from the strength of relationships with significant others, with actions which enhance the collective (as opposed to the self) being prioritised (Tassell, Flett and Gavala 2010). Maori people might use the word *whakawhanaungatanga* for this concept, which roughly translates as the practice of engaging in mutually beneficial or family-like interactions which emphasise the needs of the group, not the individual (MacFarlane et al. 2008; Tassell, Flett and Gavala 2010). The following quote is from data collected during a focus group from tribal representatives of Ngai Tahu, Ngati Mamoe and Te Whanau Apanui descent:

> Whanau [family] and the practice of whakawhanaungatanga, is an integral part of Maori identity and culture. It is a collective responsibility we have to each other. (Focus group participant)

Thus, whakawhanaungatanga is still practiced on Marae (meeting places) and at any Maori and tribal gatherings. What flows from this notion is that it is not important what job you do, what mistakes you have made or how rich or accomplished you are in a Western sense. A person's identity is understood through asking such questions as, "Ko wai au?" which means, "From which sacred waters do you come?" Related to this question is, "No hea koe?", or "Where (in relation to tribe, mountain, river and Marae) do you come from?"

Bearing this in mind, considering how young women prisoners draw on discourses of whakawhanaungatanga where the prefix *whaka* means 'to do' and *whanaungatanga* refers to kinship (Tassell, Flett and Gavala 2010) may be one step in a decolonising (Tuhiwai-Smith 2005) strategy that aids young women prisoners' well-being both within prison and beyond. As discussed by Durie (1994), well-being is a holistic concept which includes strong social/family relationships, spiritual well-being, mental/emotional well-being and physical well-being. Therefore, alongside the concept of whakawhanaungatanga are other important inter-related values which support well-being which are held dear by Maori, including reciprocity (*utu*) and spirituality (*wairuatanga*). The study demonstrated many ways that these values and aspects of well-being were sought after and enacted in the prison setting, especially between the young women and adult women prisoners (Goldingay 2007b). For the purposes of this chapter, however, I will focus on the ways young women prisoners drew on collective discourses to resist limiting subjectivities within the prison setting.

It is useful to note at this point that non-Indigenous writers overseas believe that building family-like relationships may make prisoners more likely to adhere to an antisocial prison code (Larson and Nelson 1984; Redman and Fisher 2002) and adopt a criminal identity (Larson and Nelson 1984). Paradoxically, such relationships also improve a prisoner's well-being and hence improve success in treatment (Redman and Fisher 2002), irrespective of cultural identity. This paradox suggests that prisoners adapt to prison life to survive, including adopting the 'code' which leads to their acceptance and hence social and physical safety in the prison setting. From a post-structural point of view, however, identity is not fixed, and the fact that a prisoner can adapt to the context of the prison also suggests the ability to adapt to life outside in a successful way as well. Therefore, the issue of well-being in prison will be prioritised, since, as noted by Ward, Mann and Gannon (2007), improving well-being is, by definition, likely to reduce reoffending.

There are two main ways that we observed young women prisoners position themselves as within a collective or family-like ways. The first involved seeing themselves as daughters or nieces to the adult women prisoners, which enabled them to feel a sense of being a part of a collective and as such subject to positive guidance and direction. Kowhai discusses how all the adult women prisoners are considered 'aunties' when the interviewer asks her what sort of support she receives in prison:

> In here? Maoris in here? Yeah [*laughs*], they take the aunty, you better watch out, kick you up the arse; they do that kind of thing. They keep you in line. But they're all Maori aunties to us anyway. It's all right, oh yeah, whatever. I'm the baby one here. Yep, um, it's like normal (. . .). These are all aunties to me [*laughs*]. (Kowhai)

Another prisoner went on to discuss the fact that keeping near the adult women prisoners enabled her to stay out of trouble:

> If I want to play up . . . if I get a bit fucked off and I want to play up, and I get in trouble, then I'll go straight to one of my aunties [*laughs*] and I'll just sit by them, because I know that (. . . / . . .) they'll give me a whack [*laughs*]. (Huia)

The collective experience of being parented by those who are not related biologically is different to Euro-Western norms of the nuclear family. From Huia's and Kowhai's transcripts, it appears there is no question that they see themselves as part of a collective family within the prison setting, where all adults take an interest in them. It enables the young women to feel supported in their struggle to manage themselves and their behaviour. It also demonstrates the interest older prisoners take in supporting young women to be their best self (Goldingay 2012) and resist limiting identities which may otherwise be ascribed to them by virtue of being young and in prison.

The second way that young women demonstrate their sense of being in a collective or as practicing whanaungatanga is in the kindnesses they extend to each other irrespective of the status of being offenders. Samantha draws on a discourse of unconditional positive regard which is often considered essential in a number of world religions (Roehlkepartain 2005; Topper 2003).

> We did crimes, you know; we did some crimes. But, um, when we talk with each other, it's like you see past their crimes, and, you know, they're a good person. (Samantha)

These words represent a stark contrast to the ways young women prisoners are generally constructed as outlined earlier. Miria, in another prison, notes a similar process of compassionate awareness and unconditional positive regard for prisoners less fortunate than herself:

> All the people that may have been here, that understand, you know, especially in a place like here, I reckon, and they see that you're down and out, and come along, and that's where it puts you in place, and the next person that walks through the door that's younger, that's younger than yourself, so you think, how can I help them. So you go and look after that person. It just works. (Miria)

Again, Miria constructs herself as a person with a role of actively supporting those less fortunate by virtue of having newly entered prison. She also speaks of reciprocity or utu; she is giving back because she has been given to. Such a construction of self serves to humanise and validate both herself and her fellow prisoners. Maori feminist Stewart-Harawira (2007, 134) discusses Maori notions of spirituality and notes the importance of recognising the "sacredness inherent in all things and all beings, [to recognise] the truth of our inherent interconnectedness and [the need] to act in the world and towards each other appropriately". Thus, since all people are intrinsically connected to others and the natural world irrespective of mistakes, character flaws, offences or other negative markers, all people are of intrinsic worth by virtue of their existence. From this it follows that all are worthy of dignity and respect.

Marika, in yet another prison, echoes the compassion and active care that young women extend to those who may be distressed, as can be seen from the quote below:

> Just if someone new comes in and stays in her room, we're thinking that she's scared, and if it's her first time, then we'll know how it feels like, so we just go in there and tell her to come out, and yeah, just hard out talk to her. (Marika)

Well-known Maori psychiatrist and scholar Dr. Mason Durie (2003, 62) also supports the potential for Maori to build a positive and secure identity despite their imprisonment, and notes that "the culture of the prison, with its demoralising and dehumanising forces, can be replaced with an environment which builds on the notions of positive development and the acquisition of a secure identity".

Nevertheless, not all participants observed such acts of kindness or demonstrations of a secure and healthy sense of identity. Many felt compromised by the toxic atmosphere which included bullying and stand-overs (Goldingay 2007a). The tension between collective notions of whanaungatanga and the prison subculture were expressed clearly by Huia when discussing prison processes and how it impacts on her ability to practice her cultural identity:

> Whanau [family], awhi [help and support], when we come here, we're all whanau, we're all meant to be whanau and look after each other and feel safe, you know, cos we were in that same situation. When the new bunny came in, we were in that situation (. . .) and we should think about it, but some of the women don't think about it. That's what I mean, that's whanau, treat them like whanau, don't treat them like an outsider. (Huia)

As discussed in an earlier paper (Goldingay 2007a), new prisoners in New Zealand women's prisons are termed 'bunnies' and constructed as fair game for victimisation by other prisoners. Power abuses and authoritarianism are the antithesis of the reciprocal, collective, respectful values which characterise the ideas of Tikanga Maori (Maori values).

Durie also acknowledges the difficulties inherent in attempting to bring Tikanga Maori (Maori customs and practices) into a prison setting, as described below:

> One of the difficulties in promoting a positive cultural identity within the prison environment is that the overall prison culture, even when reformed, inevitably contradicts the values and belief systems which form the basis of a Maori philosophy. Maori understandings of reciprocity, mutuality, respect for difference, space and time considerations, and the use of Maori language, find little endorsement in most prisons. (2003, 62)

IMPLICATIONS

Thus, literature and some data collected from young women prisoners indicated that prison culture and Maori culture are diametrically opposed. While Maori culture values reciprocity, mutuality and respect, an imprisoned self is one which is stripped of dignity and self-respect; the self is dehumanised, demeaned and subject to oppressive and repressive power relations. Nevertheless, some young Maori women were able to construct a sense of self which held dignity and worth as part of the process of whakawhanaungatanga—the process of building family-like relationships within the prison setting. Such a process acknowledged the intrinsic worth of all, irrespective of crime or status as prisoner. Talking about one's own role as key to collective well-being enabled young women to recognise and experience a sense of their intrinsic worth, their connections to others and the important role they have in life by nature of their relationships. Such relationships included those with adult women prisoners, where they received support and guidance in being able to behave in ways that supported the well-being of the whole group. They also included their role in being able to see the goodness and value in fellow prisoners, encompassing compassion, forgiveness and unconditional positive regard.

Nevertheless, the prison system does not belong within Maori cultural practices as it embodies separation from family and community and it alienates the offender from the victims. It inflicts suffering but does not achieve restorative justice or utu, a key process to restore balance for Maori in situations of offence or wrongdoing (Mead 2003). Gang culture and bullying also pervade women's prisons (Goldingay 2007a), and gang culture is the antithesis of Tikanga Maori, as it is built on power and intimidation (Dennehy 2006). The fledgling resistance to these limiting contexts and resulting subjectivities struggle against pervading forces which serve to construct young women in negative and demeaning ways.

CONCLUSION

There are no simple ways to ensure young women prisoners' well-being within a prison setting as imprisonment is not designed to promote well-being; it is designed to punish and separate those who have been criminalised from the rest of society. As such, it does not promote holistic health. Evidence from scholars such as Ward, Mann and Gannon (2007) suggests that promoting well-being amongst all humans, prisoner or not, is more likely to lead to them functioning well. One way to promote well-being amongst Maori in prison is to adopt a decolonising approach and foreground Indigenous cultural practices and processes. The importance of acknowledging and supporting identity as made up of social and spiritual connections, in a collective sense, to the natural and social world cannot be underestimated. Thus, identity is constructed through identifying with a tribe, with rivers, mountains and Marae. Isolation for Maori away from such connections, including whanau (family) and support systems, has shown to have negative impacts on Maori whanau (families) and individuals in all aspects of their lives.

As shown by data in this chapter, young women prisoners themselves drew on Indigenous values to resist limiting subjectivities which would compromise their well-being. As also shown, however, doing so was difficult due to imported gang culture and oppressive and repressive power relations within the prison. Oppressive discourses and practices operated both horizontally between prisoners in the form of bullying and vertically between prisoners and staff. It is therefore important that correctional departments work closely with Indigenous leaders to consider the best ways to support young Maori women who have broken the law. Considering alternatives to prison which build on notions of utu and restorative justice could be one of these possibilities. In order to avoid further colonising Maori, it is also important that control over decisions which affect Maori in various localities are made by Maori leaders who are in the role of guardians in those areas.

ACKNOWLEDGMENTS

We would like to thank SPEaR (Social Policy Evaluation and Research) for funding the research, and give special thanks to Aunty Kiwa Hutchen, Marcia Marriott and New Zealand Department of Corrections management and staff. Further, we would like to thank those who participated in focus groups and individual interviews for this study. *To rarau toku raurau ka ora te iwi.* With your knowledge and my knowledge we can grow together.

REFERENCES

Allan, E. 2008. *Policy Discourses, Gender, and Education: Constructing Women's Status.* New York: Routledge.
Belknap, J., K. Holsinger and M. Dunn. 1997. "Understanding Incarcerated Girls: The Results of a Focus Group Study." *Prison Journal* 77:381–405.
Bishop, R. 2005. "Freeing Ourselves from Neo-Colonial Domination in Research." In *The Sage Handbook of Qualitative Research*, edited by N. Denzin and Y. Lincoln. Thousand Oaks, CA: Sage Publications.
Burr, V. 2003. *Social Constructionism.* 2nd ed. London: Routledge.
Constantinople, A. 2005. "Masculinity–Femininity: An Exception to a Famous Dictum?" *Feminism & Psychology* 15:385–407.
Dennehy, G. 2006. "Working with Women (People) from Gangs: Complexity and Challenge." In *Innovative Approaches to Stopping Family Violence*, edited by K. McMaster and A. Wells. Wellington, New Zealand: Steele Roberts.
Durie, M. 1994. *Whaiora: Maori Health Development.* Auckland, New Zealand: Oxford University Press.
Durie, M. 2003. *Nga Kahui Pou: Launching Maori Futures.* Wellington, New Zealand: Huia Publishers.
Fairfax NZ News. 2008. "'Barbie Bitches' Plague School Playgrounds." http://www.stuff.co.nz/the-press/news/national/456745/Barbie-bitches-plague-school-playgrounds. Accessed 21 July 2013.
Foucault, M. 1977. "Intellectuals and Power." In *Language, Counter-Memory, Practice*, edited by D. Bouchard. Oxford: Basil Blackwell.

Foucault, M. 1979. *Discipline and Punish: The Birth of the Prison*. New York: Vintage Books.

Foucault, M. 1982. "The Subject and Power." In *Michel Foucault: Beyond Structuralism and Hermeneutics*, edited by H. Dreyfus and P. Rabinow. Chicago: University of Chicago Press.

Foucault, M. 1997. "The Ethics of Concern for the Self as a Practice of Freedom." In *Michel Foucault: Ethics, Subjectivity and Truth,* edited by P. Rabinow. New York: New Press.

Gaarder, E., N. Rodriguez and M. Zatz. 2004. "Criers, Liars, and Manipulators: Probation Officers' Views of Girls." *Justice Quarterly* 21:547–579.

Goffman, I. 1961. *"Asylums": Essays on the Social Situation of Mental Patients and Other Inmates*. London: Penguin Books.

Goldingay, S. 2007a. "The Bullying Problem: Exploring Ways Young Women Prisoners Talk about Prison Bullying." *Te Awatea Review* 5:9–13.

Goldingay, S. 2007b. "Jail Mums: The Status of Adult Female Prisoners among Young Women Prisoners in Christchurch Women's Prison." *Social Policy Journal of New Zealand* 31:56–73.

Goldingay, S. 2008. "Young Women Prisoners in Aotearoa New Zealand: Substance Abuse and Violent Offending." *Te Awatea Review* 6:17–19.

Goldingay, S. 2012. "'Without Fists': Age Mixing and Its Influence on Safety and Criminal Contamination in Women's Prisons." *Youth Studies Australia* 31:17–25.

Harrington, L., and J. Liu. 2002. "Self-Enhancement and Attitudes toward High Achievers: A Bicultural View of the Independent and Interdependent Self." *Journal of Cross-Cultural Psychology* 33:37–55.

Hogg, R. 2001. "Penalty and Modes of Regulating Indigenous Peoples in Australia." *Punishment and Society* 3:355–379.

Huriwai, T., P. Robertson, D. Armstrong, T. Kingi and P. Huata. 2001. "Whanaungatanga: A Process in the Treatment of Maori with Alcohol and Drug-Use Related Problems." *Substance Use and Misuse* 36:1033–1051.

Jeffries, S. 2001. "Gender Judgements: An Investigation of Gender Differentiation in Sentencing and Remand in New Zealand." Unpublished doctoral thesis, University of Canterbury, Christchurch, New Zealand.

Jennifer, D., H. Cowie and K. Ananiadou. 2003. "Perceptions and Experience of Workplace Bullying in Five Different Working Populations." *Aggressive Behaviour* 29:489–496.

Klare, H. 1960. *Anatomy of Prison*. London: Hutchinson.

Larson, J., and J. Nelson. 1984. "Women, Friendship, and Adaptation to Prison." *Journal of Criminal Justice* 12:601–615.

Macfarlane, A., T. Glynn, W. Grace, W. Penetito and S. Bateman. 2008. "Indigenous Epistemology in a National Curriculum Framework?" *Ethnicities* 8:102–127.

McCrone, J. 2008. "Nights of Extreme" The Press, June 28.

McLeod, R. 2006. "Pitbull Women—A New Breed." *The Press*, March 17.

Mead, H.M. 2003. *Tikanga Maori: Living By Maori Values*. Wellington, New Zealand: Huia Publishers.

Panelli, R., K. Nairn and J. McCormack. 2002. "'We Make Our Own Fun': Reading the Politics of Youth with(in) Community." *Sociologia Ruralis* 42:106–130.

Paterline, B., and D. Petersen. 1999. "Structural and Social Psychological Determinants of Prisonization." *Journal of Criminal Justice* 27:427–441.

Pollock, J. 1984. "Women Will Be Women: Correctional Officers' Perceptions of the Emotionality of Women Inmates." *Prison Journal* 64:84–91.

Pratt, J., and M. Clark. 2005. "Penal Populism in New Zealand." *Punishment and Society* 7:303–322.

Redman, T., and A. Fisher. 2002. "Sense of Community of Young Women in Custody." In *Psychological Sense of Community: Research Applications and Implications*, edited by A. Fisher, C. Sonn and B. Bishop. New York: Klever Academic/Plenum.

Roehlkepartain, E. 2005. *The handbook of spiritual development in childhood and adolescence*. Thousand Oaks, CA: Sage.

Royal Commission into Aboriginal Deaths in Custody. 1998. *Regional Report of Inquiry in New South Wales, Victoria and Tasmania. 1998*. Australian Legal Information   Institute. http://www.austlii.edu.au/au/other/IndigLRes/rciadic/regional/nsw-vic-tas/. Accessed 21 July 2013.

Sim, J. 2002. "The Future of Prison Health Care: A Critical Analysis." *Critical Social Policy* 22:300–323.

Singer, M., J. Bussey, L. Song and L. Lunghofer. 1995. "The Psychosocial Issues of Women Serving Time in Jail." *Social Work* 40:103–114.

Spivak, G. 1988. "Subaltern Studies: Deconstructing Historiography." In *Selected Subaltern Studies*, edited by R. Guha. Oxford, England: Oxford University Press.

Stewart-Harawira, M. 2007. Practising indigenous feminism: Resistance to imperialism. In J. Green (Ed), *Making space for indigenous feminism* (pp. 124–139). Black Point, Nova Scotia, Canada: Zed Books.

Tassell, N., R. Flett and J. Gavala. 2010. "Individualism/Collectivism and Academic Self-Enhancement in New Zealand Maori University Students." *Journal of Pacific Rim Psychology* 4:138–151.

Te Momo, F. 2004. "A Maori Third Way: What Does It Mean to New Zealand Today?" *Social Work Review* Winter:5–10.

Topper, C. 2003. Spirituality in pastoral counselling and the community helping professions: Expanding the horizons. Binghampton, NY: Howorth Pastoral Press.

Tuhiwai-Smith, L. 2005. "On Tricky Ground: Researching the Native in the Age of Uncertainty." In *The Sage Handbook of Qualitative Research*, edited by N. Denzin and Y. Lincoln. Thousand Oaks, CA: Sage Publications.

Ward, T., R. Mann and T. Gannon. 2007. "The Good Lives Model of Offender Rehabilitation: Clinical Implications." *Aggression and Violent Behaviour* 12:279–297.

Zimbardo, P., C. Maslach and C. Haney. 1999. "Reflections on the Stanford Prison Experiment: Genesis, Transformations, Consequences." In *Obedience to Authority: Current Perspectives on the Milgram Paradigm*, edited by T. Blass. Mahwah, NJ: Erlbaum.

Part IV

Interrogating Privileged Subjectivities

10 Transforming Privileged Subjectivities
Toward a Pedagogy of the Oppressor

Bob Pease

INTRODUCTION

Some years ago, I researched the politics and practices of pro-feminist men (Pease 2000). I argued at the time that one of the most central issues for women's prospects for gender equality is whether or not men can and will change. I put the view that changing the social relations of gender will involve changing men's subjectivities, as well as their daily practices. This research was grounded in my own experiences as a white, heterosexual man who was committed to a pro-feminist position.

I did not believe then, and I do not believe now, that heterosexual men changing their personal lives to become more equal with their female partners will in and of itself challenge the structures of patriarchy. However, I believe that men have choices as to whether they accept patriarchy or work collectively against it. If they are to work against it, some form of transformation in men's subjectivity in relation to domination seemed necessary. My research was concerned with the limits and possibilities of such transformation.

In more recent years, I have been concerned with the wider politics of change in relation to privileged subjectivities, as they relate to colonialism, white supremacy, class elitism, heteronormativity and ableism, along with male domination (Pease 2010). I have been concerned with the questions: How can members of privileged groups transform their dominant subjectivities? Under what conditions might we be able to encourage members of privileged groups to engage with the knowledge of oppression and open themselves to hearing the voices of the oppressed?

As an anti-violence activist who works primarily with men who are not identified as perpetrators of violence in a diversity of workplaces and community-based contexts, I am also interested in practical pedagogical strategies for engaging men and members of privileged groups more generally in loosening their connections to dominant subject positions. In this chapter, I set out some of the theoretical, political and pedagogical issues involved in such work.

THE INVISIBILITY OF PRIVILEGE

Most privilege is not recognised as such, by those who have it. In fact, "one of the functions of privilege is to structure the world so that mechanisms of privileges are invisible—in the sense that they are unexamined—to those who benefit from them" (Bailey 1998, 112). So not being aware of privilege is an important aspect of privilege. Johnson (2001) observes how members of privileged groups either do not understand what others mean when they refer to them as privileged or they tend to get angry and defensive. When well-meaning members of privileged groups offer to support the struggles of oppressed groups, they often cannot understand why those groups might be suspicious or even hostile towards them. Many men challenging male violence wonder why women do not embrace and applaud their efforts. Also, many whites who are opposed to racism wonder why Indigenous people are not more supportive of their stand. Members of privileged groups often just do not see how they benefit from the practices that they say they oppose.

While some men are willing to acknowledge that women are oppressed, they are less willing to recognise that they are correspondingly 'over-privileged'. Thus, much oppressive behaviour can be quite unconscious. It is easy to recognise blatant sexism or racism when someone puts another person down because of their gender or their race. But it is much harder to recognise how in our everyday interactions we may reinforce dominance just because we belong to a dominant group by birth.

Most of us seem to have some difficulty in accepting our own involvement in the day-to-day oppression of others and how many of the benefits we receive have been derived from the continued subordination of others. So members of dominant groups are taught not to see themselves as privileged or prejudiced because they are able to only identify the more blatant forms of discrimination enacted against marginalised groups. They do not recognise the ways in which society gives them privileges that come with their gender, class, race and sexuality (Pease 2010).

THE INTERNALISATION OF DOMINANCE AND PRIVILEGE

A concept that has been used to understand some of the ways in which privileged people sustain their dominant position is "internalised domination". Pheterson (1986, 147) defines internalised domination as "the incorporation and acceptance by individuals within a dominant group of prejudices against others". The concept of internalised domination may explain in part why members of privileged groups may reinforce the oppression of others without considering themselves as being oppressive.

Tillner (1997, 2) usefully takes the notion of internalised domination a little further by defining dominance "as a form of identity practice that constructs a difference which legitimises dominance and grants the agent of dominance the illusion of a superior identity". In this process, the identities of others are invalidated. Thus, I maintain that dominance is socially constructed and psychically internalised. To challenge dominant identities, we will need to explore different models of identity and construct subjectivities that are not based on domination and subordination.

It is not possible for members of dominant groups to escape completely the internalisation of dominance. Negative ideas and images are deeply embedded in the culture, and it is unlikely that men, whites and heterosexuals will not be affected by sexism, racism and homophobia.

The concept of internalised domination thus helps us to understand the seeming paradox that Minow (1990) identifies in relation to those who publicly criticise social inequality, while at the same time engaging in practices that perpetuate these inequalities. While she emphasises the task of examining and reformulating our assumptions about the social world, she acknowledges that this requires more than individuals learning to think differently, because of the ways in which the individual's thinking is shaped by institutional and cultural forces. So while it is important for individuals to acknowledge the privileges they have and to speak out against them, it is impossible to simply relinquish privilege (Pease 2010).

PRIVILEGE AND WHERE WE STAND

To address the potential for members of privileged groups to develop a critical distance from their privilege, it is necessary to turn to feminist standpoint theory. Developing knowledge grounded in the experience of oppressed groups, it provided a critical stance against Eurocentric, patriarchal, class elitist, racist, heterosexist and ableist conceptual frameworks (Harding 2004).

Feminist standpoint theory posits a direct relationship between one's structural location in the world and one's understanding of the nature of the world. While standpoint theory has been used to validate the experiences of the oppressed and encourage collective resistance against oppressors (Harding 2004), it can also be used by those in dominant groups to critically interrogate the ways in which their own world views and practices sustain the oppression of others. Harding (1995), for example, argues that standpoint theory can offer an explanation of how members of dominant groups can develop knowledge that serves the interests of subordinate groups. In this view, it is possible for members of dominant groups to develop the capacity to see themselves from the perspective of those in subordinated groups. Dominant groups do not necessarily form a homogeneous network of shared interests. Thus, it is possible for members of dominant groups to challenge the taken-for-granted self interests of their own group.

PRIVILEGE AS STRUCTURED ACTION: DOING DOMINANCE

I argue that it is through the processes of 'accomplishing' gender, race and class, et cetera, that social dominance is reproduced. That is, we live our lives trying to attain certain valued aspirations associated with these statuses. Thus, rather than seeing concepts like race, gender and class as reified categories, we should be more interested in the processes of gendering, racialising and classing. In this project, I draw upon the work of Fenstermaker and West (2002, 75) who set out to analyse how race, gender and class constitute "ongoing methodical and situated accomplishments". They analyse how people conduct themselves in specific situations to understand how people legitimate and maintain social divisions in our society.

When we act in the world, we are not just operating within structural constraints that are outside of our control. Rather, we are also determining the nature of those structures through our actions and interactions. The structures which oppress us then are not only contextual; they are also constituted through our actions. While we construct our identities through our actions, we also reproduce relations of power and domination. The implication of this view is that we can challenge those arrangements by engaging in 'inappropriate' racial or gender behaviour.

We must acknowledge the structural dimension of inequality and the importance of locating class, gender and race relations in the context of institutional structures. We must also accept, as Thorne (2002, 85) argues, that "gender, and race, class and compulsory heterosexuality extend deep into the unconscious and outward into social structure and material interests".

O'Brian and Howard (1998, 25) capture the complexity well when they say that "we are socially constituted subjects who navigate webs of opportunities and obstacles not necessarily of our own choosing". Furthermore, the concept of interlocking oppressions must involve a recognition of both 'macro-level connections' at the level of social structures and 'micro-level processes' which describes how individuals experience their positions within the hierarchies of domination and oppression. In challenging the dichotomisation of micro and macro forces, we must recognise the dynamic and reciprocal relationship between social structure and social action. While social structure is reproduced by the widespread and continual actions of individuals, it also 'produces subjects'. So individuals do not simply produce gender, race and class in a vacuum. Rather, they are reproduced and constrained by institutional settings such as families, workplaces and the state. In the remainder of this chapter, I use this framework to interrogate privileged subjectivities in three sites of domination: class elitism, gender privilege and white supremacy.

CLASS ELITISM AND CLASS DOMINATION

While I adopt a structural Marxist understanding of class in terms of its relation to the means of production, I also believe that we need to understand the way in which class is subjectively experienced and reproduced in our lives. Most class analysis is more concerned with the effects of class structures on societies as a whole and less concerned with the impact on individuals. Barone (1998) argues that class oppression needs to be extended to include an understanding of classism. This involves an understanding of both social structures and human subjectivity and agency. Thus, it is important to remember that class is not only about economics. It is internalised in our psyches and it shapes our subjectivity and identity. Class affects people on an emotional as well as an economic level (Brantley et al. 2003, 2–5).

Skeggs (1997) thus notes that it is those who have class privilege who have promoted the retreat from class, by taking attention off their own privilege. Making economic class invisible is thus a strategy for reproducing the identity of the middle class. Theorists of mobility, individualisation and identity who are displacing class are in effect reproducing their own middle-class power, and they avoid having to name it or accept responsibility for it. hooks (2000) says that class-privileged people who remain silent about economic inequality do not want to open up the issue of "where they stand", because of what they have to lose.

Gilbert (2008) asks what it means to be a person of class privilege. Dominant group members come to believe that they are more deserving, more intelligent and more articulate than working-class people. Children of middle-class and owning-class families grow up to believe that they are more intelligent and superior and are born to be in control (Leondar-Wright and Yeskel 2007). They are thus socialised into oppressor patterns of behaviour that will enable them to take on middle- and owning-class occupations and worldviews (Barone 1998).

As in other forms of privilege, middle-class experience is presented as universal. The white, heterosexual gentile middle class is presented as the normative standard that others aspire to. Skeggs (1997) talks about "respectability" as one of the key signifiers of this class positioning, as it is the basis upon which people pathologise others. Respectability is constructed as a normative standard to which others aspire. Skeggs (1997, 2) says that it "embodies moral authority" as distinct from those who need to be controlled. It is the basis upon which middle-class people position themselves against 'the masses'. Middle-class people construct their identity by distancing themselves from the working class. Leondar-Wright (2005) says that it is difficult for middle-class people to recognise their own class conditioning because they are led to believe that they represent the ideal that working-class people aspire.

Skeggs (1997) argues that to reinvigorate class analysis, we need to focus on class entitlements and the effects these entitlements have on others. Because class entitlement is produced and institutionalised, it can also be challenged and reconstructed. This is another form of class struggle at the cultural level, where class subjectivities are contested. So while class and class divisions must be understood in the context of objective structures, they are also legitimated at a subjective and cultural level by classist attitudes and beliefs. Class is internalised within the psyches of individuals who slot themselves into positions of subordination and domination.

Those who occupy positions of class dominance act in ways that are either complicit with those structures or stand in opposition to them. So while anger is an appropriate response to class-based form of exploitation (Sayers 2005), we must also address the complex feelings associated with our complicity in reproducing those structures. While class is a reflection of objective social conditions, it is also reproduced and reformulated through our actions and practices. I am suggesting here that middle-class subjectivities are constructed in ways that reproduce the oppression of working-class people.

Acker (2006) argues that social structures are embedded with social relations that are constantly constructed and reconstructed. Thus, she frames race, class and gender as racialised and gendered class practices rather than as structures. In this view, individuals are "enmeshed in complex webs of racialised and gendered practices that change over the course of the lifetime" (Acker 2006, 67). This is because identities are both fluid and contradictory.

What is missing in relation to sociological debates on class is how class constructs subjectivities and identities. The identities and subjectivities of individuals are significant in either reproducing or challenging structures of privilege and oppression. We all need to understand how we have internalised class into our psyches and address the role that we play in reproducing class-based oppression.

GENDER PRIVILEGE AND MASCULINE SUBJECTIVITIES

Mederos (1987) differentiates between the institutionalised patriarchal system, which refers to the structural advantages and privileges that men enjoy, and the personal patriarchal system, which involves men's face-to-face interactions with women both at home and in the public sphere. He makes the point that because all men are socialised within patriarchy, they will all believe to some extent that they have a right to make normative claims upon women. Men will differ in relation to what claims they believe they make and how they may enforce them. These claims include deferential treatment, unpaid domestic labour and child care, sexual services and emotional support.

Men thus come to believe that they deserve something from women, which they then experience as an entitlement. The totality of these entitlements and claims are what constitute male privilege. This sense of entitlement may not necessarily be conscious and it may only come into their awareness when they are deprived of this unreciprocated service.

We cannot overcome sexism and patriarchal arrangements if we do not acknowledge and address male privilege. If we do not recognise the unearned privileges we receive as men, we will be unable to acknowledge the impact of these privileges upon the women in our lives.

Men have to be involved in the process of challenging patriarchy. What such men can achieve in relation to reconstructing their subjectivities and challenging the cultural and structural foundations of their privilege is the subject of extensive debate within feminism and pro-feminist masculinity politics. However, I argue that it is possible for men to develop a cognisance of their gender privilege and to act in ways that challenge the reproduction of gender inequality (Pease 2000, 2002).

The concept of doing gender (West and Zimmerman 1987) focuses our attention on the interactional dynamics that men engage in to reproduce our privileges. This idea challenged the structural determinist approaches to gender that seemed to leave little room for resistance and change. Undoing gender, which describes interactions that challenge gender inequality (Deutsch 2007), allows us to identify how we can challenge the reproduction of male privilege.

In Connell's (2000) view, the primary motivating factor for men to support gender equality will come from their "relational interests" winning out over their egotistic interests. It is men's relationships with partners, daughters, mothers and sisters, et cetera, that will provide the basis upon which men will come to support change (Connell 2000, 204). Such a stance requires the development of what Kimmel (2000, 335) calls "democratic manhood", where men will take a stand against gender injustice on the basis of moral and ethical commitments. We must not underestimate, however, how difficult it is to challenge unequal gender regimes.

However, the preconditions for these actions for men have to rest on an acknowledgment that patriarchy and unearned male privileges exist, that they are reproduced by the practices of men and that men will have to develop the moral courage to act in concert with women to live a life based on reciprocity rather than unearned entitlement.

WHITE SUPREMACY AND WHITELINESS

Just as feminism has challenged men to critically reflect upon their masculinity, so anti-racism challenges white people to reflect upon what it means to be white. Just as men have been challenged to not take 'male' for granted, so white people have been challenged to not take 'white' for granted.

Frankenberg (1993) describes this as 'race cognisance', whereby racial inequality is understood as being related to social structure. This latter approach involves white people explicitly naming themselves as white because of the understanding that one of the ways in which white privilege is maintained is through white people not naming themselves in racial terms.

Once we acknowledge our whiteness and the privileges that flow from it, we then have to decide what to do about it. The strategies are often framed as either transforming or disowning whiteness. Can whiteness be reconstructed, or does it have to be repudiated? One argument is that we can construct a positive version of whiteness; that whiteness can be more than a form of domination. Flagg (1997, 629) argues that white people can develop "a positive white racial identity" that is "neither founded on the implicit acceptance of white racial domination nor productive of distributive effects that systematically advantage whites". In this view, whiteness as domination can be unlearned, just as men can unlearn hegemonic masculinity.

However, in a context where racial domination continues to exist, I do not believe that we can simply construct individual non-oppressive white subjectivities. While whiteness may be able to be reformed at the level of identity, I do not believe that this means it is able to be completely disassociated from white privilege. This aim can only ever be partially achieved under conditions of continued white domination.

Whiteness is also a process. It is one of the ways in which we 'do' social dominance. So it is not just an identity that comes out of having a white body; it is also something that is performed or practiced (Levine-Rasky 2002). Knowles (2003, 25) refers to this process as "race making". What this means is that we reproduce racial inequality through "a myriad of ordinary everyday social processes". It is thus the activities of people in their everyday lives that sustain white dominance. For those of us who are white, we make ourselves through our habitual practices. It follows that there is potential for us to 'undo' some elements of the maintenance of white privilege. Perhaps, through changing what we do in the world, we can influence both who we are and what we gain from being white.

There is debate about whether we can 'do' race in ways that do not reproduce racial hierarchy. Critics suggest that seeing whiteness as something that is simply performed fails to make connections with institutionalised dominance (Ahmed 2004). The maintenance of whiteness involves group loyalty and material interests as well as individual performance (Anderson 2003). However, to suggest that whiteness is socially constructed through everyday activities challenges the conception of whiteness as a fixed social category. White privilege is not something that can be simply rejected and denounced. White people cannot give up their whiteness. However, developing an awareness of one's whiteness and one's racial prejudice can be a part of challenging racial inequality.

While Sullivan (2006) acknowledges that racism operates on a conscious level as well, she also maintains that white privilege is sustained though unconscious practices. This means it must be resisted through transformation of the self as well as through restructuring structures and institutions. Whiteness is internalised in individual white people as 'an unconscious habit', and as such it is often outside people's experience or knowledge. In her view, white domination is located both in the world and in the individual white person.

While racism is embedded within global political and economic structures, it is people's commitment to these structures that reproduces them. We need to explore how racism takes root in people's lives. This means that changes in institutional structures need to be complemented by individual psychic changes in individuals. One cannot fully shirk racist habits, however, while conducive political and social structures are in place. Thus one needs to be working on both fronts at the same time.

Sullivan (2006) makes the distinction between being white and being whitely. While being white simply refers to white skin colour, being whitely embraces habits and dispositions that reproduce racial hierarchy and white privilege. In her view, one can be white without being whitely. So in this view, one can detach oneself from whiteliness that reproduces racism by challenging one's racist habits and disposition. The process of unlearning whiteliness is not one of transcending white privilege but rather of acknowledging it and using it to struggle against racial domination.

Bush (2004) also argues that there is an important relationship between prejudiced attitudes and racialised social structures. She believes that systemic racial inequality is reproduced through individuals' complicity with ideologies that support those structures. If you believe that you are not part of racially unequal structures, then you can enjoy the benefits of being white without having to do anything about them. We may even express anger at the injustice of those structures as long as we are not implicated in them or held personally responsible for them. By demonstrating how the everyday consciousness of people sustains those structures, we open up spaces for individuals to contribute to the elimination of white domination.

TOWARDS A PEDAGOGY OF THE PRIVILEGED

What is the role of the privileged in working for social change? Can enlightened members of privileged groups be effective allies in combating oppression? The premise underlying much progressive politics is that only the oppressed can address oppression. Many writers have portrayed the oppressor as being incapable of either personal change or activism in relation to social change. Thus there has been little attention given to how one might develop a pedagogy to transform the oppressors and the privileged. While working to challenge oppression from below should be the foundation for social change movements, such movements can be complemented by developing strategies to engage and address those who hold power that stand in the way of these movements.

So how do we move oppressors towards a critical consciousness of their oppressor status? In recent years, we have witnessed the emergence of a pedagogy for the privileged (Curry-Stevens 2004, 2007) and a pedagogy of the oppressor (Lee 2002; Breault 2003; Kimmel 2002; ; Frueh 2007; Pease 2010). These developments provide us with a conceptual and pedagogical framework for engaging members of privileged groups about their unearned entitlements. Much of this work also takes these strategies out of the university classroom and into government- and community-based forums where privilege holders can be challenged about their advantages.

The starting point is to acknowledge that oppression and privilege exist because it is privilege that blinds many people in dominant groups to the realities of oppression. This involves awakening a sense of injustice among those who do not experience the pain and hardship that is the basis for developing a critical consciousness among the oppressed. Under what conditions might we be able to encourage members of privileged groups to engage with the knowledge of oppression and open themselves to hearing the voices of the oppressed (Fine 2006)?

For oppressed groups, reconstructing one's identity is a positive and affirmative project. Members of oppressed groups need to gain a sense of self-respect and pride associated with their identity (Mullaly 2002). However, for those in privileged groups, the process by which people become conscious of their internalised domination and react against it involves the construction of a 'negative identity'.

Developing a negative identity involves challenging one's internalised moral superiority and rejecting the sense of entitlement that so many of us are socialised into. This entails refusing part of who we are and constructing a traitorous relationship with our dominant subject position (Ferguson 1998).

Many writers have described the process of coming to oppose the dominance of one's own group as becoming a traitor to their own identity group (Harding 1995; Bailey 1998; Lee 2002). Traitorousness involves being disloyal to the parts of ourselves that are privileged and rejecting the expectations that having such privilege entails (Heldke and O'Connor 2004). Bailey (1998) discusses traitorous identities as developing a cognisance of one's privilege and refusing to be faithful to the world views that members of privileged groups are expected to hold.

Harding (1995) believes that members of privileged groups can reinvent themselves by learning about their own social location and by taking responsibility for their dominant subject position. She argues that privileged traitors can develop liberatory knowledge by being critically reflective of their privilege rather than being oblivious to it. The aim for traitors is to search for ways to disrupt the process of coercion into dominant subject positions. Bailey (1998) regards the process of becoming traitorous as similar to Aristotle's idea of acquiring moral virtue.

We all need to recognise the multiple subjectivities we inhabit and to locate ourselves in relation to privilege and oppression in our lives. Those of us who are most unmarked, white, heterosexual, middle-class, able-bodied men, need to understand how our subjectivities are constructed through the marking of others (Fellows and Razack 1998).

Bailey (1998) believes that to develop a traitorous identity, one must become a "world traveller" to learn about the lives of those who are oppressed.

"World travelling" is an idea developed by Lugones (1987) to describe the process of locating oneself outside of one's comfort zone and immersing oneself in other worlds where our privileged identities will be challenged.

RELINQUISHING PRIVILEGE?

Some radical critics will no doubt see a project such as this as fitting within a neoliberal agenda and will question what potential there is for privileged activists to contribute anything meaningful to progressive social change. Some critics doubt that members of privileged groups will voluntarily commit themselves to challenge their own privilege (Curry-Stevens 2007). They certainly raise the issue of not expecting the privileged to do so. One of the forms of privilege is the ability to ignore calls for involvement in social justice campaigns. Those who do make a commitment still have the privilege at any point of changing their minds and allowing their commitment to wane. Awareness of privilege can be reversed. But my experience in campaigns tells me that there is a point of no return for allies. Significant reconstruction of subjectivities can occur to the point where turning away from activist involvements is no longer viable.

Furthermore, if oppressed groups continue to maintain pressure on privileged groups to transform themselves and to take responsibility for action against their privilege, they will not be taking this course of action solely from internalised motivations (Curry-Stevens 2007).

Even if one is sceptical of the ability of the privileged to transform themselves and relinquish their privilege, how might they respond more positively to the demands of the oppressed? We need to understand their resistance to change and how they can be encouraged to lessen the obstacles they create that work against change. For if those with privilege do not yield power, then the gains achieved by the oppressed can be more easily co-opted (Curry-Stevens 2004).

It is unlikely than anyone brought up in a patriarchal, racist, class-elitist, heterosexist, ableist Western society is ever likely to fully eliminate oppressive attitudes and practices. It is also clear that the privileged cannot fully relinquish privilege. While the structural relations that advantage the privilege remain, they will always gain unearned benefits from them. This leaves privilege-cognisant members of dominant groups in the difficult position of knowing that they cannot get rid of their privilege and that they cannot use it without perpetuating the dominant–subordinate relations they are opposed to (Bailey 1999).

While some aspects of privilege cannot be renounced or given up because it is structurally conferred, a socially just society would take conferred dominance away from privileged groups, and this will be experienced as a loss by them. When members of privileged groups say that they want everyone else to have privilege but do not want to relinquish the privileges they have, they often want to hold on to their conferred dominance.

Unsettling privilege is difficult because it is the privileged who make the rules and construct the norms that govern our actions. It would be utopian to suggest that the structures of privilege can be dismantled solely by actions from within. Challenging privilege has to be a project from below as well. However, I argue that members of privileged groups do not have to maintain their internalised commitment to dominance, that they can be responsive to the claims of the oppressed and that they can loosen their connections to dominant subject positions.

ACKNOWLEDGMENTS

Some sections of this chapter were adapted from an earlier version of these ideas in Pease (2010).

REFERENCES

Acker, J. 2006. "Inequality Regimes: Gender, Class and Race in Organisations." *Gender and Society* 20 (4): 441–464.

Acker, J. 2006. *Class Questions, Feminist Answers*. Lanham, MD., Rowman and Littlefield.

Ahmed, S. 2004. "Declarations of Whiteness: The Non-Performativity of Anti-Racism." *Borderlands E-Journal* 3 (2).

Anderson, M. 2003. "Whitewashing Race: A Critical Perspective on Whiteness." In *White Out: the Continuing Significance of Racism*, edited by A. Doane and E. Bonilla-Silva. London: Routledge.

Bailey, A. 1998. "Privilege: Expanding on Marilyn Fry's Oppression." *Journal of Social Philosophy* 29 (3): 104–119.

Bailey, A. 1999. "Despising an Identity They Taught Me to Claim: Exploring a Dilemma of White Privilege Awareness." In *Whiteness: Feminist Philosophical Reflections*, edited by C. Cuomo and K. Hall. Totowa, NJ: Rowman and Littlefield.

Barone, C. 1998. "Political Economy of Classism: Towards a More Integrated Multilevel View." *Review of Radical Political Economy* 30(2):1–30.

Brantley, C., D. Frost, C. Pfeffer, J. Buccigrossi and M. Robinson. 2003. *Class: Power, Privilege and Influence in the United States*. New York: Wetware, Workforce Diversity Network.

Breault, R. 2003. "Dewey, Freire, and a Pedagogy for the Oppressor." *Multicultural Education* 10 (3): 2–7.

Bush, M. 2004. *Breaking the Code of Good Intentions: Everyday Forms of Whiteness*. Oxford: Rowman and Littlefield.

Connell, R. 2000. *The Men and the Boys*. Sydney: Allen and Unwin.

Connell, R. 2003. "The Role of Men and Boys in Achieving Gender Equality." Consultant's paper for the Role of Men and Boys in Achieving Gender Equality Expert Group Meeting, United Nations Development Program, Brasilia, Brazil, October 21–24.

Curry-Stevens, A. 2004. "Pedagogy for the Privileged: Building Civic Virtues in Political Leaders." Unpublished paper, University of Toronto.

Curry-Stevens, A. 2007. "New Forms of Transformative Education: Pedagogy for the Privileged." *Journal of Transformative Education* 5 (1): 33–58.

Deutsch, F. 2007. "Undoing Gender." *Gender and Society* 21 (1): 106–127.

Fellows M., and R. Razack. 1998. "The Race to Innocence: Confronting Hierarchical Relations among Women." *Journal of Gender, Race and Justice* 1:335–352.

Fenstermaker, S., and C. West. 2002. "Introduction." In *Doing Difference, Doing Gender: Inequality, Power and Institutional Change*, edited by S. Fenstermaker and C. West. New York: Routledge.

Ferguson, A. 1998. "Resisting the Veil of Privilege: Building Bridge Identities as an Ethico-Politics of Global Feminisms." *Hypatia* 13 (3): 95–113.

Fine, M. 2006. "Bearing Witness: Methods for Researching Oppression and Resistance: A Textbook for Critical Research." *Social Justice Research* 19 (1): 83–108.

Flagg, B. 1997. "Was Blind but Now I See: White Race Consciousness and the Requirement of Discriminatory Intent." In *Critical White Studies: Looking behind the Mirror*, edited by R. Delgado and J. Stefancic. Philadelphia: Temple University Press.

Frankenberg, R. 1993. *White Women, Race Matters: The Social Construction of Whiteness*. Minneapolis: University of Minnesota Press.

Frueh, J. 2007. "Pedagogy of the Oppressors: Challenging Nationalism from a Position of Privilege." Paper presented at the International Studies Association Conference, Chicago, Illinois, March.

Gilbert, R. 2008. "Raising Awareness of Class Privilege Among Students." *Diversity and Democracy* 11 (3): 7–9.

Harding, S. "Subjectivity, Experience and Kowledge: An Epistemology for Rainbow Coaltion Politics". In *Who Can Speak? Authority and Critical Identity*, edited by J. Roof and R. Wiegman. Chicago, Il., Illinois Press.

Harding, S. 2004. "Standpoint Theory as a Site of Political, Philosophical and Scientific Debate." In *The Feminist Standpoint Theory Reader: Intellectual and Political Controversies*, edited by S. Harding. New York: Routledge.

Heldke, L., and P. O'Connor, eds. 2004. *Oppression, Privilege and Resistance: Theoretical Perspectives on Racism, Sexism and Heterosexism*. New York: McGraw-Hill.

hooks, b 2000. *Where We Stand: Class Matters*. New York: Routledge.

Johnson, A. 2001. *Privilege, Power and Difference*. Mountain View, CA: Mayfield Publishing Company.

Kimmel, M. 2000. *The Gendered Society*. New York: Oxford University Press.

Kimmel, M. 2002. "Toward a Pedagogy of the Oppressor." In *Privilege: A Reader*, edited by M. Kimmel and A. Ferber. Boulder, CO: Westview Press.

Knowles, C. 2003. *Race and Social Analysis*. London: Sage Publications.

Lee, R. 2002. "Pedagogy of the Oppressor: What Was Freire's Theory for Transforming the Privileged and the Powerful?" Paper presented at the annual meeting of the American Educational Research Association, New Orleans, LA. April 1–5.

Leondar-Wright, B. 2005. *Class Matters: Cross-Class Alliance Building for Middle-Class Activists*. Gabriola Island, BC: New Society Publishers.

Leondar-Wright, B., and F. Yeskel 2007. "Classism Curriculum Design." In *Teaching for Diversity and Social Justice*, 2nd ed., edited by M. Adams, L. Bell and P. Griffin. New York: Routledge.

Levine-Rasky, C. 2002. "Critical/Relational/Contextual: Toward a Model for Studying Whiteness." In *Working through Whiteness: International Perspectives*, edited by C. Levine-Rasky. Albany: State University of New York Press.

Lugones, M. 1987. "Playfulness, 'World' Travelling and Loving Perception.' *Hypatia* 2 (2): 3–19.

Mederos, F. 1987. "Patriarchy and Male Psychology." Unpublished manuscript.

Minow, M. 1990. *Making All The Difference: Inclusion, Exclusion and American Law*. New York: Cornell University Press.

Mullaly, B. 2002. *Challenging Oppression: A Critical Social Work Approach*. Toronto: Oxford University Press.

O'Brian, J., and J. Howard. 1998. "Introduction: Differences and Inequalities." In *Everyday Inequalities: Critical Interrogations*, edited by J. O'Brian and J. Howard. Malden, MA: Blackwell.

Pease, B. 2000. *Recreating Men: Postmodern Masculinity Politics*. London: Sage Publications.

Pease, B. 2002. *Men and Gender Relations*. Melbourne: Tertiary Press.

Pease, B. 2010. *Undoing Privilege: Unearned Advantage in a Divided World*. London: Zed Books.

Pheterson, G. 1986. "Alliances Between Women: Overcoming Internalized Oppression and Internalized Domination." *Signs: Journal of Women, Culture and Society* 12 (1): 146–160.

Sayers, A. 2005. *The Moral Significance of Class*. Cambridge: Cambridge University Press.

Skeggs, B. 1997. *Formations of Class and Gender: Becoming Respectable*. London: Sage Publications.

Sullivan, S. 2006. *Revealing Whiteness: The Unconscious Habits of Racial Privilege*. Bloomington: Indiana University Press.

Thorne, B. 2002. "Symposium on West and Fenstermaker's 'Doing Difference.'" In *Doing Gender, Doing Difference: Inequality, Power and Institutional Change*, edited by S. Fenstermaker and C. West. New York: Routledge.

Tillner, G. 1997. "Masculinity and Xenophobia: The Identity of Dominance." Paper presented to the UNESCO conference Masculinity and Male Roles in the Perspective of a Culture of Peace, Oslo, Norway.

West, C., and D. Zimmerman. 1987. "Doing Gender." *Gender and Society* 1 (2): 125–151.

11 Moving from One Place to Another within a Coloniser Positioning

Clare Land

INTRODUCTION

Recent research with a particular political community of Indigenous people from southeast Australia and some of the non-Indigenous supporters of their ongoing struggle for survival and justice demonstrates the political importance of transforming the subjectivities of the privileged. This chapter will discuss some ways in which non-Indigenous people involved in this struggle are attempting to understand and resist dominance. Excerpts from interviews with non-Indigenous people who accept that they are positioned as 'colonisers' will give insight into how they have developed critical distance from their positioning and how this has felt—how they have experienced a sense of moving from one place to another within their positioning.

The research involved interviewing Indigenous people from southeast Australia who have pursued land rights, community control and sovereignty and non-Indigenous people who were nominated as being reflective about the practice of solidarity in this context. It focused on the work of both Indigenous people and non-Indigenous supporters to forge productive relationships in a context in which these structural categories are the focus of critical attention both at the level of the state and between individuals. It discerned and engaged with the apparent politics of non-Indigenous solidarity with southeast Indigenous struggles. The research described was inspired by questions generated through the personal experiences of the author as a non-Indigenous person who has worked in solidarity with these southeast Indigenous struggles.

Indigenous people from the community already mentioned have contested the nature of non-Indigenous people's solidarity with their struggles in the settler-colonial context of Australia (Foley 2000). They have exhorted non-Indigenous people to practice critical self-reflection and to organise publicly and collectively to challenge white privilege and structural injustice (Land 2011). Further, they have challenged would-be supporters to reconstruct understandings of interests,[1] in an attempt to generate recognition of the need for societal change "not just for us (Aboriginal people] but for everybody" (Foley, as cited in Land 2011, 51). Finally, Indigenous people have encouraged learning and questioning that would lead non-Indigenous people to confront complicity with colonialism. Whether or not this last challenge is something that has been wholeheartedly taken up is a question I will return to later in this chapter.

The larger project out of which the material for this chapter is drawn is underpinned by the conviction that in order to change colonising relations in Australia, there will need to be both redistribution (land rights, including compensation) and changes in the way non-Indigenous people see and experience themselves. As Nancy Fraser (1995; see also Lake 2003, 145–160, on the Australian context) has argued, 'race' is one of the axes of injustice that are simultaneously cultural and socio-economic, and in which recognition and redistribution struggles are intertwined. A particular responsibility to act is placed on those who are "multiply" or "relatively" privileged (Pease 2010, 23; Young 2011, 181), such as non-Indigenous people who also accrue white privilege and/or class privilege. This chapter will be devoted to showing how non-Indigenous participants in the research apparently make sense of their subjectivity as they are constructed and reconstructed within colonialist and other relations of power.

THEORISING PRIVILEGED SUBJECTIVITIES

Understandings of subjectivity in colonising contexts still refer to the important contributions of Albert Memmi (1965) and Frantz Fanon (1968), who both wrote from and about North Africa (on Fanon, see Mansfield 2000). Memmi in particular provides insight into the subjectivities of colonisers who either embrace or come to refuse the colonialist project.[2] Much more recently, in a study of a political subculture that developed in late nineteenth-century London, Leela Gandhi (2006, 6) has brought to light the political sensibilities of those who had nothing to gain materially from undoing the dynamics of empire, yet who 'stood with' the colonised. Memmi's description of the contradictions faced by the 'coloniser who refuses' speak to the experiences of those I interviewed. Emma Kowal (2011, 318) is concerned with a similar group, "white anti-racists" employed in the "Indigenous improvement" sector (specifically, a health institute in northern Australia), who "readily acknowledge their privilege". Bob Pease (2010), Frances Kendall (2006) and Stephen Burghardt (1982) have addressed would-be allies and community and social workers who, in cognisance of privilege, are keen to find new ways of acting and organising politically. Adam Barker (2010) and Jennifer Margaret (2010) speak specifically to would-be allies of Indigenous people in settler colonies. In combination, these works speak to the project of confronting colonialism as a non-Indigenous person from within a colonising society such as Australia.[3] The implication for non-Indigenous people involved in supporting Indigenous struggles is parallel with Ruth Frankenberg's advice for conscientious white people: that "we must always remember that we act from within the social relations and subject positions we seek to change" (Frankenberg 1993, 5; see also McIntosh 2006; Tamasese and Waldegrave 1996).

There is a complex, partial overlap between the dynamics of settler colonialism and whiteness in Australia. For white non-Indigenous people in particular to understand relationships to Indigenous people from a structural view is to learn from Indigenous critiques of systems of white supremacy, and the privilege that accrues to white people (Bailey 1998; Foley 1998; McIntosh 2006). This is not intended as an argument to accept a view of non-Indigenous and white people as homogenous, but as a strategy for bringing unacknowledged white privilege into view and informing strategies for challenging it. To Alison Bailey (1998, 30, 36), "insiders" to white privilege who learn from the knowledge and critical social theories generated by people outside of white privilege but who are familiar with its workings "are said to have 'traitorous identities'" because they use that knowledge to "forge traitorous scripts."[4]

Shannon Sullivan (2006) takes a more pessimistic view of the project of learning to think and act out of different scripts: she dedicates her book, *Revealing Whiteness*, to showing how the unconscious habits of racial privilege "make up the very beings that humans are [whatever race a particular self may be]".[5] Sullivan (2006, 44) also argues that these habits resist conscious efforts to transform them. Yet her account of race and white privilege allows these to be viewed as both hard to change and possible to change (Sullivan 2006, 185). Sullivan affirms the need to act, to produce a 'hyper- and pessimistic activism'. The necessity of pessimism here reflects Sullivan's attentiveness to the possibility that "efforts to improve the world" could end up making it "worse", or that "new dangers will be created in place of the old" (2006, 185).

The possibility that efforts to improve the world could end up making it worse is, for Sullivan, a paradox that "cannot be completely eliminated", but "rather than despairing or giving up, a person needs to engage in an ongoing struggle to find ways to use white privilege against itself. A significant part of that struggle involves trying to understand one's own complex relationship—and complicity—with white privilege, and this is true whatever one's race" (2006, 11).

INTERVIEWS WITH SELF-REFLEXIVE NON-INDIGENOUS PEOPLE

This chapter draws on responses to a certain line of questioning that I pursued in interviews I undertook with a select group of independent non-Indigenous activists who understood themselves to be positioned as colonisers and displayed cognisance of their privilege. The line of questioning was about whether or how people experience themselves as non-Indigenous, and about self-consciousness as being privileged and/or oppressed and how this shapes lives and interactions (Land 2012, 269).

Non-Indigenous people's responses were often rich, reflective and personal, at times speaking to current theoretical debates. These included reflections on learning about difference (Jones and Jenkins 2008) and experiencing a transformation of a sense of self or subjectivity. Further, a set of reflections across several interviews illustrated non-Indigenous people's personal experiences of intersections between privilege and oppression. This underscores the importance of adopting an intersectional approach to research into coloniser subjectivity.

The examples of transforming subjectivities explored below include land rights supporter Sally's account of her journey through wanting to escape coloniser positioning; the reflections of members of a group of solidarity activists (the Melbourne Kungkas) who were conscious of their desire to be known to those Indigenous people they were toiling to support; and pro-sovereignty environmental activist Cam Walker's experience of an activist "apprenticeship" to an elder that shifted his understanding of himself.[6] Further, the interviews spoke to the possibility that ally work could become integral to a transformed sense of self, undermining the choice for members of privileged groups to walk easily away from social justice commitments.

COLONISER SUBJECTIVITY: MOVING FROM 'ONE SPACE TO ANOTHER WITHIN IT'

Sally—a middle-class, tertiary-educated Australian of Anglo-Irish descent who is a practicing artist and a single parent—spoke during our interview about listening for and finding out how Indigenous people saw white culture. Having tested this against herself and her culture, Sally was convinced that "their analyses are basically right!" Sally felt the "tag of whiteness" very keenly in terms of shame, and in addition felt isolated in her journey of dealing with it. One of the things she laughs about now is one of her fantasies about escaping whiteness:

> Well, look, I used to fantasise that I would have—I would find a black, an Aboriginal ancestor. You know, so I could *legitimise* my feeling that I wasn't white. But there wasn't any Aboriginal ancestor! And I wasn't going to make it up! So I had to stay on this side of the reality. But, uh, that was one way, but that was very real for me, psychologically. And of course, who could I talk to about that? It was embarrassing!

Sally also talked about her anger and her disgust at white society, verging on self-hatred. Even though she admitted to strong urges to disavow her membership of white society and find a way to escape it, Sally was very clear about owning her structural location. As shown in the following excerpt from our interview, she spoke clearly and articulately about her relationship with her identity as an Australian, a coloniser. Sally's changing relationship with her identity was effected through critical self-reflection alongside her twenty years of activism in relation to particular Indigenous struggles in southeast Australia:

> I find my identity as an Australian very, very problematic. And I can't say I'm proud to be Australian because I have an identity as an Australian who is a coloniser. And I'm gonna be stuck with that. I'm going to move, you know, from one space to another within it. Irish people that I'm connected to, they just love being Irish. But I can never ever be like that about being an Australian . . . but I accept it. Cos that is, you know, who I am in this time and place, in this lifetime.

In this excerpt Sally points to the importance of the political and historical context in her relationship with her identity, an attentiveness I also find compelling in the work of Sullivan (2006, 123), for instance. However, it is the former insight—Sally's disposition towards coloniser identity being one of accepting it, but *moving from one space to another within it*—that I will engage with at more length. The sense of an inescapable contradiction and the possibility only of moving 'from one space to another within it' speaks to the continued relevance of Memmi's (1965) insights about coloniser and colonised subjectivities in the contemporary Australian context. It also connects to theorising about transforming privileged subjectivities as Pease (2006) discusses.

For Sally, following the step of developing a self-consciously articulated white identity came an ongoing struggle to reshape that white identity, or to move to another space *within* that identity (i.e. explicitly *not* to escape from or to disavow the tag of whiteness). Notably, as Memmi (1965, 86) has argued, tranquillity is lost forever when the reluctant coloniser perceives the illegitimacy of his or her status. The pain of this loss and of this difficulty, this burden that conscientious non-Indigenous people carry, Sally reminds me, is: "a very fucking light burden in comparison to what *they* [Indigenous people] had to carry."

Just as Sally talked about moving from one space to another, one of the members of the Melbourne Kungkas, in a group interview, recounted a changing sense of self, this time in relation to a move towards a collective identity. This development was connected with a struggle with what the Melbourne Kungkas members that I interviewed saw as the problem of 'wanting something' out of their support work. In discussing the Melbourne Kungkas's reflections, I will note how they resonate in rich and interesting ways with theoretical insights.

MELBOURNE KUNGKAS: MOVEMENT FROM INDIVIDUAL TO COLLECTIVE IDENTITY

Ali, Cath and Belinda worked for several years as members of the Melbourne Kungkas. The Melbourne Kungkas was a Melbourne-based collective of young, non-Indigenous, educated women which supported the campaign of the Kupa Piti Kungka Tjuta (KPKT or Kungkas, Senior Aboriginal Women of Coober Pedy) in northern South Australia. Most of the members of the Melbourne Kungkas travelled to Kupa Piti (Coober Pedy) one or more times during the life of the campaign (which they saw through to its successful end), meaning that their political support of the KPKT was carried out largely in the absence of face-to-face contact with the senior women. During our interview, Ali spoke about what it was like to spend "all my spare time, you know, working really hard on a campaign I really believed in, but then you'd meet or re-meet the Kungkas, and you really didn't know if they knew who you are." Belinda and Cath both shared this experience of asking themselves whether the KPKT remembered them personally. As Ali said:

> You didn't want to assume they'd forget you either . . . but then it was strange, like, that you had to reintroduce yourself or check that they knew you, and there wasn't always clear messages from some of the women that they actually knew who you were, or wanted to build up more of a relationship, because they had met lots of greenies, and young people, and they've got these long lives with lots of people in them.

I asked if things changed over time. As part of her response, Cath said:

> I guess it changed things for me in terms of: at least the experience of when I *was* there and spending time with them, feeling much more comfortable with that myself, and so being able to enjoy it more, rather than I think, at first, being much more self-conscious about this idea of wanting things. Wanting them to recognise me, wanting to be somebody that they know, and then simultaneously being like, "Oh no, it's not important that they know who I am, because what's important is the work, and the bigger picture, and, you know, it's not about me."

Here, Cath made a connection between the issue Ali raised and another pre-occupation about her levels of self-consciousness when she spent time with the KPKT. While for Cath one thing that didn't change was "having this deference to some sort of authority", what did change was "being able to be more cheeky or . . . less uptight and concerned about the implications of everything I did". Belinda framed her sense of these preoccupations, and the tension over "wanting things, wanting them to recognise me" as about the:

> paradox of trying so hard to be the good anti-racist, and being quite deferring always, and . . . saying, "It's not important if they don't recognise me, or don't want to see me, even though I've travelled about two thousand Ks just for the privilege."

So for Ali, Cath and Belinda, there was some similarity in the experience of the character of their relationships with the KPKT, whom they only saw intermittently, particularly the feeling of "wanting to be somebody that they know". However, there were contrasting ways of dealing with this. Belinda saw the effacement of such wants as an instance of deference, as complex and problematic. Cath expressed self-consciousness "about this idea of wanting things, wanting them to recognise me", and over time "became more comfortable with that tension" and was able to better enjoy spending time with the KPKT in more "contained moments" rather than as an expression of long-term relationship. Ali's approach, based on her feeling it would be understandable if the Kungkas didn't remember her, ended up being that she would "focus on a couple of the Kungkas . . . it became more of trying to build those relationships than getting to know the whole group".

However, towards the end of the interview, when I had finished asking questions and asked if anyone had anything they wanted to mention, Belinda spoke again about the tension between wanting recognition as an individual and feeling it was not okay to want something. What she said I saw as a coming to terms with this tension politically:

> I think we all have expressed feeling more and more relaxed in growing into the relationships. Like, [recently] we went to visit Mrs. Lacey in Port Augusta. And driving there I was like, "Oh, will Mrs. Lacey remember who I am?" And I was like, "Oh, actually I don't think it matters". And I knew that Melbourne Kungkas meant enough . . . So I just rang and was like, you know, "Two Melbourne Kungkas are coming to visit you". And she was so happy. And we went around. And you know, who knows if she . . . placed us at all or where or when she'd met us, but we were two Melbourne Kungkas, and that was a solid basis for us to spend you know, half an hour having afternoon tea and looking at family photos, like. Yeah. So the Melbourne Kungkas did come to mean something that meant that you could—you know, which was really nice. Yeah.[7]

This is crucial: Belinda talks about letting go of the "wanting to be somebody that they know" ("Oh, will Mrs. Lacey remember who I am?") and realising "Melbourne Kungkas meant enough". She was happy to be known as a member of this collective, and only as a member of that collective, not as a particular individual. This suggests that members of the Melbourne Kungkas collective had developed trust in each other to identify in that way, and that they had developed relationships of collective responsibility for each other's behaviour and actions. Such relationships of responsibility are encouraged by Kendall (2006) and Tamasese and Waldegrave (1996). The excerpt also suggests that Belinda had confidence in how Mrs. Lacey (and other members of the KPKT, presumably) regarded the Melbourne Kungkas.

Belinda's reflections seem to show her shift from wanting to be loved for being particular (as in friendship; see Vernon 2005) to being happy to be loved more generically as a political ally, in common with those of the same ilk. Belinda's suspicion of the desire to be recognised as a known individual seemed to be resolved over time through her acceptance of a collective identity as a non-Indigenous supporter of the KPKT. This suggests that for Belinda, at least, there was shift in her relationship with her activist identity: a 'move from one space to another' within it. Elsewhere in the interview, Cath in particular spoke about a sense that she was involved with the KPKT for the purposes of supporting a campaign, not in order to develop personal relationships with the KPKT. Here, the distinction Kendall (2006, 145–146) makes between being an ally to issues, not to people, is important: "focusing my alliance on a person leads me to relationship and friendship", and to the logic of one's actions being directed by the relationship and possibly being directed away from the work necessitated by building an alliance around issues. Intellectually, Cath had critical distance from the desire to be recognised, and over time felt a shift in an emotional sense towards deriving satisfaction elsewhere; Belinda came to feel it was enough to be recognised by the KPKT as a member of the Melbourne Kungkas. For both, the sense of fulfilment from their involvement was reformulated so that it did not rely on individual relationships. The Melbourne Kungkas's suspicion of their own desires speaks to their self-conscious grappling with a dynamic around "solidary incentives" that Karl-Erik Paasonen (2007, 90) discusses, of political supporters wanting something from Aboriginal people in exchange for their support work.

SELF-UNDERSTANDING THROUGH SOLIDARITY

In our interview, Cam Walker, campaigns coordinator for Friends of the Earth, Melbourne, described an important time early on in his activist life of being a "slave"—or, better, an "apprentice"—"for various people":

> You know, the driving, the kind of, the looking after individual people. I probably did about two years of that . . . You just had a really intense relationship with someone, they were clearly the boss, you were the youngster who was learning, and you were kind of the gofer. And that was a fantastic experience to have and—especially as a young activist from the realm where effectively we're anarchists in our philosophy and we're all equal, and we all should have equal say in our decision making, and consensus rules—to be in a classic, age-old, you know, mentor–disciple kind of relationship where they're the boss and you're not the boss. I think that was a fantastic experience.

Cam talked about the many things he learned from this experience. These included, as in the excerpt above, learning to be comfortable with putting aside his political philosophy of "equal say" and accepting an Indigenous person having "some sort of power over me." Further, it gave Cam insight into his "role in the universe", and specifically his role in a relationship whose terms were set by the culture of the person he worked with in which young men are valued differently from the way young men are valued in white society. Cam's discussion of this insight speaks to the importance of an intersectional approach to oppression and how cross-cultural contexts complicate it.

Cam's experiences as an "apprentice" also provided an opportunity for "understanding the reality of living life as an Aboriginal person", and for deepening the quality of his understanding of what the wars and the invasion in Australia have meant for Aboriginal people:

> You know, you can read about oppression and the wars and the invasion. But when you hang out with people, as you know, the past keeps splashing over into the present, and instead of understanding that intellectually, you kind of get it more a sense in your bones. So I just think it's a really useful thing to do.

In this and the previous excerpt from the interview with Cam, it can be seen that public political action and self-understanding work are inextricable—or rather that they feed each other. Cam's apprentice work changed him personally, changed his ways of relating (giving him insights that enabled 'more real' relationships) and deepened his understanding of the relationship of the past to the present reality of Aboriginal people's lives: his sense in his bones. However, Cam did make sure to point out that he was "not saying every relationship like that's going to be healthy". Cam himself talked about how his experience of a servant-like role was radicalising because it cut across the male privilege he was accorded in white culture. By contrast, for some white non-Indigenous women I interviewed, the servant-like role was congruent with the servile role accorded to young women in white culture.

"A POINT OF NO RETURN FOR ALLIES"

For some members of privileged groups, involvement in supporting struggles for justice begins to reconstruct their subjectivity. This can be permanent, so that a new sense of self makes it impossible not to remain committed to supporting struggles for justice (Pease 2010). Pease's claim (2010, 184) about a "point of no return for allies" is shared by critical whiteness scholar Fiona Nicoll (2000), who knows she can't get back to the time and place 'before' she had confronted colonialism and white privilege.

I also found this sense of a point of no return expressed by some non-Indigenous people I interviewed. For instance, in an answer to my question about whether she'd had experiences of "finding this kind of work too difficult . . . like you don't want to continue", Ali (of the Melbourne Kungkas) said:

I kind of found by that stage like, most of my friends or networks were involved in Indigenous issues or were Indigenous, um, yeah. And it was—even though I sort of wanted to escape from it all, I found it was such a part of my life I couldn't really! . . . I went [travelling] to try and, sort of, separate myself from people or issues or something, but it didn't really work . . . the formative years of growing up were so preoccupied with those issues, so, felt quite hollow not being more active on it.

This speaks to the political project of reconstructing the interests of members of dominant groups (Pease 2002, 2006), as well as to the notion that there may be a personal or other cost to members of dominant groups for ignoring Indigenous and antiracist struggles. In the context of my study, these costs could include the deeply felt sense that to tolerate racism and inequality is to be diminished as an ethical being; that empire does its work on non-Indigenous people too; that ecocide is proceeding and environmental collapse is imminent; that the majority of people—'black or white'—have common cause against capitalism; and that white people give something up to become white (Land 2012, 174–189).

NON-INDIGENOUS PEOPLE'S RESISTANCE TO REALLY CHANGING

The previous section gave some cause for optimism about the possibility of members of dominant groups making long-term commitments to justice activism. However, observations and challenges from Indigenous people point to non-Indigenous people's entanglement in and attachment to existing forms of privilege. In our interview, Yorta Yorta woman Monica Morgan, whose struggle for her community has included activism, community development and collaborative work with 'whitefellas', expressed frustration that "everyone" even "the ones that were supposed to be the most, you know, proactive on Indigenous rights" were still prejudiced; "they're also wedded to the system because that's their existence". I interpreted Monica as saying that being "wedded to the system" both culturally and economically produces a fundamental reluctance among non-Indigenous people to change the system. Monica is frustrated by this but also suggests, generously, that it is understandable; that: "for them to abandon their system, they're abandoning themselves. Maybe it's hard for them. . . . Yeah, I think so." Thinking this, Monica is no less convinced that the system needs to change. However, her reflections give insight into the depth of non-Indigenous people's attachments to the structures of a colonially organised society. Goenpul woman and academic Aileen Moreton-Robinson (2000) poses a question with the potential to bring the shape and detail of such attachments to the fore. In the introduction to her influential book, *Talkin' Up to the White Woman: Aboriginal Women and Feminism*, Moreton-Robinson (2000, xvii) describes an interaction she had with a white feminist professor who seemed intent on offering "unsolicited advice about what we should do [about the denial of Indigenous rights in this country] and wanted us to advise her about what we might want her to do." Moreton-Robinson's response was to ask the white feminist herself to "tell us what the limits were to what she would do". It appears as a question that non-Indigenous people more broadly could consider.

CONCLUSION

This chapter has discussed notions of subjectivity, privilege and intersectionality by engaging with reflections generated in interviews with non-Indigenous supporters of Indigenous land rights and related struggles in southeast Australia. It speaks to the importance for social justice struggles broadly, and alliances within them, of transforming the subjectivities of members of privileged groups.

The excerpts from interviews included in this chapter illustrate how non-Indigenous people reflected on the workings of their own privilege, and on experiences of transformation in a sense of self, through involvement in supporting Indigenous struggles. It considers how some of the rich and complex stories and practices of reflection by non-Indigenous people speak to key theoretical debates, such as Sally's response to (her perceptions of) Indigenous views of white people and white culture; the Melbourne Kungkas's movement from desire for individual recognition to, in one case, being happy with being recognised through a collective 'ally' identity; and Cam Walker's reflections on how his time in an 'apprentice' role changed his self-understanding. Indebted to Sally, I described some of these processes of reflection as an experience of 'moving from one space to another' within coloniser positioning. I note that non-Indigenous people I focused on here did not indulge (for long) any desires to escape from this positioning. However, I also highlight the question of what the limits are to what members of dominant groups would do to resist dominance. To consider the ways in which non-Indigenous people are attached to and complicit with colonialism is also to attend to the urgent question of redistribution. As Lake (2003, 160) argues:

> Aboriginal peoples' struggle for recognition as the first owners and custodians of the country now called Australia has far-reaching economic implications, as their call for the redistribution of national resources, not least, land, is central to their political claim . . . [Aboriginal peoples'] recognition and redistribution struggles have necessarily been intertwined.

This discussion of the way some non-Indigenous people are reflecting on their non-Indigeneity and activist practice is offered as an engagement with Indigenous peoples' challenge to interrogate whiteness and privilege. It seeks to illustrate that non-Indigenous people are reflecting deeply, and what the content of some of these reflections are. To listen to Indigenous peoples "talking back" to empire (Ashcroft, Griffiths and Tiffin 1989) but not answering seems inadequate, but this answering should not be read as demanding that Indigenous people answer in turn. It shows in particular detail some instances in which critical self-reflection and collectivist and public political action have fed each other, and that activists are engaged in theorising Indigenous—non-Indigenous alliances.

NOTES

1. See Foley's (2000) discussion of the dynamics produced by varying or common interests. Any person or peoples' sense of what constitutes his, her or their own interests is a political issue (Molyneux 1985; Pease 2002; Valiente 2003).
2. Memmi distinguished between a colonial, a coloniser and a colonialist. He observed that "if every colonial immediately assumes the role of colonizer, every colonizer does not necessarily become a colonialist" (1965, 85). A colonialist is enthusiastic about colonialism. The non-colonialist coloniser is the coloniser who 'refuses' or resists the 'general effect of actual conditions' in colonial life. For this coloniser-who-refuses, "It is impossible . . . not to be aware of the constant illegitimacy of his status" (Memmi 1965, 74), and in knowing this illegitimacy, the coloniser-who-refuses has two options, each fraught with dilemmas. "To refuse means either withdrawing physically from those conditions, or remaining to fight and change them" (Memmi 1965, 85).
3. As Moreton-Robinson argues (2003, 37), colonising power relations have not been discontinued in Australia; Balint and Evans (2011) discuss the significance of the fact that there has never been a 'point of rupture' or 'point of conclusion' to the process of settler-colonialism in Australia.
4. The word 'traitorious' evokes 'race traitor' politics, although Bailey's approach is distinct from this.
5. This is reflective of an argument Sullivan makes about the social construction of the unconscious.
6. Where people I interviewed expressed the wish, I have used their real names in the research. Some people have chosen to remain anonymous; in these cases I have provided a changed first name and omitted the last name.
7. Names in this excerpt have been changed.

REFERENCES

Ashcroft, B., G. Griffiths and H. Tiffin. 1989. *The Empire Writes Back: Theory and Practice in Post-Colonial Literatures*. London: Routledge.

Bailey, A. 1998. "Locating Traitorous Identities: Toward a View of Privilege-Cognizant White Character." *Hypatia* 13 (3): 27–42.

Balint, J., and J. Evans. 2011. "Transitional Justice and Settler States." In *The Australian and New Zealand Critical Criminology Conference Proceedings*, edited by M. Lee, G. Mason and S. Milivojevic. Sydney: Institute of Criminology, the University of Sydney.

Barker, A. 2010. "From Adversaries to Allies: Forging Respectful Alliances between Indigenous and Settler Peoples." In *Alliances: Re/Envisioning Indigenous-Non-Indigenous Relationships*, edited by L. Davis. Toronto: University of Toronto Press.

Burghardt, S. 1982. *The Other Side of Organizing: Resolving the Personal Dilemmas and Political Demands of Daily Practice.* Cambridge, MA: Schenkman Publishing.

Fanon, F. 1968. *Black Skin, White Masks.* 1st Evergreen Black Cat ed. New York: Grove Press.

Foley, G. 1998. "The Power of Whiteness." *Farrago* 77 (7): 18.

Foley, G. 2000. "Whiteness and Blackness in the Koori Struggle for Self-Determination: Strategic Considerations in the Struggle for Social Justice for Indigenous People." *Just Policy* 19–20:74–88.

Frankenberg, R. 1993. *White Women, Race Matters: The Social Construction of Whiteness.* Minneapolis: University of Minnesota Press.

Fraser, N. 1995. "From Redistribution to Recognition?: Dilemmas of Justice in a 'Post-Socialist' Age." *New Left Review* I (212): 68–93.

Gandhi, L. 2006. *Affective Communities: Anticolonial Thought, Fin de Siècle Radicalism, and the Politics of Friendship.* London: Duke University Press.

Jones, A., and K. Jenkins. 2008. "Rethinking Collaboration: Working the Indigene-Colonizer Hyphen." In *Handbook of Critical and Indigenous Methodologies,* edited by N.K. Denzin, Y.S. Lincoln and L.T. Smith. Los Angeles: Sage Publications.

Kendall, F.E. 2006. *Understanding White Privilege: Creating Pathways to Authentic Relationships across Race.* New York: Routledge.

Kowal, E. 2011. "The Stigma of White Privilege: Australian Anti-Racists and Indigenous Improvement." *Cultural Studies* 25 (3): 313–333.

Lake, M. 2003. "Woman, Black, Indigenous: Recognition Struggles in Dialogue." In *Recognition Struggles and Social Movements: Contested Identities, Agency and Power,* edited by B. Hobson. New York: Cambridge University Press.

Land, C. 2011. "Decolonising Activism/Deactivating Colonialism." *ALAR Action Learning and Action Research Journal: Decolonising Action Research Special Edition* 17 (2): 42–62.

Land, C. 2012. "The Politics of Solidarity with Indigenous Struggles in Southeast Australia." Unpublished PhD thesis, Deakin University, Geelong.

Mansfield, N. 2000. *Theories of the Self from Freud to Haraway.* Sydney: Allen and Unwin.

Margaret, J. 2010. *Working as Allies, Winston Churchill Fellowship Report.* Accessed August 30, 2010. http://awea.org.nz/allies_north_america.

McIntosh, P. 2006. "White Privilege and Male Privilege: A Personal Account of Coming to Correspondences through Work in Women's Studies." In *Race, Class, Gender: An Anthology,* edited by M.L. Andersen and P.H. Collins. Belmont, CA: Wadsworth/Thomson Learning.

Memmi, A. 1965. *The Colonizer and the Colonized.* New York: Orion Press.

Molyneux, M. 1985. "Mobilization without Emancipation? Women's Interests, the State, and Revolution in Nicaragua." *Feminist Studies* 11 (2): 227–254.

Moreton-Robinson, A. 2000. *Talkin' Up to the White Woman: Aboriginal Women and Feminism.* Saint Lucia: University of Queensland Press.

Moreton-Robinson, A. 2003. "I Still Call Australia Home: Indigenous Belonging and Place in a White Postcolonizing Society." In *Uprootings/Regroundings: Questions of Home and Migration,* 1st ed., edited by S. Ahmed. New York: Berg Publishers.

Nicoll, F. 2000. "Indigenous Sovereignty and the Violence of Perspective: A White Woman's Coming Out Story." *Australian Feminist Studies* 15 (33): 369–386.

Paasonen, K.-E. 2007. "Between Movements of Crisis and Movements of Affluence: An Analysis of the Campaign against the Jabiluka Uranium Mine, 1997–2000." Unpublished PhD thesis, University of Queensland, Brisbane.

Pease, B. 2002. "(Re)Constructing Men's Interests." *Men and Masculinities* 5 (2): 165–177.

Pease, B. 2006. "Encouraging Critical Reflections on Privilege in Social Work and the Human Services." *Practice Reflexions* 1 (1): 15–26.

Pease, B. 2010. *Undoing Privilege: Unearned Advantage in a Divided World.* London: Zed Books.

Sullivan, S. 2006. *Revealing Whiteness: The Unconscious Habits of Racial Privilege.* Bloomington: Indiana University Press.

Tamasese, K., and C. Waldegrave. 1996. "Cultural and Gender Accountability in the 'Just Therapy' Approach." In *Men's Ways of Being,* edited by C. White, C. McLean and M. Carey. Boulder, CO: Westview Press.

Valiente, C. 2003. "Mobilizing for Recognition and Redistribution on Behalf of Others?: The Case of Mothers against Drugs in Spain." In *Recognition Struggles and Social Movements: Contested Identities, Agency and Power,* edited by B. Hobson. New York: Cambridge University Press.

Vernon, M. 2005. *The Philosophy of Friendship.* New York: Palgrave Macmillan.

Young, I.M. 2011. *Responsibility for Justice.* New York: Oxford University Press.

12 Educating Men for Gender Equality

The Potential and Limitations of Remaking Masculine Subjectivities

Stephen Fisher

Involving men in efforts to improve gender equality and eliminate violence against women is an important goal, and many countries' governments and NGOs develop policies and programs to address this issue. While there have been some writers urging caution in this area (White 2000; Pease 2008), Flood (2006) argues for men's involvement for three reasons. First, given that men are the vast majority of perpetrators of violence against women, they are responsible for ending it. Second, dominant views about masculinity are the cause of violence. And, third, men care about the issue and have a stake in improvement in gender relations.

If engaging men is understood as an important, or even necessary, aspect of social change, it is essential to elaborate what such engagement might involve. Some approaches call for men to 'speak out' against men's violence against women, which at face value sounds laudable but may carry some risks. It is too simple to request men to 'speak out' as it is a socially awkward or challenging request and so unlikely to result in men responding positively. Also, there is often little guidance on what the content of such speaking should include.[1] Crooks et al. (2007, 222) point out that engaging men is often ill-defined and tends to revert to an individualising position, where individual men are being asked to be non-violent and show respect in their interactions with women rather than effect any broader social change.

> At the individual level, it is much harder to identify the end state toward which we hope men and boys will progress. Are we simply looking for all men to commit to nonviolence? Are we looking for all men to renounce male privilege and commit to gender equality? Are we looking for men to organize rallies and marches? Without this clear end goal in mind, prevention initiatives are often constrained to the absence of violence perpetration. The expanded notion of violence prevention in terms of advocacy and personal commitment to being part of the solution is relegated.

Without clear guidance, unhelpful or misleading messages may be communicated (Fisher 2011).

'Speaking out' may also, somewhat paradoxically, actually reinforce rather than diminish men's status and power. For example, Rich et al. (2010) found that men liked the idea of speaking out or making a stand as they reinforced traditional masculine leadership roles, and Spark (1994) argues that so-called pro-feminist men are often pro-male in their rush to take the "centre-stage" on the issue of violence against women.

Using the frame of 'violence prevention' (see Pease 2011 for an extended critique), Flood (2006, 27) argues that work involving men must occur at many levels to be successful and include "programs in schools and among youth, media campaigns, interventions among particular groups of men such as athletes, and grassroots mobilisations such as the White Ribbon Campaign, an effort to invite men to wear a white ribbon to show their opposition to violence against women". The description of White Ribbon's work as 'grassroots mobilisations' is perhaps not the most accurate way to describe a social marketing campaign. Through extensive interviews, Moore (2010) uncovered the essentially narcissistic and apolitical nature of the ribbon-wearing phenomena over the past decade. Following her analysis, White Ribbon could more accurately be regarded as a blend of fashion trend and a form of cause-related marketing. King (2008, 2) highlights the issue of reducing political action to "a lifestyle choice, through which individuals can attain self-actualisation and self-realization". In terms of the impact on government policy and legislative reform, perhaps one of the most effective political mobilisations of men in Australia in the area of gender politics has been the fathers' rights challenges to family law that have undermined women's and children's safety (Flood 2004).

It is apparent that the strategies identified by Flood are essentially all of the one kind—community education, which are broadly of two types, group training or mass media campaigns. While there has been some writing (Drezin and Lloyd-Laney 2003) about the value or otherwise of mass media approaches, there are numerous examples of training from short workshops to more extended training programs (Ricardo and Veran 2010). Some of these programs have gained international prominence as models of effective practice, such as Stepping Stones from South Africa (see also Sonke Gender Justice 2006; Promundo and The ACQUIRE Project 2008; and Welbourn 2010). My own work for the Pacific Women's Network has resulted in the development of a training handbook designed to educate men to become advocates for the elimination of violence against women (Fisher 2011).

Most of these curricula imply, rather than explicitly discuss, their educational rationale. There is a tension between an emphasis on male participants learning skills or knowledge versus an intention to shift men's subjectivities. The focus of this chapter is to examine this tension in terms of the pedagogical frameworks commonly employed with men in promoting gender equality and eliminating violence against women.

ANALYSING THE GOALS OF GENDER JUSTICE
TRAINING PROGRAMS FOR MEN

When educating for social justice, three goals appear to underpin the range of approaches to training potential advocates. While not necessarily discrete, they appear as definite points of emphasis. Some programs emphasise the goal of developing a more moral sense of self, that is, a change in subjectivity. Another very common goal of many curricula targeted at men is to achieve a measurable and substantive change in attitudes. A smaller number of programs aim to address the third goal, which is to directly influence men's actions positively towards gender equality.

In terms of the above-mentioned first goal about changing subjectivity, Goodman's (2011) approach to training people from privileged groups tends to focus on developing a person's empathy and ethical sensibilities. Similarly, other programs targeted at men emphasise the need to investigate and take on new forms of masculinity or masculine subjectivity.

The change in men's attitudes towards women was the focus of study by Pulerwitz and Barker (2008) examining the effectiveness of a group education program for young men in Brazil. Using a psychometric gender equitable men scale, they found that the training interventions successfully influenced the young men's attitudes towards gender roles. While some programs focus exclusively on attitudes as the target for change, most tend to use the phrase 'attitudes and behaviour' when describing their key focus (Ataya 2010; Berkowitz 2004; Centerwall and Laack 2008; MRI 2009; Promundo and The ACQUIRE Project 2008) and when describing their aims. However, the training tends to focus on the former in the implicit belief that this will result in a change in the latter. While there is no clear connection between a changed subjectivity and shifts in attitudes, many programs appear to assume that a renewed 'mind-set' maintains continuity with renewed personhood. However, Flood and Pease (2006, 14) recognise that most attitudes do not represent stable dispositions, but can be highly contextual and contingent and "just because an attitude is expressed on one occasion, does not mean that the same attitude will necessarily be expressed on another occasion".

Thus, the assumption that a man with a changed sense of self or a renewed set of attitudes will consistently demonstrate this through his active support for gender is not self-evidently true. The link between 'teaching' progressive attitudes or advocating new forms of masculine subjectivity and men's agency is complex and contested. Some argue that behaviour does not arise from but forms identity and attitudes. For example, Butler (2006, 33) explains that gendered action and identity are inextricably linked. She argues that masculinity is performative and "gender is always a doing, though not a doing by a subject who might be said to pre-exist the deed". This insight undermines the essentialist premise of many liberationist approaches to changing men that claim a 'good man' can be found once the layers of social conditioning have been removed or men are taught to take off the mask. This brings into question the very project of attempting to create new men in the sense of some permanently achieved, reborn subjectivity. While one's sense of self appears to have a certain biographical consistency, I believe the pedagogical focus needs to be more firmly on the particular skills and knowledge men need in order to enact gender equality advocacy, rather than remoulding masculine identity on its own.

Many programmatic evaluations of success rest on evidence of changed attitudes among male participants in spite of a lack of evidence to suggest such changes translate into improved ways of relating to women. Some programs appear to improve the measure by evaluating behavioural intentions rather than simply attitudes, although questions are raised about the supposed action that will follow:

> programs . . . claim success in demonstrating that participants knew more about relationship violence. However, the more relevant and difficult question to answer is how knowledge about relationship violence translates into actual violent behavior and the likelihood that one will engage in such behavior. Only a few of the programs demonstrated additional changes in participants' attitudes and patterns of thought. (Meyer and Stein 2004, 201)

Therefore, there appears to be a lack of clarity or focus within men's advocacy training programs on how they intend to equip men to challenge gender inequality and support women's rights beyond merely gaining their agreement that such a change should occur. At issue is the underlying pedagogical rationales that either prevent or support such action.

PROBLEMATISING PEDAGOGICAL RATIONALES OF TRAINING MEN AS ADVOCATES

Education for men as anti-violence advocates can also be examined by focusing on the two common pedagogical rationales that are explicitly grounded in social justice frameworks: democratic Freirian humanism and stages of self-hood development. I suggest that they are both open to criticism, and instead I offer a more appropriate rationale for training men as advocates of violence elimination.

While there are many books that deal with the pedagogy of the oppressed (Freire 1973; Kincheloe 2008; McLaren and Lankshear 1994; Shor 1992), few have attempted to employ Freirian principles to educate those from the oppressor class. While Kimmel (2002) titles an article "Toward a Pedagogy of the Oppressor", it is more an exhortation for white, middle-class men of privilege to be willing to see our unearned privilege than a philosophical or practical engagement with pedagogy to bring this about.[2] He does recognise the commonly cited pedagogical risk that men who hear about their complicity in patriarchy will become immobilised by guilt rather than spurred to action. Rather than offering a teaching strategy in response, he suggests the remedy is collective organising.

Perhaps recognising the potential risk of alienating men, Schapiro (2001, 1) outlines a Freirian approach that seeks to "help people to grow and change in regard to such issues without subjecting them to coercion, indoctrination, or other forms of political correctness". He is keen to take a "student-centred" approach that involves learners in "genuine inquiry", and using the concept of transformation is firmly centred on men's selfhood.

Schapiro takes two key elements from Freire to apply to his own pedagogical rationale. First is the task of assisting learners to work towards a state of critical consciousness involving a systemic and structural analysis of individual problems. To achieve this outcome, learners must travel from the 'magical-conforming' phase, where social reality is accepted as either unproblematic or unchangeable, and through the 'naive-reforming' phase, where problems are inappropriately individualised. While this sounds progressive, and indeed is invaluable, it can be more prosaically understood as developing sociological thinking (Mills 2000). This raises the question as to whether learning sociological analysis requires such staged personal transformation. While in my own teaching I am aware that students who begin to see beyond the individual do indeed speak of shifts in their sense of self, I regard this as secondary to the pedagogical goal of developing skills and knowledge to critically analyse their social world.

The second element employed by Schapiro is the pedagogical technology to achieve this staged transformation, namely, dialogic education. Repeating Freire's critique of banking education, where knowledge, beliefs and ideas are pre-determined and deposited by the teacher in the democratic classroom, he argues that knowledge is something people can discover for "themselves in their struggle to understand and change their world" (Schapiro 2001, 9). This is an understandable moral stance given the context Freire critiqued, where educated and privileged teachers were teaching poor peasants knowledge about their world in a way that maintained their oppression. This concern with the inequality in such didactic teaching is valid regardless of whether it is an empirically effective way to learn to think structurally about social problems. However, there is no such moral imperative in the case of training male learners to support gender equality, where they themselves are confident and privileged beneficiaries of gender inequality. Of course if the training were to focus on racism, or issues of class oppression, then the men's social location in these areas would be very important.

It is important to critically investigate the idea of the dialogic, democratic classroom as an important way to train men to be advocates for gender equality. Some argue that the notion that teachers can ever simply be facilitators of students' collective knowledge creation is misleading, as we are constantly faced with conflicting value positions and understandings that require a clear moral choice. From this perspective, it is actually our moral imperative as teachers to actively promote particular progressive worldviews with our students. Other writers (Knight and Pearl 2000; Ellsworth 1994) are critical of the notion of a democratic classroom to the extent that it masks the actual unequal power dynamics occurring within the learner group. Or worse, the dialogic tools are practiced in a way that increases oppressive practices and understandings rather than the purported opposite.

Critiquing the naive humanism inherent in the work of moral adult educators such as Shapiro, Baptiste (1998) argues that we are unwilling to consider the possibility of a progressive pedagogy designed to disempower rather than simply support. Somewhat controversially, in the context of training for pro-feminism, he suggests that three sorts of caring get in the way of recognising the need to directly challenge power and privilege. Caring as human capital formation is based on the view that teaching is simply about building people skills and talents while denying there are any fundamental structural conflicts in society, while caring as self-improvement occurs when the educational process is primarily about altering the learner's state of being. He cites Mezirow (1981) as a progressive educator who is keen to change individual perspectives through transformative learning, but notes that "although positive social change might be a serendipitous outcome, it is not a requirement of the theory". He notes that Newman (1994) calls this introspective activism, where the idea of starting with changing ourselves usually also ends there, and no collective coordinated political action is undertaken. Thus the pedagogical value of the goal of changing men's subjectivity is further weakened.

Finally, caring as empowering our allies refers to efforts to develop critical consciousness among marginalised or oppressed groups. In this case, all the effort and focus goes on those with least power, while the powerful, whom he refers to as our enemies, remain unchallenged. Baptiste (1998) is critical of Freire, who writes at length about oppression and yet seems to imply that "critically conscious allies will eventually transform their enemies into friends"; thus everyone will win in a world where the powerful are allowed to connect with their true humanity. The proposed path to a liberated society is to free oppressors by giving them the ability to think critically about social relations. Schapiro (2001, 11) draws on socialisation theory to suggest that "because everyone in the society, oppressors as well as oppressed, is socialized to believe that the present social reality is essentially unchangeable . . . Freire's process can and should be experienced by members of both social groups", therefore completely removing the notion of structural power relations.[3] The risk here is identified by Allen (2002), who, based on his experience as a teacher, recognises that most who encounter Freire tend to imagine themselves as the oppressed and the understanding of oppressive global hierarchies disappears.

Baptiste (1998) is concerned that oppression is inappropriately conceived as being due to ignorance, and that simply ensuring oppressors are thinking critically will result in progressive action. He considers Freire's stages of development schema as being uncritically naive as it rests on the belief that once an oppressor has an understanding of the nature of oppression, reformed ethical behaviour will automatically follow. Thus, in recognising that inequality in structural power and privilege cannot simply be overcome through empowering the oppressed, nor appealing to the enlightened good nature of oppressors, he proposes the development of a pedagogy of disempowerment of the privileged.

In a subsequent article, Baptiste (2000) advances his proposal with a suggestion to move beyond reason and personal integrity and towards a pedagogy of coercive restraint. Here he goes directly against the invitational, non-threatening and democratic approach commonly adopted within not only the transformative learning field, but more particularly within gender equality programs for men. For example, Fernandes (Fernandes, et al. 2005) explains that her training manual is produced from a male-centred and male-sensitive perspective to ensure participants feel affirmed rather than threatened. Similarly, Esplen (2006, 12), in describing lessons learned in training men, has at the top of her list the importance of using only positive messages and avoiding blaming men for "things they were taught to do",[4] or being made to feel guilty for the actions of the violence of other men.[5] Psychologisation of the oppressor allows Curry-Stevens (2005, 95) to note "that superiority is embedded in one's self concept and that efforts to undo it may induce the privileged learner to feel threatened. We need to avoid imperilling such learners".

Within Freirian humanism, men become recast not as privileged and powerful, but as fragile beings requiring support and care. For example, in one report describing promising practices of engaging men around gender-based violence, MRI (2009, 15–16) recommends creating "a safe environment where personal feelings and experiences can be shared, thus making the reality of gender violence visible and showing how it affects everyone in society". This concern for 'poor men' is supported by a wealth of anti-feminist and men's liberation literature (Biddulph 2002, 2003; Bly 1992; Farrell 1974, 1993; Parker 2008).

Allen (2004) supports Baptiste's pedagogy of coercive constraint by arguing that educators need to hold privileged learners clearly on track to prevent or challenge resistant or avoidant responses. Ellsworth (1994) is similarly concerned with the naive humanism in current discourses on critical pedagogy, asserting that many of the key concepts such as empowerment, student voice, dialogue "and even the term critical, are repressive myths that perpetuate relations of domination". She notes that, in spite of its political intent, the literature on critical pedagogy rarely explains how particular teaching methods will actually alter specific power relations. This is possibly due to a reluctance by proponents to recognise the tension inherent in teaching supportively while simultaneously wishing to undermine the power of men.

Ellsworth (1994) is troubled by the techniques of dialogue and promoting student voice, arguing that they are based on the constraining rationalist assumption that students will engage in reasoned debate and that each student's position on an issue is equally valid. This false neutrality does not take into account the varied cultural backgrounds and social locations of students that privileges some over others in such discursive settings. Similarly Huber and Cale (2002, 1) refer to Brookfield (2001) in criticising democratic teaching as it "allows for the voicing and acceptance of intolerant perspectives creating an environment that Marcuse (1965) calls repressive tolerance". Thus, there is a potential risk in following the advice of writers of gender equality training programs, such as Haas (2009, 101), who suggests a "crucial step for promoting behavioural change is creating spaces for dialogue and reflection", adding that men-to-men dialogue offers the opportunity to reconsider views and attitudes. On the contrary, it is often homosocial men-to-men dialogue that maintains patriarchal privilege (Bird 1996).

In a related field of anti-racism training, Srivastava (2007, 305) critically refers to the dialogic method as the "let's talk" technique, which tends to have a more self-development intention than organisational or structural change. Her main concern is that this pedagogical model of personal exploration of feelings and perspectives is "influenced by trends towards individualization, discussions of experience (which) often glide over any close examination of social relations". Further, challenging the focus on developing the individual moral character, she agrees with Newman (1994) in suggesting that "these preoccupations with morality and self are common obstacles to a fuller discussion of antiracism" and social change. She similarly argues for a more explicitly activist approach to training "formed around particular political objectives, community or organizational projects, or tasks; which would focus on sharing the analyses, skills, and strategies required to promote and support action on racism" (Srivastava 2007, 309).

The common themes among these criticisms of the application of Freirian principles to training the privileged to be advocates for social justice is the lack of a clear political position on the part of the trainer and a lack of emphasis on skills and analysis for community organising or political action. A further concern is the individualistic underpinning of such training evident in a number of works that employ a stages of development pedagogical rationale. Goodman (2011) and Curry-Stevens (2005) both draw on models of stages of development of social justice allies. They refer to a range of different selfhood development models, including Adams, Griffin and Bell (2007), Bishop (2002), Kegan (1983), Lawrence and Tatum (1997). One of the more commonly employed is Hardiman and Jackson's (1997) concept of white identity development to explain the steps undertaken by people of privileged groups. The stages include: naive, passive or active acceptance, passive or active resistance, redefinition and internalisation.

Based on in-depth interviews with allies of privilege, Curry-Stevens (2007) develops her own alternative set of developmental stages, starting with a confidence-shaking process: awareness of oppression, oppression as structural, locating oneself as oppressed, understanding the benefits that flow from privilege, understanding oneself as implicated in the oppression of others and understanding oneself as an oppressor. These are followed by a confidence-building process: building confidence to take action and knowing how to intervene; planning actions for departure from the course; finding supportive connections to sustain commitments; and declaring intentions for future action.

This could be seen as either a set of steps of self-hood development, or as a series of staged learning goals, followed by an action-planning process. This scheme seems to meet the challenges previously identified that privileged learners: (a) are clearly directed in their learning; (b) understand the structural basis of inequality; and (c) are required to identify specific actions towards social justice. The only questionable stage perhaps is the requirement that students see themselves as oppressed. Based on the belief that it is easier to accept this position and the affirmation that accompanies it, Curry-Stevens (2007) argues that without such recognition, learners will be resistant to accepting their oppressor status. This idea that feeling heard and understood as a victim is a necessary pre-condition to learning about one's own privilege is contentious and runs the risk of allowing men to divert attention away from an analysis of gender inequality back onto themselves. Notwithstanding the range of men's subordinate race and class locations, that men would much rather position themselves as victims of societal pressures does not necessarily translate into their understanding of their oppressor location vis-à-vis women. In discussing the politics of the ways women and men are approached in gender and development (GAD) discourses, White (2000, 35) notes:

> 'GAD for women' is robustly materialist, concentrating on social relations particularly as they define rights and responsibilities in work, consumption and households. That is, it has not been characterised by the exploration of female subjectivities. 'GAD for men' is by contrast much more individualistic and personal, much more preoccupied with the self.

Thus, it is important to develop a pedagogical framework that responds to the danger of moving away from a feminist focus and turning attention to men in an apologetic way (White 2000). There may thus be value in exploring a pedagogy of coercive restraint.

THE POTENTIAL OF A PEDAGOGY OF COERCIVE CONSTRAINT

As previously discussed, Baptiste (2000) is concerned that education for social justice should not focus on the development of learners from the oppressor class but on coercively restraining the perpetrators of injustices. Based on his recognition that in the real world people harm others not out of ignorance but freely and knowingly, the role of the educator is primarily to reduce the likelihood of them committing such acts. He thus proposes negative pedagogy in opposition to the weaknesses of a positive developmental approach with men.

Arguing further in favour of the requirement of educators to promote clear and strong directions on students' learning, Baptiste (2008, 8–9) exposes fallacies associated with the practice of 'educational niceness' centred around the refusal to recognise and use one's power as a teacher that contribute to the maintenance of unethical student behaviour or learning. Following Dykstra and Law (1994) in conceptualising a pedagogy of mobilisation that develops political actors who are willing to acknowledge and challenge power relations, Baptiste is arguing that it is consistent to also confront students' actions and views within the classroom that reproduce inequality. As a result, he supports the use of manipulation by educators as there are times when maintaining neutrality or being completely open and honest about one's actions means one is unlikely to be very effective in achieving training for social justice goals. For example, it is not uncommon for trainers to tease out a particular resistant student's misogynist stance for the purpose of trapping (and even publicly chastening) them in their contradictory or inconsistent stance. This would be a form of 'ethical' manipulation designed to thwart support for a dominant sexist worldview.

While I agree with Baptiste's antidote to the discourse of reassurance of men, I maintain that it is important and possible to hold both a firmly critical stance on patriarchy and masculine practices within a training context, while also working towards developing necessary skills and knowledge required for men to become effective pro-feminist allies. Thus far, the pedagogical discussion has presented a dichotomy of the ethics and politics of training men. On one hand are the perspectives that men, even as oppressors, need the opportunity to develop themselves, and privileged social justice allies need to go through a series of transformative stages, while on the other hand, any training of the privileged must primarily focus on constraining their likely oppressive and harmful actions.

This dualism is represented by Redman (1996), who writes of the contradiction of empowering men to disempower themselves. Connell (2005, 82–83) argues that "the politics of masculinity cannot concern only questions of personal life and identity; it must also concern questions of social justice". Accordingly, Greig (2000) argues that while attempts to 'fix' a masculine identity are politically problematic due to the dynamic flux of "identities-in-the-making", it is equally inappropriate to falsely separate out personal life from questions of social justice. He proposes a possible way through this impasse by focusing on 'identification as relation', meaning that men experience a constant series of making and remaking identity as they relate to others (men and women) throughout daily life. Thus, awareness of the agency men employ in deploying a range of relational strategies can become an effective pedagogical strategy that avoids a focus on 'developing' men and yet provides something more constructive than Baptiste's coercive constraint.

CONCLUSION

There are many potential pitfalls in a focus on developing men's subjectivity as a pathway to involving men in gender justice activism. I argue that Freirian pedagogy, while revered as central to any project of teaching for social justice, does not appear to be an appropriate framework when dealing with men as learners. Similarly, too strong an emphasis on taking men through stages of ally development risks an individualism that diverts attention away from a feminist structural analysis.

Recognising "the vested interest many men have in resisting change" (Cornwall and Lindisfarne-Tapper 1994, 34) does not mean, however, that teachers must avoid confronting or alienating men. Nor does it mean that an educator's only option is to implement a pedagogy of coercive constraint. While it is necessary to be ready to directly challenge men's misunderstandings and defence of patriarchy, it is also possible to implement a pedagogy of pro-feminist activism that equips men with the capacity to critically analyse taken-for-granted gender relations and act as effective allies to the women's rights movement.

NOTES

1. For example, in an article titled "Men Speak Out against Violence", the following appears with little elaboration, "I got to talk with a number of men who have signed on as White Ribbon ambassadors and have taken the pledge to speak out against violence towards women" (Penberthy 2011, 49).
2. Rasmussen (2005) is similarly philosophical in tone, while Curry-Stevens (2007) is much more focused on teaching and learning processes.
3. Socialisation theory is now largely discredited by sociology of gender writers (see, for example, Connell 1987).
4. Social learning theory is commonly employed to both individualise violence and excuse men of a range of anti-social and misogynist behaviours (Hicks 2008).
5. Pease (2008) highlights the importance of recognising men's responsibility not just as perpetrators of direct violence against women, but also as perpetuators of a violence-supporting society.

REFERENCES

Adams, M., P. Griffin and L.A. Bell. 2007. *Teaching for Diversity and Social Justice*. Vol. 1. New York: Routledge.

Allen, R.L. 2002. "Pedagogy of the Oppressor: What Was Freire's Theory for Transforming the Privileged and the Powerful?" Paper presented at the annual meeting of the *American Educational Research Association*, New Orleans, Louisiana, April 1–5. Accessed November 15, 2012. http://www.eric.ed.gov/PDFS/ED467424.pdf.

Allen, R.L. 2004. "Whiteness and Critical Pedagogy." *Educational Philosophy and Theory* 36 (2): 121–136.

Ataya, O. 2010. *Women and Men: Hand in Hand against Violence: Strategies and Approaches of Working with Men and Boys for Ending Violence against Women*. Oxford: Oxfam International.

Baptiste, I. 1998. "Towards a Pedagogy for Disempowering our Enemies." In *39th Annual Adult Education Research Conference*. San Antonio, TX: University of the Incarnate Word. Accessed November 12, 2012. http://www.adulterc.org/Proceedings/1998/98baptiste.htm.

Baptiste, I. 2000. "Beyond Reason and Personal Integrity: Toward a Pedagogy of Coercive Restraint." *Canadian Journal for the Study of Adult Education* 14 (1): 27–50.

Baptiste, I. 2008. 'Wages of niceness: the folly and futility of educators who strive to not impose'. New Horizons in Adult Education and Human Resource Development 22 (2).

Berkowitz, A.D. 2004. "Working with Men to Prevent Violence against Women: An Overview (Part One)." *VAWnet: The National Electronic Network on Violence against Women*. Accessed December 15, 2012. http://www.alanberkowitz.com/articles/VAWNET.pdf.

Biddulph, S. 2002. *Manhood: An Action Plan for Changing Men's Lives*. 3rd ed. Lane Cove, NSW: Finch Publishing.

Biddulph, S. 2003. *Raising Boys: Why Boys Are Different—and How to Help Them Become Happy and Well-Balanced Men*. 2nd ed. Sydney: Finch Publishing.

Bird, S.R. 1996. "Welcome to the Men's Club: Homosociality and the Maintenance of Hegemonic Masculinity." *Gender and Society* 10 (2): 120–132.

Bishop, A. 2002. *Becoming an Ally: Breaking the Cycle of Oppression*. Sydney: Allen and Unwin.

Bly, R. 1992. *Iron John: A Book about Men*. Shaftesbury, Dorset: Element.

Brookfield, S. 2001. "Traveling from Frankfurt to La La Land: Marcuse, Repressive Tolerance and the Practice of Learner-Centered Adult Education." Presented at the 31st Annual Standing Conference on University Teaching and Research in the Education of Adults, University of East London, London, July 3–5.

Butler, J. 2006. *Gender Trouble: Feminism and the Subversion of Identity*. New York: Routledge.

Centerwall, E., and S. Laack. 2008. *Young Men as Equal Partners Handbook*. Stockholm: Swedish Association for Sexual Education (RFSU). Accessed November 8, 2012. http://www.rfsu.se/Bildbank/Dokument/ymep-pdfer/YMEPguidebookapril08.pdf.

Connell, R.W. 1987. *Gender and Power: Society, the Person, and Sexual Politics*. Cambridge: Polity.

Connell, R. W. 2005. Masculinities: Second Edition. 2nd ed. University of California Press.

Cornwall, A., and N. Lindisfarne-Tapper. 1994. *Dislocating Masculinity: Comparative Ethnographies*. London: Routledge.

Crooks, C.V., G.R. Goodall, R. Hughes, P.G. Jaffe and L.L. Baker. 2007. "Engaging Men and Boys in Preventing Violence against Women: Applying a Cognitive–Behavioral Model." *Violence against Women* 13 (3): 217–239.

Curry-Stevens, A. 2005. "Pedagogy for the Privileged: Building Theory, Curriculum and Critical Practices." Doctoral dissertation, University of Toronto.

Curry-Stevens, A. 2007. "New Forms of Transformative Education Pedagogy for the Privileged." *Journal of Transformative Education* 5 (1): 33–58.

Drezin, Jenny, and Megan Lloyd-Laney, ed. 2003. Making a Difference Strategic Communications to End Violence Against Women. New York: United Nations Development Fund for Women (UNIFEM).

Dykstra, C., and M. Law. 1994. 'Popular Social Movements as Educative Forces: Towards a Theoretical Framework'. In Proceedings of the 35th Annual Adult Education Research Conference, (pp. 121–126). Knoxville: University of Tennessee

Ellsworth, E. 1994. "Why Doesn't This Feel Empowering? Working through the Repressive Myths of Critical Pedagogy." In *The Education Feminism Reader*, edited by L. Stone. London: Routledge.

Esplen, E. 2006. *Engaging Men in Gender Equality: Positive Strategies and Approaches Overview and Annotated Bibliography.* Brighton: Institute of Development Studies, University of Sussex.

Farrell, W. 1974. *The Liberated Man: Beyond Masculinity. Freeing Men and Their Relationships with Women.* New York: Random House.

Farrell, W. 1993. *The Myth of Male Power: Why Men Are the Disposable Sex.* New York: Simon and Schuster.

Fernandes, A., R. Khanna and A. Pawar. 2005. *Working with Men on Gender, Sexuality, Violence and Health (Trainers' Manual).* Alkapuri, India: Sahaj. Accessed November 8, 2012. http://www.hsrc.ac.za/Document-2359.phtml.

Fisher, S. 2011. *Male Advocates for Women's Human Rights Handbook.* Fiji: Fiji Women's Crisis Centre. Suva, Fiji.

Flood, M. 2004. 'Backlash: Angry Men's Movements'. In The Battle and Backlash Rage on: Why Feminism Cannot Be Obsolete, edited by Elin Rossi, 261–278. Philadephia: Xlibris.

Flood, M. 2006. "Changing Men: Best Practice in Sexual Violence Education." *Women against Violence: An Australian Feminist Journal* 18:26–36.

Flood, M., and B. Pease. 2006. *The Factors Influencing Community Attitudes in Relation to Violence against Women: A Critical Review of the Literature.* Carlton South, Victoria: Victorian Health Promotion Foundation.

Freire, P. 1973. *Pedagogy of the Oppressed.* London: Penguin.

Goodman, D. 2011. *Promoting Diversity and Social Justice: Educating People from Privileged Groups.* The Teaching/Learning Social Justice Series. London: Routledge.

Greig, A. 2000. "The Spectacle of Men Fighting." *IDS Bulletin* 31 (2): 28–32.

Haas, J-W. 2009. *Steps for Action to Promote Gender Equality.* Esohborn, Germany, Gesellschaft für Technische Zusammenarbeit (GTZ) publisher.

Hardiman, R., and B. Jackson. 1997. "Conceptual Foundations for Social Justice Courses." In *Teaching for Diversity and Social Justice*, edited by M. Adams and L.A. Bell. New York: Routledge.

Hicks, S. 2008. "Gender Role Models . . . Who Needs 'Em?!" *Qualitative Social Work* 7 (1): 43–59.

Huber, C., and G. Cale. 2002. "(Dis)Empowering Pedagogies: Repressive Tolerance and Democracy in the Adult Education Classroom." Paper presented at the Midwest Research-to-Practice Conference in Adult, Continuing and Community Education, Northern Illinois University, DeKalb, October 9–11. Accessed

November 12, 2012. http://www.cedu.niu.edu/reps/Document/Midwest_Conference_Papers_part1_pdf.pdf#page=101.

Kegan, R. 1983. *The Evolving Self.* Cambridge, MA: Harvard University Press.

Kimmel, M. 2002. "Toward a Pedagogy of the Oppressor." *Tikkun* 17 (6): 42–45.

Kincheloe, J.L. 2008. *Critical Pedagogy Primer.* New York: Peter Lang.

King, S. 2008. *Pink Ribbons, Inc.: Breast Cancer and the Politics of Philanthropy.* Minneapolis: University of Minnesota Press.

Knight, T., and A. Pearl. 2000. "Democratic Education and Critical Pedagogy." *Urban Review* 32 (3): 197–226.

Lawrence, S.M., and B.D. Tatum. 1997. "White Educators as Allies: Moving from Awareness to Action." In *Off White: Readings on Race, Power, and Society,* edited by M. Fine. New York: Routledge.

McLaren, P., and C. Lankshear. 1994. *Politics of Liberation: Paths from Freire.* New York: Routledge.

Meyer, H. and N. Stein. 2004. "Relationship Violence Prevention Education in Schools: What's Working, What's Getting in the Way, and What Are Some Future Directions." *American Journal of Health Education* 35 (4): 198–204.

Mezirow, J. 1981. "A Critical Theory of Adult Learning and Education." *Adult Education Quarterly* 32 (1): 3–24.

Mills, C.W. 2000. *The Sociological Imagination (40th Anniversary Edition).* New York: Oxford University Press.

Moore, S.E.H. 2010. *Ribbon Culture: Charity, Compassion and Public Awareness.* Basingstoke, UK: Palgrave Macmillan.

MRI. 2009. *Engaging Men in Ending Gender-Based Violence in Liberia; Case Study and Promising Practices: Male Involvement Project—Year One.* Springfield, MA, USA: Men's Resources International publisher.

Newman, M. 1994. *Defining the Enemy.* Sydney: Stewart Victor Publishing.

Parker, K. 2008. *Save the Males: Why Men Matter, Why Women Should Care.* New York: Random House.

Pease, B. 2008. *Engaging Men in Men's Violence Prevention: Exploring the Tensions, Dilemmas and Possibilities.* Sydney: Australian Domestic and Family Violence Clearinghouse, Issues Paper 17. Accessed November 12, 2012. http://www.adfvc.unsw.edu.au/PDF%20files/Issues%20Paper_17.pdf.

Pease, B. 2011. "Governing Men's Violence against Women in Australia." In *Men and Masculinities around the World,* edited by E. Ruspini, J. Hearne and K. Pringle. New York: Palgrave Macmillan.

Penberthy, D. 2011. "Men Speak Out against Violence." *Sunday Mail (Brisbane),* November 20, 49.

Promundo and The ACQUIRE Project. 2008. *Engaging Boys and Men in Gender Transformation: The Group Education Manual.* New York: The ACQUIRE Project publisher.

Pulerwitz, J., and G. Barker. 2008. "Measuring Attitudes toward Gender Norms among Young Men in Brazil." *Men and Masculinities* 10 (3): 322–338.

Rasmussen, D. 2005. "Cease to Do Evil, then Learn to Do Good . . . (a Pedagogy for the Oppressor)." In *Rethinking Freire: Globalization and the Environmental Crisis,* edited by C.A. Bowers and F. Apffel-Marglin. Mahwah, NJ: Lawrence Erlbaum Associates.

Redman, P. 1996. "Empowering Men to Disempower Themselves: Heterosexual Masculinities, HIV, and the Contradictions of Anti-Oppressive Education." In *Understanding Masculinities: Social Relations and Cultural Arenas,* edited by M. Mac an Ghaill. Buckingham: Open University Press.

Ricardo, C., Verani, F. (2010). Engaging Men and Boys in Gender Equality and Health: A Global Toolkit for Action—Gender Based Violence. New York: UNFPA publisher. Retrieved January 25, 2011, from http://www.unfpa.org/public/home/publications/pid/6815

Rich, M.D., E.A. Utley, K. Janke and M. Moldoveanu. 2010. "'I'd Rather Be Doing Something Else': Male Resistance to Rape Prevention Programs." *Journal of Men's Studies* 18 (3): 268–288.

Schapiro, S. 2001. *Toward a Pedagogy of the "Oppressor."* Fielding Graduate Institute. Accessed November 3, 2012. http://legacy.oise.utoronto.ca/research/tlcentre/conference2003/Proceedings/Schapiro.pdf.

Shor, I. 1992. *Empowering Education: Critical Teaching for Social Change.* 1st ed. Chicago: University of Chicago Press.

Sonke Gender Justice. 2006. "What Is the One Man Can Campaign?" Accessed November 12, 2012. http://www.genderjustice.org.za/onemancan/introduction/download-the-introduction-to-the-one-man-can-action-to-2.html.

Spark, R. 1994. *Gift-Wrapping the Men's Movement: Canada's White Ribbon Foundation Campaign.* Kingston, Ontario: Queen's University.

Srivastava, S. 2007. "'Let's Talk': The Pedagogy and Politics of Anti-Racist Change." In *Utopian Pedagogy*, edited by M. Côté R. Day and G. de Peuter. Toronto: University of Toronto Press.

Welbourn, Alice. 2010. Stepping Stones: A Training Manual for Sexual and Reproductive Health Communication and Relationship Skills. III. CERSA, Medical Research Council, Pretoria and the Planned Parenthood Association of South Africa.

White, S.C. 2000. "'Did the Earth Move?' The Hazards of Bringing Men and Masculinities into Gender and Development." *IDS Bulletin* 31 (2): 33–41.

Part V

Creating New Spaces of Resistance in Everyday Life

13 Resisting Age Conformity in Everyday Life

Tina Kostecki

INTRODUCTION

Western notions of identity are typically aligned with categories of gender, class, sexuality, race and age. Of these, age is the least theorised (Krekula 2007, 158) and yet it is an axiomatic experience for each of us. Age markers determine broad experiences of living in terms of the effects of social, employment, housing and health policy, as well as personal experiences with respect to how others will respond to us and make summations about competency and character (Westerhof and Tulle 2007, 246; Sontag 1997).

Most attitudes and approaches toward older citizens are negative. The origins and effects of ageist stereotypes as an institutionalised practice in Western society have been discussed elsewhere (Nelson 2004). Calasanti and Slevin (2001) also explore the nature of age-related stereotypes in terms of the social construction of aging. Recently, I noticed an online newspaper segment regarding older men and women. The photographic compilation consisted of a set of images of older individuals in various poses within settings of family life. Without exception, all portrayed older members of the family as amusingly awkward, incompetent, weak, ugly, childish, aggressive or as passive grandparents. The photographs consisted of scenarios such as a baby asleep in a pram, with the grandparent—who is presumably caring for the infant—nearby in a chair, also asleep. Other images showed older bodies juxtaposed alongside extraordinarily fit young ones, an older person riding a child's tricycle; older people in unflattering attire—including underpants and matching "snuggies"—and sporting egregious hairstyles. And, finally, in a revealing depiction of exclusion, a photograph showing a grandmother seated some distance from the rest of the family, who are hugging each other closely. Each image assumed permission to use age stereotypes to demean and trivialise older people.

This chapter is based on a study I conducted in 2009, in which I interviewed sixteen older women about their experiences of childhood sexual abuse. Their insights were enlightening regarding how older women might manage the impact of abuse throughout their lives and how they might conceptualise the notion of recovery. The women also highlighted the assorted ways in which they express themselves and resist normative discourses about age identity. Their views reflect how they enact their identity with respect to their age: each with a different expression but all in juxtaposition to assumed stereotypes of aging. In speaking about themselves and the issue of childhood sexual abuse, the women demonstrated how their powerful and nuanced subjectivity works to resist and contradict dominant discourses regarding gender and age. In unexpected ways, they emancipate themselves from normative social expectations. The following discussion explores how these women cross traditional lines and resist age conformity in their everyday lives.

Powell and Wahidin (2006, ix) identify how the construct of age has developed through a series of institutionalised practices and how a Foucauldian analysis can seed "spaces of resistance and artistic practices of the self." Further, Irving (2006, 20) has theorised ways in which a Foucauldian analysis can disrupt fixed constructions of age that can be "brutal and destructive" and move toward "a world of contingency, a world of imagination and story, a world not of finding but of making." In contrast to the period of the Enlightenment, which sought to establish a precise version of humanity, Foucault demonstrated the possibility of the transformation of the self by understanding the "technologies" of the self used in particular historical epochs alongside particular forms of rationality. Irving (2006, 21–23) identifies three discourses of age that have come to represent the category of 'old'. First, there is the development of essentialist binary categories, such as young–old, and a subsequent 'industry' of social practices and bodies of professional knowledge that sketch out the borderlines, thus managing the boundary of 'old age'. Second, there is a discernible array of imagery associating old age with decay and decline. The final age discourse constructs cultural measurement systems aimed at 'ordering' the 'old' body. In a similar vein, Westerhof and Tulle (2007) discuss in relative detail the discursive context of aging with respect to the medicalisation of the aging process, social policy and mass media.

In terms of identity, Foucault resists inherited totalities to go beyond dominant prescriptions of identity. Who we are should always be unanswered and allow a plurality of subjectivities: "Being human for Foucault means resisting identifying truth(s), thereby creating spaces for being-different . . . inventing new kinds of relationship and imaginative ways of life" (Irving 2006, 28). The women in my study are reconstructing what it means to be them. They resist dominant discourses of age constructions and demonstrate what it can be to question constituted experience endlessly (Rajchman 1985, 7). Akin to Calasanti and Slevin (2001, 10), I use the term 'old' here despite its negative associations in everyday language to "naturalize and neutralize" (Calasanti and Slevin 2001, 10) its conventional meaning, as well as to re-contextualise dominant meanings and to reconstruct a new possibility for sense making.

THEORISING AGE SUBJECTIVITIES: ON INTERSECTIONS OF AGE AND GENDER

In theorising the experiences and subjectivities of the women in my study, the notion of 'intersectionality' is useful. Meekosha (2007) extends understandings of the complex nature of identity by using an inter-categorical analysis that assembles identity constructs of race, gender, class and disability. Such an approach is aligned with intersectional analyses that theorise subjectivities in more holistic and elaborate ways than insouciant approaches that rely on mutually exclusive categories. Similarly to other identity formations, age denotes a social relationship (Meekosha 2007, 162) and the inclusion of gender as an aspect of identity formation can assist in understanding subjectivity as a more "complex web of cultural interpretation" (Meekosha 2007, 170). To understand the complexity of identity is important for critical social analysis because all markers of identity are "social constructions of exclusion and processes of naming and classifying who does and who does not constitute a full citizen" (Meekosha 2007, 172). McCall (2005) also advocates an intersectional approach to subjectivity in order to understand its complexity. Intersectionality can account for the contradictory nature of single categories and kindles unlimited, nuanced, flexible and inconstant possibilities for the nature of subjectivity—possibilities that are contingent on every moment (McCall 2005). This chapter employs a strategic use of the identity categories of age and gender.

In her detailed analysis of the discourse on family, race and nation, Collins (1998) discusses intersectionality in terms of how the categories mutually construct one another:

> As opposed to examining gender, race, class, and nation, as separate systems of oppression, intersectionality explores how these systems mutually construct one another . . . certain ideas and practices surface repeatedly across multiple systems of oppression and serve as focal points or privileged social locations for these intersecting systems. (63)

Ross-Sheriff (2008) aims to apply an intersectional approach to address oppression. She argues for critical insights to the experience of aging as has been done for gender and race. Identity is always interwoven with other indicators such as gender, ethnicity, religion, sexual orientation, socio-economic status and age (Ross-Sheriff 2008, 309). Narratives and life histories are important tools used to help explain complexity in the

> Older women have been relatively less visible in gender theory, and their voices have not been heard in research. As social work professionals and feminist theorists, we need to conduct more research that examines elderly women's lives within the context of the women's

diverse positions and further develop feminist theories that provide a more nuanced understanding of elderly women's complex conditions. (Ross-Sheriff 2008, 310)

In discussing the theory of intersectionality, Wilinska (2010) outlines the nature of discourses and the patterns of power creating social relations that include and exclude (thus creating social inequality for men and women) on the basis of the social categories of age and gender. She aims to understand the intersection of age and gender to recognise patterns of social inequality in dominant discourses. In respect of social policy discourse and media, the intersection of age and gender produces subject positions that are one-dimensional and reproduce inequality, such as "older women can only be grandmothers" (Wilinska 2010, 892). This analysis serves to make visible dominant discourses and the technicalities of governance as well as the ways in which a *political* subjectivity can enact change or alternative positions for social actors.

Krekula (2007) advocates for more complex understandings of the experiences of older women and supports approaches that include exploration of the intersection of age and gender. Gender is located along with identity positions such as age, race, sexuality and class: "Gender cannot be understood without including its intersections with these other positions" (Krekula 2007, 157). With age being the least problematised category construction in the field of social gerontology, she argues that older women have been objectified and have become part of a dominant and simplistic discourse, namely, the "misery perspective" (Krekula 2007, 163). In terms of understanding subjectivities, older women's experiences and views are made invisible and it is only through foregrounding, at the micro level, the 'voices' of older people and the narratives of individual women that a finer complexity of perspectives and diversity can be expressed. Krekula's own research counters simplifying meta-narratives on the experiences of women growing older and, while acknowledging the importance of structural analysis to shed light on inequality, contends that it is at the level of the individual that an intersectional approach can explore subjectivities that reconstruct dominant discourse:

> Even though the interplay between power relations shows a double jeopardy on a structural level, when it comes to the micro level, individuals are actors, who interpret and define their reality and also work out strategies to change structures and societies. (Krekula 2007, 167)

It is at the level of the everyday that this research explores the subjectivities of older women. The everyday personal responses of the women constitute acts of quiet and loud resistance, and their particular experiences of living with the impact of childhood sexual abuse present alternative, nuanced narratives and perspectives on aging. Rose (1999) describes the everyday, unseen action in the lives of individuals as highly significant in terms of future possibilities for change and as minor engagements with resistance:

> Something might be learnt from those insurgent, minority or sub-altern forces that have often refused to codify themselves . . . that have taken shape in the shadows, interstices and oversights of conventional politics and that so often acted as laboratories for alternative futures . . . These minor engagements . . . are cautious, modest, pragmatic, experimental, stuttering, tentative . . . They frequently arise in 'cramped spaces'—within a set of relations that are intolerable, where movement is impossible, where change is blocked and voice is strangulated. And, in relation to these little territories of the everyday, they seek to engender a small reworking of their own spaces of action. (279–280)

As I talked with women in older age groups and heard them speak about their "own spaces of action," I saw that they, too, contribute in a modest way to the process of creating alternative possibilities for recognition of their subjectivities as older women.

RESISTANCE: BEYOND 'OLD' FORMULAS

Resistance in a normative sense is mostly perceived as anti-social and public. However, this study demonstrates that there are many permutations of what it means to resist. In this context, 'resistance' describes the ways the women in my study use their 'cramped spaces' at the level of the everyday to define or reconstruct themselves. It is a conceptualisation of how the women create alternative subject positions and reconstruct the misrecognition of their identities.

Turiel (2003) has theorised how resistance is a part of everyday life aimed at transforming the social system, while Rose (1999, 279) has distinguished resistance as a varied demonstration of what is made of the self in the private realm, at the interpersonal level, in "cramped spaces." Specifically, Wang (1999) demonstrates how social constructions of older age are characterised by qualities of passivity, devaluation and non-production. He describes how these constructions have been resisted by the American seniors' movement, whose activities produce new experiences of existence and thus new subject positions. The views of the women in my study also signal a resistance and challenge to dominant ageist and gender constructions of older women.

RESISTERS, REBELS AND ACTIVISTS: RECONSTRUCTED SUBJECTIVITIES

During the process of interviewing the women, I was struck by the fervency and dynamism of their desire to help others and to contribute to social change. All believed in the importance of achieving social justice, for themselves and others. The women were passionate about preventing childhood sexual abuse and wanted to address the issue of how society reacts in the aftermath of abuse. In speaking about their experiences of childhood sexual abuse, the women illustrated how they resist normative views of how older women should think and act and demonstrated plurality in the lived expression of those views. They spoke about what they see as ethical wrongs and how they actively pursue issues when they believe they can make changes. The construction of this subject position is a counterpoint to discourses of aging that are characterised by passivity, insouciance and decrepitude.

Activism and resistance tend to be viewed as collective activities with a social justice agenda that take place in public. The women in the study certainly revealed a strong sense of being resisters, rebels and activists in public forums. However, their activities also occurred in unexpected, unseen and unorthodox ways, and I interpret these activities as resistance through the reconstruction of subjectivities. Involvement in my research was a significant resistive act for most of the women because they perceived the study as an important activity in which their involvement could contribute to change in terms of better understandings of abuse. This was the dominant motivation for their involvement. All the women expressed ideas about their desire to be a force to assist younger generations.

The women spoke about their efforts to achieve justice for everyone across a number of issues, including childhood sexual abuse itself and managing its impact as well as aging and the role of women. Marjorie (seventy-one years of age) has written and continues to write many letters, articles and public-issue texts, and she makes herself available for interviews and reflections regarding wide-ranging public matters, such as the management of sexual abuse complaints by religious institutions from congregation members, nursing home care, government budget implications for Australians receiving pensions and the critical perspectives on the recent introduction of 'smart' electricity meters into Australian households. Her activism has informed opinion, insight and direct action and has been of great benefit to the broader community. Marjorie has contacted heads of state, church authorities, human rights organisations and the legal profession regarding the judgments on contemporary legal cases. Her contributions to difficult issues in the public realm are insightful, informative and refreshing.

One issue on which Marjorie has been campaigning for many years is mental health advocacy and, in particular, the accountability practices of specific professionals, institutions and systems. She is concerned about the way information was recorded in the past by mental health professionals.

For instance, as a result of the right to access her personal medical records, she discovered that when she described the sexual abuse she had experienced as a child, inverted commas were used in her disclosure, making her experiences appear as allegations. She feels that she was not granted the opportunity to relate her truth and be heard:

> You know, all I want is an acknowledgment that I was telling the truth . . . It's negated my childhood. These people, they were aware of . . . well, that I was "allegedly" sexually abused as a child. I *alleged* this. He wrote [this] on the very first page of my medical, and I'd never even met him before.

For Marjorie, the consequences of not being believed by professionals have been immense. Further, she is appalled by the way she was described, judged and constructed: "You know, they described me as being manipulative."

Marjorie also feels she was constructed as unreliable and that her perspectives were dismissed. She spoke about an instance when the state of her marriage was described by professionals. The conclusions reached were stated as factual; however, for Marjorie, they were incorrect assumptions. For example, comments included in her personal documents described the marriage as a "happy" one, while Marjorie's experience of the marriage was, in her estimation, far more complex and certainly not inconclusively "happy." Further, Marjorie spoke about material that was written about her without her being consulted.

Marjorie expressed her deep anger about these issues and is unafraid to speak out, despite often having experienced rejection or dismissal of her claims. She rallies against labels and continues to advocate on social justice matters, including legal reform for women who have experienced sexual abuse.

Marjorie does not accept that the dominant discourses constructing older women as frail, retiring and unproductive are relevant to her current way of being. In many ways—publically and privately, quietly and loudly, and always with precise intent and strategic direction—she thinks with foresight and beyond the normative social constructions of aging women. She rallies against the inaccuracy of her mental health assessments. She disputes the manner and content of these reports and lives her life in ways that disrupt familiar social constructions of what it is to be a woman growing older. Marjorie says she does not care how others perceive her.

Bernardez (1991) explains the experiences of women such as Marjorie as a function of structural oppression, in which the pathologising of women is an outcome of non-conformity:

> Diagnosis and treatment in the cases of women who are unconsciously resisting conformity represent an acceptance of the status quo and indicate blindness to the potential strength in the woman who is acknowledging and challenging a state of oppression. (219–220)

Certainly, throughout her life, Marjorie has experienced what it is like to be labelled and constructed as 'ill', not credible, lacking judgment and in need of silencing. In spite of this, she is re-creating her identity in ways that disrupt and confront dominant age and gender constructions.

In her study on emotions and aging, Woodward (2002) argues that the cultural expectation with respect to aging, or the emotional standard for older people, is "wisdom." This assigns a discourse and establishes the stereotype of the older person as detached, calmly dispassionate or someone who has a measured and balanced view. Woodward believes that this assigned wisdom is also regarded as useless and irrelevant. In later life, "we need to change what has been called an affect script for older people in our culture" (Woodward 2002, 207). Aging discourse encourages suppression, particularly of anger. Woodward argues that the ideal older woman is viewed as wise and without anger. Women who express anger are often labelled hysterical and irrational and, particularly for older women, the emotion of anger is "outlawed" (Woodward 2002, 206).

Irni (2009) concurs, stating that when older women express anger, they are seen as "cranky old women." The value of their views is minimised, and older women might be seen as "difficult." By expressing her anger and forging on, despite the obstacles presented by a cultural discourse that marginalises her perspectives, Marjorie is an "outlaw" living "new scripts" for age and gender subjectivities.

Another woman in the study, Edith (seventy-two years of age), believes social justice is vitally important to her life. Edith belongs to animal rights groups and regularly attends rallies, stalls and events promoting animal welfare. Her overarching reason for her activism is a commitment to social justice: "Social justice . . . for everybody and animals." Edith explained that she values her connection to all creatures and believes it is her responsibility to change anything she views as unethical: "I think that people or animals who haven't got a voice are the vulnerable ones and I think because I felt so vulnerable all my childhood that I relate to that feeling." Edith also spoke about why she is regularly involved in activities such as providing food to homeless people: "I think it helps me to feel stronger because sometimes . . . when they know somebody cares, it possibly helps them so it makes me feel stronger."

She rejects the idea that her aim and actions to create positive change for animals and others arose from any sense of altruism or 'maladjustment' to past trauma:

> I think it's the sort of thing you come to yourself . . . I guess I just felt sorry . . . seeing that I was able to look after myself after a certain age, I felt sorry for people who could have had a dreadful childhood and not got skills to live how we're expected to live. And I thought, well, perhaps I can make a difference somewhere.

Edith has possessed a keen sense of justice all her life:

I was one of the people against the Vietnam War and . . . yes, I was one of the early ones that . . . have gone on from there. We supported what we could . . . We were involved in the Aboriginal strike that was on at the time . . . It's a long while ago now . . . I think that opened up my eyes to lots of things that were happening.

Similarly, as a result of her past experience, another interviewee, Lily (fifty-seven years of age), expressed the view that her commitment to social justice arose out of an understanding that communities needed to address the issue of sexual abuse differently to how she had experienced the aftermath in her own community:

Once I realised that no one gave a shit in hell about us children . . . then I realised that also the community was involved in that . . . that they were there and although in those times nobody got involved, they were aware. I came to accept that no one gave a crap about us kids. From that, I can see that this is a society that is really very dysfunctional . . . That none of us were getting the support that we needed . . . the care we needed. And society itself had neglected us. And that's when I realised that this is a problem that needs to change.

Other women in the study, such as May (fifty-seven years of age), also expressed their commitment to making positive social changes. May's impetus came from a simple comment made by her mathematics teacher:

She used to say, "Nothing is impossible," and that really stuck with me and somehow the way she lived those words . . . was very empowering for me. Even though I felt so atrocious . . . and was still very much trying to puzzle out what on earth the world was about and all these inconsistencies . . . I knew that justice is important . . . that sort of justice is important.

Rose (sixty-six years of age) describes how speaking out when she saw injustice has had implications for her:

I'm a very just person and I don't tolerate injustice to myself or other people, and that's caused me some confrontations where I've seen other people just hide under the table . . . In the work area, I think people get rewarded for being "yes men" . . . where, despite not being happy about a situation, they did not speak out . . . whereas I . . . not rudely or anything . . . have always spoken my mind, even if it's had the potential to not be helpful to me. So that's sometimes an issue. I also have an issue with people who are incompetent. And unfortunately in the government, incompetence is what gets promoted. If you say "yes" to certain people, you get promoted. So that, I feel, has been a problem.

So, where other people couldn't have cared less, I've felt I've been the one to go in there and do battle . . . That has been an issue for me and I've reared all my children like that, too. I would never want them to be downtrodden . . . I mean, they're not rude or abusive or use foul language, but they're confident.

CONCLUSION

Allen (2008) suggests a tension between agency and the possibility of transformation of the self due to the reality of subjection and the patterns of power as a feature of social life. However, the development of new cultural understandings that broaden the "choices" of the self as well as of notions such as "democracy" and "equality" can lead the way to social transformation (Allen 2008, 184). In addition to change that might emerge from the "social and cultural imaginary" (Allen 2008, 183), Allen suggests that the presentation of narratives is also important in the process:

> Such narratives can envision and make possibilities for recognition, patterns of attachment and identification, and ways of living together . . . We have no choice but to start from where we are, as gendered subjects who are constituted by power relations. (184)

The women in the study, through their narratives, *are* creating new possibilities. They *are* in the process of reconstructing gendered and aging subjectivities over and over in each moment. They enact agency for transformation of the self in spite of the self being constructed by patterns of power. The women, in transforming subordinated identities, resist conformity to age and gender norms.

Westerhof and Tulle (2007, 254) believe the individual reconstruction of identity can be seen as resistance, but they add that this must occur alongside structural change in order to address the inequitable power imbalance among older age groups. However, Krekula (2007, 163) argues that it is a simplification to assume that dominant paradigms of aging and women always prevail. The narratives of the women presented here demonstrate their dynamism, strength, will and passion, and resist discourses that construct aging as frail, weak, ugly and ineffective. Alongside their ideas, ideals and pursuits that are unashamed, angry, joyful and crushing, the women's perspectives on their experiences are instructive in terms of gender and aging. They are resisting 'age-old' stereotypes and redefining mis/conceptions of 'old'. In this way, they are politicising patterns of structural power.

A transversal politics incorporates "the complexity of the lived experience" (Meekosha 2007, 172). The women's narratives occupy various identity positions within our conversations. In working with the women, I witnessed the mundane become monumental, and the hidden become known. The perspectives of the women in this study demonstrate many new possibilities for the resonance of subjectivities. In reconstructing their selves, the women interrogate "the process of boundary-making" (Meekosha 2007, 172).

The narratives of these women resist normative ideas on what it is to be an older woman. Often, women are pathologised and marginalised for speaking out, being angry and objecting to violence against women. These women are outlaws when they resist dominant discourses that trivialise, demean or hide women growing older. These women resist ideas that support an inequitable *status quo* and speak forcefully about the issue of childhood sexual abuse and about what they believe needs to change in respect of societal attitudes and responses. By resisting conformity to dominant age and gender misconceptions in everyday life, these women are creating revolutions in the reconstruction of their identities "because, so often in our history, events, however major their ramifications, occur at the level of the molecular, the minor, the little and the mundane" (Rose 1999, 11).

REFERENCES

Allen, A. 2008. *The Politics of Our Selves*. New York: Columbia University Press.

Bernardez, T. 1991. "Adolescent Resistance and the Maladies of Women: Notes from the Underground." *Women & Therapy* 11 (3–4): 213–222.

Calasanti, T.M., and K.F. Slevin. 2001. *Gender, Social Inequalities and Aging*. Walnut Creek, CA: AltaMira Press.

Collins, P.H. 1998. "It's All in the Family: Intersections of Gender, Race, and Nation." *Hypatia* 13 (3): 62–82.

Irni, S. 2009. "Cranky Old Women?: Irritation, Resistance and Gendering Practices in Work Organizations." *Gender, Work and Organization* 16 (6): 667–683.

Irving, A. 2006. "The Relentlessness and the Ruin: Beckett, Foucault and Aging." In *Foucault & Aging*, edited by J. Powell and A. Wahidin. New York: Nova Science.

Krekula, C. 2007. "The Intersection of Age and Gender: Reworking Gender Theory and Social Gerontology." *Current Sociology* 55:155–171.

McCall, L. 2005. "The Complexity of Intersectionality." *Signs* 30 (3): 1771–1800. Accessed August 30, 2012. http://www.jstor.org/stable/10.1086/426800.

Meekosha, H. 2007. "What the Hell Are You?: An Intercategorical Analysis of Race, Ethnicity, Gender and Disability in the Australian Body Politic." *Scandinavian Journal of Disability Research* 8 (2–3): 161–176.

Nelson, T.D., ed. 2004. *Ageism: Stereotyping and Prejudice against Older Persons*. Cambridge: Massachusetts Institute of Technology.

Powell, J., and A. Wahidin, eds. 2006. *Foucault and Aging*. New York: Nova Science.

Rajchman, J. 1985. *Michel Foucault: The Freedom of Philosophy*. New York: Columbia University Press.

Rose, N. 1999. *Powers of Freedom: Reframing Political Thought*. New York: Cambridge University Press.

Ross-Sheriff, F. 2008. "Aging and Gender, Feminist Theory, and Social Work Practice Concerns." *Affilia* 23:309–310. Accessed October 11, 2011. http://aff.sagepub.com/content/23/4/309.

Sontag, S. 1997. "The Double Standard of Aging." In *The Other within Us: Feminist Explorations of Women and Aging*, edited by Marilyn Pearsall. Boulder, CO: Westview Press.

Turiel, E. 2003. "Resistance and Subversion in Everyday Life." *Journal of Moral Education* 32:115–130.

Wang, F. 1999. "Resistance and Old Age: The Subject behind the American Senior's Movement." In *Reading Foucault for Social Work*, edited by A.S. Chambon, A. Irving and L. Epstein. New York: Columbia University Press.

Westerhof, G.J., and E. Tulle. 2007. "Meanings of Ageing and Old Age: Discursive Contexts, Social Attitudes and Personal Identities." In *Ageing in Society*, edited by J. Bond, S. Peace and F. Dittmann-Kohli. London: Sage Publications.

Wilinska, M. 2010. "Because Women Will Always Be Women and Men Are Just Getting Older: Intersecting Discourses of Ageing and Gender." *Current Sociology* 58:879–896. http://csi.sagepub.com/content/58/6/879. Accessed October 11, 2011.

Woodward, K. 2002. "Against Wisdom: The Social Politics of Anger and Aging." *Cultural Critique* 51:186–218.

14 Residues and Resistance

The Chafe of Working Class Girl to Academic

Norah Hosken

INTRODUCTION

> Nowhere is there a more intense silence about the realities of class differences than in educational settings. (hooks 1994, 177)

This chapter uses threads of a larger current PhD institutional ethnographic research project, "Searching for Recognition and Social Justice in Tertiary Education" (Hosken 2012b), that explores classed, gendered and racialised practices in a Western university. Auto-ethnographic narratives from this study are combined with the literature to foreground a class analysis of relationships between class, agency and social injustice in education. I argue that discourses of equity and diversity have displaced social justice and class in many Australian institutional and policy contexts, including education (Blackmore 2007). This displacement facilitates continued silence about class in Australian higher education, and is one of the reasons that universities continue to be primarily about, and for, the middle class, and are not as successful as hoped in widening participation.

A GENDERED THEORY OF CLASS, WORK AND THE ECONOMY

Sociological theories, research and narrative have identified the role of education in reproducing middle-class privileges and working-class disadvantages (for example, hooks 1994; Preston 2007; Gorski 2010). Different theories have varied approaches to defining class membership (Pease 2010, 64), emphasising objective or subjective aspects of social class. In contrast to conventional understandings of class, I adopt Acker's gendered theory of class and the economy, and Smith's (2005) broad definitions of work. In Acker's theory, class refers to "enduring and systematic differences in access to and control over resources for provisioning and survival" (Acker 2006a, 444), which includes the unpaid work of women as "the activities for provisioning human life or providing the material goods and processes for provisioning and survival" (Ackerb 2006, 170). In this gendered view of the economy, Acker's definition allows those activities required to link paid work and the rest of life to come into view (Acker 2006, 170).This approach aligns with Smith's broad concept of work that includes everything that takes 'time, effort and intent', allowing us to see "what people need to do their work as well as what they are doing" (Smith 2005, 151–154). This has been useful in the larger study, and in this chapter, to understand what makes up the work of being a student and academic at the university and to see how practices of the university may be classed.

In this chapter, I focus on revealing some of the practices that shape the gendered, working-class experience of education. I use four passages of autobiographical narrative to explicate not the truth or universality of those experiences but, rather, possible patterns of gendered-classed practices that inhere in Western patriarchal, capitalist institutions and organisations. The narratives, analysis and the literature indicate that Western universities continue to operate, usually without overt intent or active design, on the historically entrenched norm of a white, middle-class, able-bodied, unencumbered student and staff member (Pearce, Down and Moore 2008; Goldingay and Hosken 2012; Hosken 2012b). The solutions to attraction and attrition of those staff and students who differ from this norm lie as much with changing the culture, pedagogy, policy and practices of the university as they do with recognition and support (Hosken 2012b).

THE UNIVERSITY'S PROBLEM WITH CLASS AND DIFFERENCE

Categorisations both form and are a product of the rhetoric that tends to locate lack of success in widening participation in the students', rather than in the university's subjectivities, aspirations and agency. The "failure to capture the complexity" beyond market-driven category-based plans is, I suggest, one of the reasons institutional plans do not quite work (Lea 2008, 227). University workers are pressured and seduced via "performativity . . . when we come to want for ourselves what is wanted from us" (Ball 2010, 126) to deliver the strategic goals of the organisation. University staff members contribute to the creation of easily defined categories in response to, and are shaped by, the parameters of the latest available funding. These are translated into short-term 'innovative' pilots and projects, required to link with university strategic plans and to market a successful and attractive 'university brand'. As found in research about widening participation in England, despite a superficial focus on innovation, "at a deeper more impenetrable level certain structures of privilege remain impervious to change" (Reay, David and Ball 2005, 106).

The Problem with Equity and Diversity for Class

The Australian Federal government set a national target that by 2020 the percentage of students participating in higher education from low socio-economic backgrounds (low SES) should increase from the current 15 percent to 20 percent (Commonwealth of Australia 2009). This push for widening participation has been made on the basis of an economic case, rather than on the grounds of social justice. Widening participation, as implemented by universities through the language and practices of equity and diversity, sits within the logic of the market. This diversity management for productivity perspective (Blackmore 2006) tends to disregard, or only superficially engage with, the classed, racialised and gendered practices of universities themselves and broader societal discriminations and inequities.

Recent Australian research has identified that not addressing the wider social inequities that 'ration' (Preston 2007) life opportunities, including good quality education, is a key flaw in the plans of government and universities to widen participation. Students in lower socio-economic contexts are less likely to complete secondary school, and those who do complete secondary school tend to have lower levels of attainment than students from higher socio-economic contexts (Chesters and Watson 2012).

Discussion or dissent as a university employee regarding the ethics of widening participation is not easily accommodated or tolerated in this business climate focused on market share, consumer satisfaction and promoting the corporate brand name. Codes of conduct, workloads, performance appraisals, promotional risk, for example, can be operationalised to discipline those who are vocal within their own institution about the impacts of corporate models on education and social justice (Blackmore 2007; Hill 2012).

Pressures for Homogeneity Hide Working-Class Subjectivities

Being working class is conflated to low SES or first in family at university. Many universities use geographic measures of low SES which concentrate "on the general level of educational and occupational skills of people within an area" (Price-Robertson 2011, 7). Some researchers warn against the:

> pitfall of ecological fallacy when using any measure of area-based advantage/ disadvantage . . . when one makes assumptions about specific individuals, families, or even minority populations based on the characteristics of the overall population of the area in which these individuals or groups live . . . relying on the assumption that communities are homogenous. (Price-Robertson 2011, 8)

This ecological fallacy of homogeneity is evident in an inability, unwillingness or non-recognition of the need for universities to complicate their categorisation of 'low SES students' with other aspects of subjectivity for working-class students that may be equally or more important, particularly in an educational context. Research indicates that compared to higher-class individuals, working-class people may possess a greater sense of social engagement, interdependence and social connection (Kraus and Stephens 2012, 643); high empathic accuracy (Kraus, Côté and Keltner 2010); adaptive agency, communal styles of helping, greater desires for conformity and respect for superiors, different conceptions of morality, higher ethical standards, less sense of personal control and greater attention to context (Côté 2011); and high levels of generosity (Piff et al. 2010). In addition, two small-scale Australian studies have shown that students do not separate being low SES or working class from other aspects of subjectivity, of similar or greater importance to themselves at different times, such as, for example, being a South Sudanese Australian, being a mature-age woman, being a sole parent, being a survivor of abuse, being a carer or having a disability (Hosken 2010; Hosken et al. 2012).

Although many university academics may use intersectional theory and approaches in their research, this is not generally the approach that informs, or is enacted in, Australian university human resources, managerial and student policy and practice. This often leads to organisational policy that sounds progressive but is subtly discriminatory and/or unethical, in practice, for those most marginalised in universities and in the broader society.

Misrecognition

I argue that this sort of misrecognition or "withdrawal of social recognition, in the phenomena of humiliation and disrespect" (Fraser and Honneth 2003, 134) occurs, for example, in the language and enactment of policy based on aspiration that can pathologise and homogenise working-class students. Misrecognition in the university is acted out in concert with, but rarely acknowledges the existence and impact of, inter-dependence with broader historical, political and economic contexts.

FOUR NARRATIVES OF CLASS

I often feel torn about my white, working-class background, and current middle-class positioning as a university social work educator and community worker. These conflicted feelings link to my gendered working-class-shaped desires for: down-to-earth practicality and materiality; normative middle-class male approval of the rational and of the body; and subversive, covert-connected and relational ways of knowing, behaving and surviving. These feelings and ways of acting in the world were formed in my era, location and context of gendered, classed and racialised Western patriarchal, colonial capitalism.

Four passages comprise auto-ethnographic narrative excerpts, written using the methods of Muncey (2010) from different time periods (delineated by three separating dots) about working-class childhood and adulthood. The narrative passages are used to assist in developing and providing examples of the formation and endurance of gendered, working-class subjectivity, and how it chafes in the university.

NARRATIVE PASSAGE ONE: LEARNING TO BE A WORKING-CLASS GIRL

My father, controlled and contained, always physically separate to me, sits on his vinyl chair at the head of our small laminate family dinner table. Our dining room just fits the table in our war-service loan asbestos house in Dog Swamp. It is summer, and boiling, Mum sweats, but Dad doesn't. Mum says Dad has discipline, honour and duty; he will always do the right thing. He went to university, my mother did not. He talks in a calm, rational, objective manner about things, books, world events, and the news. When my Mum talks, she is often put down, for trying to make points using what she knows from our life, or the lives of people in our street, or from people at her work. Mum does not have time to read newspapers or see the news, she is too busy cooking, cleaning, looking after me, my brothers and sister, and my father, when she gets home from her full-time paid job . . . I feel a traitor at times because I want, and try, to join the rational conversations, to get approval, and turn my back on our life and experiences. I want to be recognised as being smart by my father and brothers, and also to side with, and emotionally protect, my mother. I get confused and disappointed at myself when, at times, I feel embarrassed of my mother's efforts to join the rational head conversations . . . I am ashamed when I see pity on her face when my own efforts fail . . . I learn as I watch, over many dinners, our attempts to use experience as a basis to join the conversation, are dismissed . . . My mother always tries to smooth or hide things in the family so that they do not upset, or come to the attention of, Dad. My older sister is also good at this. There are many things we do not tell Dad . . . I hear through the wall . . . my father tells my mother they cannot afford the washing machine she wants. I feel sad and angry for her, for us. I will never be asking any man for my own money so I can keep washing his clothes . . ."Why can't Norah be more like Sandra, more graceful and feminine?" Dad tells Mum to do something about this. Sandra lives up on the hill, in the better area. I look, and act like, my Mum. Why doesn't Mum defend me? I feel ashamed, and angry. They made me, but I am not what my father thinks I should be. (Hosken 2012a,3)

The father in narrative passage one is "calm, rational, objective . . . evidenced to 'facts', books, news", not to experience. Like other separate knowers, he applies Western Enlightenment-informed objective knowledge standards with regard to what the is trying to know, relying on "disinterested reason" (Plowman and Smith 2011, 74). I suggest more women, compared to men, in working-class and middle-class white Australia develop and maintain relational and connected ways of knowing and being. This occurs through gendered socialisation practices, mediated by cultural, political and economic systems, as influenced by social and, to some extent, biological reproduction. The main differences between relational and connected ways of knowing and being, compared to separate ways of knowing and being, derive from the relationship the knower has with what is to be known. "People who are separate knowers maintain distance from the object of knowing, they use doubt and suspicion to develop arguments, all the while maintaining personal distance from the object and the argument" (Plowman and Smith 2011, 74).

The girl in this passage learns and watches her mother's connected and relational ways of knowing and being, women's knowledge, repeatedly 'dismissed' by the father and brothers. The girl learns that the 'world' to which her father is connected is more powerful; it is the father who has the power to decide on the mother's desire to purchase a washing machine. The girl notices that "Mum sweats, but Dad doesn't". Control over one's body is "a potent symbol of the extent to which their 'owners' possess self-control" (Muncey 2010, 13). The Western academic male epistemology (knowing), ontology (being) and axiology (doing), predicated on a Cartesian split between mind and body that requires self-control to remove body and emotion from intellect, was what the girl observed and learned. Practices and judgments of middle-class universities reach from their sandstone buildings into this family's dinner table.

The mother in the passage, like many connected and relational knowers, wants a closer relationship with what is to be known. This is shown when the girl recounts the way in which the mother uses knowledge gained in relationships with people to try to make points at the dinner table. In the use of the possessive 'our' rather than 'her', and the singular 'life' instead of the plural 'lives', the girl already demonstrates a more relational way of being and knowing, not separating her own life from that of the mother. The mother trusts that others have something useful to say, and that knowledge can be gained by doing and listening with them. These narratives resonate with research suggesting connected knowing more often represents women's way of knowing, while separate knowing more often characterises the male way of knowing (Plowman and Smith 2011, 74).

The Daily Concert of the Cycles of Misrecognition

The girl is both recipient and made an active member of the daily concert of misrecognition. Playing out in the dining room are historically entrenched gendered and classed dominations and material and symbolic violence. Although the child is clearly less powerful, the processes of misrecognition also sow the need, and the tools, for her survival, resistance and agency as shown in this sentence: "I will never be asking any man for my own money so I can keep washing his clothes".

The child also becomes, in a sense, bicultural, learning when and where to use, or cover, her connected and relational ways of knowing and being, and when to use the knowledge and language of the more powerful, the separate ways of knowing and being. Like the knowledges and languages of many discriminated against groups, they are used in covert ways as shown in the secrecy of conversation and action between the mother and the child in this section of the narrative, which indicates both subversion of and complicity in the cycle of misrecognition, "there are many things we do not tell Dad". The complicity of patriarchal, classed, capitalist society, schools, suburbs, richer families, mothers, fathers, brothers, sisters and her own 'self', in misrecognition, is a complete cycle in the moment of the child's realisation of the worth of herself, of girls and women, in relation to men; she feels ashamed and angry in not being what her father wants her to be.

These covert and subversive knowledges, languages and skills of discriminated against groups are used and hidden, at the same time, in different ways for different purposes. Sometimes used and covered to enable the joining with, and attempts to pass for, the "mythical norm" (Samuels 2007), here of middle-class white male rationality and middle-class femininity; used to please and placate the normative and the more powerful; and used to undermine, manipulate or challenge those with more power. This sort of agency, born from need and survival, is complicated, shaped by and shaping its creative forces.

Working-Class Girls and 'Emotion-Scaping'

The girl child in the narrative passage was trained in subtle and overt ways to observe and learn her place; she learned the 'rule of rational men' in daily family life. The narrative also reveals a version of "cruelling" (Sutton 2009). Grandmothers and mothers reportedly practice(d) 'cruelling', pinching the cheeks of babies in a hard manner, in some Australian Aboriginal communities to increase the speed of visceral reactions in children to potential danger to enhance their chances of survival in hunting and gathering tribal life (Sutton 2009). In working-class white families, this cruelling involves mothers and sisters training young girls in the necessity of 'reading' men, in order to abide by, please or not displease them. I call this version of cruelling 'emotion-scaping', as I cannot find an existing word that is right. The mother and sister's ability to 'smooth and hide' things from the father in narrative passage one is demonstrated on a daily basis, to the girl. The girl is co-opted by the mother and the sister, to learn the need, and the skill, to read emotional and physical cues that culminate in an always-on radar seeking out emotional and physical signs, a radar alert to the needs of men.

Femininity Is Classed

"Why can't Norah be more like Sandra, more graceful and feminine?" When the girl in the passage hears the father say this, and notes the lack of defence from the mother, the girl feels "ashamed and angry". The girl starts to learn that femininity is classed. The sort of femininity the father valued, and wanted for his daughter, was the sort of normative femininity, decorum and beauty portrayed and required of respectable middle- and upper-class women (Skeggs 1997). The father's need to comment to the mother about a perceived lack of femininity is perhaps explained by Skeggs (1997), who demonstrated femininity and respectability as tied and important issues for working-class women, as they are more vulnerable to assessment based on their appearance and sexuality (rough/respectable/slut). Skeggs (1997) explains being labelled as rough or a slut would reduce the possibility of girls' entry into upward mobility through their ability to appear worthy of marriage to a middle-class man.

The girl in the passage believes she is like her mother, and in hearing the father's comment, realises that neither she nor her mother are good enough. The femininity the father judges the mother and the girl for lacking, and wishes the girl to have, "lives up on the hill, in the better area", presumably with the money and cultural capital necessary to produce (at least aspects of) middle-class femininity (clothes, hair, teeth, makeup, knowledge and desire for tastes expressed in 'high' culture, experiences of theatre, plays, art, etc.). The impossibility of the father's desire is expressed when the girl identifies her mother and father as working-class people, and that they 'made' the girl who she is in her not good enough working-class femininity: "They made me, but I am not what my father thinks I should be."

NARRATIVE PASSAGE TWO: A 'WHITE' WORKING-CLASS GIRLHOOD

There are a few Aboriginal kids at my high school. Mum says most of them stay at the hostel, because their families live a long way away. There aren't any Aboriginal families in our suburb. I saw on television that in Balga, eight kilometres from our house, there is a lot of state housing, Aboriginal families and problems. There is one Aboriginal girl in my district basketball team who lives with her family in Balga. I wonder what her life is like. My older sister teaches in Norseman.

She has brought two Aboriginal girls home for a week's holiday in the school break. Mum said Dad is not at all happy about this, and I see his discomfort, every day the girls are here . . . I do not say it to my family, but I think my mother bears a resemblance to a famous Aboriginal woman in Australia that I have seen on television (Hosken 2012a, 8).

In this narrative passage, although only eight kilometres separated Dog Swamp and Balga, they were racially segregated suburbs. The white girl wondered, but did not know, what the life of the Aboriginal girl she played basketball with might be like. Within this working-class family, neighbourhood and school, reinforced by television, people absorb and re-create a wealth and "race hierarchy" (Gorski 2010, 8). This is evident in the separation of the family in the narratives, the 'us' seeing themselves in the middle, different from the richer families on the hill, at the top of the hierarchy, and from the 'them' comprising the Aboriginal and state-housing families in Balga with problems, being seen as on the bottom of the wealth and race hierarchy. The fact that the girl does not ever raise her curiosity about any possible Aboriginal heritage with her family is perhaps related to the father's discomfort with the visiting Aboriginal children, and indicative of the normative racist societal attitudes particularly prevalent in the Australia of the 1960s and 1970s that would make Aboriginality shameful for a 'white' working-class family.

Collective Reproduction of Memories

Overwhelmingly, women still provide the majority of care for children in Australia (Craig and Mullan 2011). Gendered socialisation and reproduction processes that devalue girls and women are still evident in Australia's version of Western, patriarchal, colonial capitalism. It is hard to imagine a society that equally values women and men producing, or tolerating, systemic abuse of its female population, where over a third of women who had a current or former intimate partner report experiencing physical and/or sexual violence since the age of sixteen (Mouzos and Makkai 2004). I suggest this socialisation, produced and reinforced in Australia's economic, political and cultural schema, creates a collective reproduction of memories for white working- and middle-class women. The collective reproduction of memories is a not a uniform process, but rather comprises "complex and often contradictory ways in which the reproduction of memories shapes the social and biological reproduction of people" (Cole 2005, 1). I suggest this explains aspects of the gendered nature of classed subjectivity, and feelings of being shaped, not determined, by a collective memory that links individual to collective feelings and experiences of oppression, joy, survival and agency.

NARRATIVE PASSAGE THREE: MEMORIES
OF UNIVERSITY IN THE 1980S

I am speaking at a university conference as part of our project team about how to teach low SES students. What does it mean to be low SES? Is that all I was? . . . I walk out of my dysfunctional high school, 15 years old, no one notices or stops me. I want something more . . . As a junior clerk I am not sure what upsets me more, the sexual harassment or the mind numbingly boring, repetitive work . . . Working at the restaurant, the chef harasses me, I feel shame, it must be me . . . I watch out, always . . . I save, go back and do an intensive year at TAFE . . . I get in to the best University, work part-time. I am lonely; the other students have come here already with friends. Someone said . . . the kids walking across from the nice buildings opposite the uni are the rich kids who stay at colleges . . . I had no idea . . . they all have nice teeth, the girls are really pretty . . . I watch out here when I walk the few blocks to where I park after a late class to drive to work . . . I am devastated, my first essay, ever, at University back . . . 51%, but why . . . all he has written on my paper is 'This is a non-event' . . . just like at home, at the dining room table. At the end of the year I change universities, move to the more practical one. Even here, I did not know that you could try and get special prizes, like honours. I thought it was enough to pass. (Hosken 2012a, 11)

Like many other young working-class adolescents, the girl attended a 'dysfunctional' state high school where no one noticed she left; she does not complete her secondary education, 'wanting something more'. The girl's experience of sexual assault as a young female worker is not unusual. Australian research finds that 22 percent of women reported have experienced sexual harassment in the workplace (Australian Human Rights Commission 2008); that young women are particularly vulnerable; and that feelings of blame, shame and self-doubt linger (Purdy and Levy 2010). Experiences of interrupted schooling and sexual harassment, assault or abuse are common for working-class girls and women (Purdy and Levy 2010; Hosken et al. 2012). The girl's experiences create "the female fear" (Popkin, Leventhal and Weismann 2010, 717) that impedes women's lives as shown when she 'watches out' walking to the car park. Without any peers from her high school, the girl has to manage loneliness, gendered self-doubt about her femininity compared to the rich girls at the college and lack of intellectual 'rationality' as evidenced in the poor mark on her first assessment. The girl has to figure out on her own how the university works and manage her part-time job, where sexual harassment is normalised. There is a disciplining of working-class girls into doubting their abilities that occurs at the emotional, intellectual and physical levels, normalised and naturalised in Western patriarchal society.

NARRATIVE PASSAGE FOUR: A WORKING-
CLASS BACKGROUND ACADEMIC

I am happy and uneasy in the university. Daily emails or meetings express and confirm university values and ways of working, centred on excellence, merit, and competition. I do not like competing, and know merit is a damaging discourse. I fail at explaining the connected ways of knowing to male academics . . . I love learning, feel amazingly privileged, not quite real, to be in my own office with my name on the door . . . I have never had that before. I know I am coming to want what is wanted from me; I feel pride at publishing; I feel more important . . . I am torn . . . hear and see 24/7 everywhere, on the website. I try, but do not think it is possible to be a good teacher and researcher. There is no time . . . Everyone at the major meetings have computer tablets now. They can keep working on other things. It seems rude to not pay attention to people speaking . . . The women staff have once again organised, bought the cake, and made sure everyone can come . . . Is my challenging, my on-guardedness, what I see as disregard, poshness and pomposity, my discomfort with ceremony and awards, just examples of rejecting what was already rejected for me? I am not sure now how much I exercise agency or play out gendered-classed survival. The understandings I have of myself, and the world, that are based on experience and relationships, are again scrutinised and questioned here at the university . . . I feel that familiar defensive reaction in me, a girl at the dining table, a quiet tingling sensation creeping up from my gut, along my back, up my throat and to the back of my head. My heart slows, and my vision and other senses calm into a tunnel. My body . . . ready to physically, mentally and emotionally defend itself, to resist, and when necessary, to fight. (Hosken 2012a, 13)

There is a continuation of the existence and process of these connected and relational feelings and behaviours and mixed desires, shown to transition from girl to mature woman in narratives three and four. Desire for validation from the 'disinterested reason' of the middle- classed male-centred university and the desire for the subversive connection, from the individual to a collective memory, conflict and compete. This is an example of the residue of gendered working-class girlhood continuing to influence into womanhood, even in the context of the adult enjoying much greater economic and employment privilege. I suggest the difficulty of maintaining, and the accompanying need to defend, connected and relational ways of knowing and being, even with those sympathetic to the ideas of epistemological equity (Dei 2000; Goldingay et al. 2012) as a component of social justice, are partly explained by Ien Ang's (1997, 59) "gulf of incommensurability".

Profound Moments of Incommensurability

The words that Ien Ang uses, poignantly, to convey the nature of the gulf between her and white feminists, I think, also captures the nature of this gulf between Anglo working-class and middle-class people, and between Anglo working-class women and men. I have deleted "white feminists" and made an insertion in brackets in the following passage using Ien Ang's quote to change its meaning for this purpose.

> time and again she finds herself in 'profound moments of incommensurability' and in 'the uncomfortable position of being unable to bridge the gulf' separating herself from [men and middle-class people] . . . 'no matter how willingly they engage in conversation', 'because there is always a residual personal truth . . . which I cannot share and the impact and repercussions of which they cannot ever fully understand'. (1997, 59)

I suggest that although bridging the gulf may not be possible, there is great value in acknowledging its existence, respectfully exploring and partially understanding its contours.

CONCLUSIONS

For the girl and woman in these narratives, 'being working class' as an aspect of subjectivity cannot be separated from 'being a girl and a woman' in the context of Western colonialist, capitalist society. Gendered working-class experiences provided the reasons for, and tools of, resistance. The inability to separate class from gender, and from race/ethnicity, supports the call by some intersectional (Christensen and Jensen 2012) and institutional ethnography (Smith 2006) scholars and practitioners to use everyday life as the point of departure, or standpoint, from which to explore links between subjectivity and structure as one way "to circumvent the problem of non-additivity" (Christensen and Jensen 2012, 117) that troubles intersectional analysis. Real life is not experienced in a non-additive way.

I have endeavoured to show the value in using explorations grounded in the views and experiences of those who experience marginalisation. This sort of approach invites movement of focus from, and between, those who are discriminated against and discriminatory practices. In examining this from a privilege-oppression (Pease 2010) lens, it is possible to appreciate one's own complicity. Realisations of complicity can form feelings, places and ways to produce the empathy, collective aspiration and agency needed to progress social justice. Studies of organisational equity and widening participation reform indicate greater success when there is an exchange between bottom-up activism and top-down policy (Kift, Nelson and Clarke

2010). Infrastructure, resources and a policy framework that invites moving beyond categories to empathic social justice reform is needed.

REFERENCES

Acker, J. 2006. "Inequality Regimes Gender, Class, and Race in Organizations." *Gender & Society* 20 (4): 441–464.

Acker, J. 2006. Class Questions: Feminist Answers, The Gender Lens. Rowman & Littlefield, Lanham, MD.

Ang, I 1997, 'Comment on Felski's "The Doxa of Difference": The Uses of Incommensurability', *Signs*, vol. 23, no. 1, pp. 57–64.

Australian Human Rights Commission. 2008. *Sexual Harassment: Serious Business: Results of the 2008 Sexual Harassment National Telephone Survey*. Sydney: Australian Human Rights Commission.

Ball, S. 2010. "New Voices, New Knowledges and the New Politics of Education Research: The Gathering of a Perfect Storm?" *European Educational Research Journal* 9 (2): 124–137.

Blackmore, J. 2006. "Deconstructing Diversity Discourses in the Field of Educational Management and Leadership." *Educational Management Administration & Leadership* 34 (2): 181–199.

Blackmore, J. 2007. "Equity and Social Justice in Australian Education Systems: Retrospect and Prospect." In *International Handbook of Urban Education*, edited by W. Pink and G. Noblit. Dordrecht, Netherlands: Springer.

Chesters, J., and L. Watson. 2013. "Understanding the Persistence of Inequality in Higher Education: Evidence from Australia." *Journal of Education Policy* 28 (2): 1–18.

Christensen, A., and S. Jensen. 2012. "Doing Intersectional Analysis: Methodological Implications for Qualitative Research." *NORA—Nordic Journal of Feminist and Gender Research* 20 (2): 109–125.

Cole, J. 2005. "Foreword: Collective Memory and the Politics of Reproduction in Africa." *Journal of the International African Institute* 75 (1): 1–9.

Commonwealth of Australia. 2009. *Transforming Australia's Higher Education System*. Canberra: Commonwealth of Australia.

Côté, S. 2011. "How Social Class Shapes Thoughts and Actions in Organizations." *Research in Organizational Behavior* 31:43.

Craig, L., and K. Mullan. 2011. "How Mothers and Fathers Share Childcare: A Cross-National Time-Use Comparison." *American Sociological Review* 76 (6): 834–861.

Dei, G. 2000. "Rethinking the Role of Indigenous Knowledges in the Academy." *International Journal of Inclusive Education* 4 (2): 111–132.

Fraser, N., and A. Honneth. 2003."*Redistribution or Recognition? A Political-Philosophical Exchange*. London: Verso.

Goldingay, S., and N. Hosken. 2012. "Affirming That Everyone Belongs: Practical and Philosophical Issues in Teaching Students from Low Socio-Economic Status Backgrounds." Paper delivered at HERDSA & Deakin, Teaching Diverse Students: A Deakin University Teaching and Learning Forum (TLF), Deakin University Burwood Campus, Victoria.

Goldingay, S., S. Macfarlane, D. Hitch, N. Hosken, G. Lamaro, D. Farrugia, C. Nihill and J. Ryan. 2012. *A Multidimensional Framework for Embedded Academic Skill Development: Transition Pedagogy in Social Work*. Geelong: Deakin University Faculty of Health.

Gorski, P. 2010. "Unlearning Deficit Ideology and the Scornful Gaze: Thoughts on Authenticating the Class Discourse in Education." In *Assault on Kids: How Hyper-Accountability, Corporatization, Deficit Ideology, and Ruby Payne are Destroying Our Schools*, edited by R. Ahlquist, P. Gorski and T. Montaño. New York: Peter Lang.

Hill, R. 2012. *Whackademia: An Insider's Account of the Troubled University.* Sydney, NSW: NewSouth.

hooks, b. 1994. *Teaching to Transgress: Education as the Practice of Freedom.* New York: Routledge.

Hosken, N. 2010. "Social Work and Welfare Education Without Discrimination. Are We There Yet?" *Practice Reflexions* 5 (1): 3–16.

Hosken, N. 2012a. "Auto-Ethnographic Narrative for Searching for Recognition and Social Justice in Tertiary Education." Unpublished paper, Geelong, Deakin University.

Hosken, N. 2012b. "Searching for Recognition and Social Justice in Tertiary Education." Thesis in progress, Geelong, Deakin University.

Hosken, N., C. Land, S. Goldingay, P. Barnes and K. Murphy. 2012. "It's My Dream to Be a . . . : Building Bridges between Gordon TAFE and Deakin University Staff and Students." In *Deakin University Participation & Partnerships Program, End of Year Forum.* Melbourne, Deakin University.

Kift, S., K. Nelson and J. Clarke. 2010. "Transition Pedagogy: A Third-Generation Approach to FYE: A Case Study of Policy and Practice for the Higher Education Sector." *International Journal of the First Year in Higher Education* 1 (1): 1–20.

Kraus, M., S. Côté and D. Keltner. 2010. "Social Class, Contextualism, and Empathic Accuracy." *Psychological Science* 21:1716–1723.

Kraus, M., and N. Stephens. 2012. "A Road Map for an Emerging Psychology of Social Class." *Social and Personality Psychology Compass* 6 (9): 642–656.

Lea, T. 2008. *Bureaucrats & Bleeding Hearts: Indigenous Health in Northern Australia.* Sydney, NSW: UNSW Press.

Mouzos, J., and T. Makkai. 2004. "Women's Experiences of Male Violence: Findings from the Australian Component of the International Violence Against Women Survey (IVAWS)." In *Research and Public Policy Series.* Canberra: Australian Institute of Criminology.

Muncey, T. 2010. *Creating Autoethnographies.* London: Sage Publications.

Pearce, J., B. Down and E. Moore. 2008. "Social Class, Identity and the 'Good' Student: Negotiating University Culture." *Australian Journal of Education* 52 (3): 257–271.

Pease, B. 2010. *Undoing Privilege: Unearned Advantage in a Divided World.* London: Zed Books.

Piff, P., M. Kraus, S. Côté, B. Cheng and D. Keltner. 2010. "Having Less, Giving More: The Influence of Social Class on Prosocial Behavior." *Journal of Personality and Social Psychology* 99:771–784.

Plowman, D., and A. Smith. 2011. "The Gendering of Organizational Research Methods: Evidence of Gender Patterns in Qualitative Research." *Qualitative Research in Organizations and Management: An International Journal* 6 (1): 64–82.

Popkin, S., T. Leventhal and G. Weismann. 2010. "Girls in the 'Hood: How Safety Affects the Life Chances of Low-Income Girls." *Urban Affairs Review* 45 (6): 715–744.

Preston, J. 2007. *Whiteness and Class in Education.* Dordrecht: Springer.

Price-Robertson, R. 2011. *What Is Community Disadvantage? Understanding the Issues, Overcoming the Problem.* Melbourne: Australian Institute of Family Studies.

Purdy, A., and N. Levy. 2010. "Experiences of Sexual Harassment amongst Young Women Workers: An Exploration of Power and Opportunity", *in Women and IR Conference*. Darwin, August 2010.

Reay, D., M. David and S. Ball. 2005. *Degrees of Choice: Social Class, Race, Gender and Higher Education*. Stoke-on-Trent: Trentham Books.

Samuels, D. 2007. "Connecting to Oppression and Privilege: A Pedagogy for Social Justice." In *Race, Gender, and Class in Sociology: Toward an Inclusive Curriculum*, edited by B. Scott and M. Texler Segal. Washington, DC: American Sociological Association.

Skeggs, B. 1997. *Formations of Class & Gender: Becoming Respectable*. London: Sage Publications.

Smith, D. 2005. *Institutional Ethnography: A Sociology for People*. Lanham, MD: AltaMira Press.

Smith, D. 2006. *Institutional Ethnography as Practice*. Lanham, MD: Rowman and Littlefield.

Sutton, P. 2009. *The Politics of Suffering: Indigenous Australia and the End of the Liberal Consensus*. Melbourne: Melbourne University Press.

15 Recognition and Redistribution as Situated Practices
Reflections on Some Experiences as a Social Work Academic

Heather D'Cruz

INTRODUCTION

Activism that involves action to challenge subordination and social and material inequality tends to address the intersection of identities and distribution of rewards, opportunities and burdens: for example, "justice and the politics of difference" (Young 1990); "justice interruptus" (Fraser 1997); resisting the colonisation of Indigenous lands and knowledge (Gray, Coates and Yellow Bird 2008); and "resistance" to the "regulation of people of color" in the United States (Schiele 2011). This chapter aims to investigate recognition and redistribution as situated "concrete social and political practices" (Young 1990, 5). In particular, it focuses on the practical construction of 'activism' as a response to (mis)recognition that has the potential to affect (mal)distribution of rewards (Fraser 2000) in an academic context.

The chapter examines activism where I am the activist, and as narrator/writer tell of my activism, on behalf of individual students who were *not* aware of their (mis)recognition by others, that had potentially significant consequences for the allocation of rewards (marks and grades) to them. The meaningfulness of focusing on people who are objects of injustices by others, yet remain unaware of events transpiring around, them may be justified:

> because moral theories tend to focus on deliberate action for which they seek means of justification, they usually do not bring *unintended social experiences of oppression* under judgement. *A conception of justice that fails to notice and seek institutional remedy for these cultural sources of oppression . . . is inadequate.* (Young 1990, 11; emphasis added)

These aims differ from accounts of activism where narrators claim full exercise of their agency, collectively (Gray, Coates and Yellow Bird 2008; Schiele 2011), or in case studies about the co-construction of resistance with individuals and groups through feminist practice (Crinall 1999; Morley 2009) and community development (Lane 1999), where the activist is also narrator/writer.

CONCEPTUAL FRAMEWORK: RECOGNITION AND REDISTRIBUTION

Recognition is associated with identity. It has emerged as the politics of new social movements, where social groups mobilised politically for "recognition of difference" within societies to assert their claims where they have felt their differences to be marginalised or suppressed (Young 1990; Fraser 1997, 11–13; 2000). Contemporary theorising of identities has moved beyond structural, modernist ideas of monolithic homogeneity associated with descriptive categories of affiliation. Post-modern and post-structural conceptualisations of identity are informed by social and cultural theorists (Roseneil and Seymour 1999, 2–8) and assert the potential for transformation of the self, the instability of individual and group identities and heterogeneity within identity-categories (Butler 1990; Young 1990; Fraser 1997, 2000).

Theories of subjectivity are fundamental to identity (Young 1990, 131–133; Cranny-Francis et al. 2003, 9–13) and aim to understand the dynamics between individual and collective, structure and agency, determinism and autonomy. Subjectivity is important in appreciating how the 'I' asserts him- or herself as a subject, and in doing so, differentiates from 'others' within multiple affiliations (Fraser 2000). Young (1990, 122–155) conceptualises the social processes by which identities are differentiated and judged as "normals" and "abnormals", as "a scaling of bodies" within "the politics of identity". Such processes have a "cultural logic" that creates a politically-important hierarchy between bodies through a "normative gaze" (Young 1990, 10–11), corresponding with "interactive dynamics and cultural stereotyping of racism, sexism, homophobia, ageism, and ableism" (Young 1990, 11).

Young (1990, 131–132), captures the tension between "discursive consciousness" and "a need for basic ontological security" related to "unconscious motives", stating that:

> aversive or anxious reactions to the bodily presence of others contribute to oppression. Such cultural reactions are usually unconscious. . . . often exhibited by liberal-minded people who intend to treat everyone with equal respect. (1990, 10–11)

This tension is conceptualised as "practical consciousness", which examines:

> those aspects of action and situation which involve often complex reflexive monitoring of the relation of the subject's body to those of other subjects and the surrounding environment, but which are on the fringe of consciousness . . . [it] is the habitual, routinized background awareness that enables persons to accomplish focused, immediately purposive action. (131)

Redistribution is associated with the allocation of material resources, power and participation (Young 1990; Fraser 1997, 11–13). Young (1990) and Fraser (1997, 2000) advocate different approaches to identity (recognition) in their remedies for redistribution.

Young (1990, 10) promotes the recognition of difference, arguing that "a denial of difference contributes to social group oppression". She gives examples within public and organisational life, of the "ideals of impartiality" and "merit" that are based on unquestioned criteria assumed to be neutral, and that inform the distribution of rewards, opportunities and burdens (Young 1990, 96–121, 192–225)—such as the allocation of marks and grades to students in academic institutions. Instead, acceptance of these ideals as universal principles of "equal treatment" maintains and legitimates "cultural imperialism" and an "authoritarian hierarchy" by privileged groups (Young 1990, 10, 122–124). Affirmative action programs (Young 1990, 192–200) are therefore:

> important means for undermining oppression, especially oppression that results from unconscious aversions and stereotypes and from the assumptions that the point of view of the privileged is neutral. (Young 1990, 12)

In rejecting affirmative remedies that rely either on equality as sameness or assertions of fundamental differences between groups, Fraser (1997, 11–39) proposed transformative remedies: socialism as "transformative redistribution", and deconstruction to achieve "transformative recognition [of identities]". Deconstruction destabilises privileged identities represented as normative, for example, "androcentrism" (29), and "opposes the sedimentation or congealing of . . . difference . . . [as essentialism]" (30). Transformative remedies would not generate the problems associated with affirmative remedies, such as claims of "special treatment" (29). Transformative remedies attend to intersectionality (30–33), 'interlocking oppressions' (Yeatman 1995) and 'interlocking privileges' (Nash 2008), and propose dismantling of the deep structures that construct and perpetuate the binaries and hierarchies between identities preventing "parity of participation" (Fraser 2000).

Practical consciousness allows an exploration of *how* social actors participate in discursive practices, such that they maintain and/or transform social dynamics and subjectivities (D'Cruz 2007, 43–53; Nash 2008). It allows us to examine micro-practices as "an *ascending* analysis of power" (Foucault 1980, 99; original emphasis) by which identities are constructed through "dividing practices", as "normal" and "abnormal" bodies, with associated disciplinary practices to achieve normalisation. Through an analysis of situated micro-practices, we may understand how identities and subjectivities are constructed, *and* the boundaries between identities of privilege and subordination that are implicated in the politics of recognition and redistribution (Naples 2008, 1–3; Nash 2008).

The chapter aims are achieved through a methodology that I characterise as an 'uneasy autoethnography', being mindful of critical debates as to its ethical and methodological soundness (Delamont 2009; Ellis, Adams and Bochner 2011). I represent two 'critical' incidents—'Representing Reality, Re-presenting 'Critical' Incidents'—that emerged from my experiences over thirteen years as an academic (1996–2009) in social work programs at various Australian universities. I next examine, in "'Activism' as Contingent on Recognition and Distribution", the rhetorical devices by which I have constructed the re-presented incidents, with activism contingent on the situated constructions of identities and the potential and actual consequences of such constructions. "(Mis)recognition and (Mal)distribution?" reflects upon the two re-presented incidents, to move beyond the "atomisation" and "re-ductionism" (Atkinson 2009; Delamont 2009) associated with personal narratives. To what extent, for example, might the deconstruction of 'critical' incidents increase understanding of the articulations between recognition and redistribution? How might the (mis)recognition of identities as situated practices offer insights into their articulation with distributive processes, without asserting monolithic views of identities, power and distributive justice? I do not offer conclusions, but I reflect on the potential of 'writing', 'reading' and 'activism', as opportunities presented by situated interpretations of texts (Richardson 2006; Ellis, Adams and Bochner 2011).

QUESTIONS OF METHODOLOGY

The methodology sits uneasily between "autoethnography" (Ellis, Adams and Bochner 2011) and "reflexive ethnography" (Delamont 2009, 58), being mindful of the critiques of approaches focusing on personal experiences as "narcissistic", "unethical" and methodologically unsound (Delamont 2009, 59–60). The re-presented 'critical' incidents are somewhere between 'personal narratives' and 'therapeutic writing' (Ellis, Adams and Bochner 2011, paras. 24–27).

They are 'personal narratives' because I:

> propose to understand . . . some aspect of a life as it intersects with a cultural context . . . invite readers to enter the author's world and to use what they learn there to reflect on, understand, and cope with their own lives. (Ellis, Adams and Bochner 2011, para. 24)

They are a form of "therapeutic writing" because I:

> seek to improve and better understand . . . relationships. . . . reduce prejudice . . . encourage personal responsibility and agency . . . raise consciousness and promote cultural change. (Ellis, Adams and Bochner 2011, para. 25)

Writing the incidents for this chapter allows me to make public what has been private for a long time, with the aim of bearing witness, "allowing [me], a researcher, an author, to identify other problems that are cloaked in secrecy" (Ellis, Adams and Bochner 2011, para. 27).

Methodologically, the re-presented 'critical' incidents are not the outcomes of formalised interviews and recorded observations (Delamont 2009; Ellis, Adams and Bochner 2011, paras. 7, 13–14). They have emerged from my lived experience. These re-presentations about others' experiences that I have witnessed have remained with me as troubling and memorable "epiphanies" (Ellis, Adams and Bochner 2011, paras. 8–9) and seem legitimate for reflection and critical analysis for their broader potential significance.

Writing from experience necessitates "relational ethics" that include protecting the privacy and safety of others by altering identifying characteristics, using pseudonyms and masking dates and places (Ellis, Adams and Bochner 2011, para. 31). There may be considerations of whether or how to get informed consent, even from unidentified people. There may be criticisms of methodological trustworthiness of writing from experience, related to alteration of details for ethical reasons and the fallibility of memory (Ellis, Adams and Bochner 2011, paras. 32–35). However, I am hoping that the re-presented incidents have sufficient credibility, through being recognisable to readers, especially if the writing and reading are to generate knowledge about hidden forms of oppression (Ellis, Adams and Bochner 2011, paras. 33–35).

Recognition of "positioned subjectivity" (Riessman 1994, 133–138) is the norm by which the influence of identities on "how I know, what I know, and what I do" is acknowledged. However, Butler (1990, 142) destabilises this apparent determinism between identity, epistemology and action. While I can list my embodied, intersecting and situated identities—as (Eur)asian woman of colour, immigrant to Australia, middle class, heterosexual by inclination, able-bodied, educated academic, social worker, 'etc.'—the 'et cetera':

> strives to encompass a situated subject while being a sign of exhaustion *and* the illimitable process of signification [that] offers . . . a new departure for . . . political theorizing. (Butler 1990, 143; original emphasis)

REPRESENTING REALITY, RE-PRESENTING 'CRITICAL' INCIDENTS

The re-presented 'critical' incidents cannot be reified or easily detached from the continuity of lived experience and the multiplicity of incidents that occur simultaneously with differing demands for attention. The incidents are the surface of a confluence of unknown histories, biographies and subjectivities of participants and complex dynamics between identities, perspectives (unconscious or hidden), motives and practices. The incidents became 'critical' through my intention to prevent perceived injustices; they are not objectively 'critical', and others might perceive them as merely 'coincidental'.

The re-presented incidents involve students enrolled in Bachelor of Social Work degrees at Australian universities and their engagement within the university community, with academics and peers.[1] The incidents and my part in them have been emergent and unexpected, and my activism was both reflexively responsive at the time and now re-presented to meet the aims of this chapter.[2]

Ashley (either a new migrant or an international student) was a student from China [A2]. He was self-conscious about being Chinese [A3], for example, being embarrassed to be called by his Chinese name [A3a], instead asking to be called by an English first name [A3b] he had legally adopted [A3c]. He lacked confidence in his English-language skills [A4], so he rarely spoke in classes [A4a] *unless* he was asked a direct question [A4b]. However, he would consult with me regularly [A5a], after having read the literature recommended for the subject he was enrolled in [A5b]. I was amazed at the quality of the analysis of his reading [A6a], and his ability to articulate and discuss complex questions and issues he had prepared [A6b], that were relevant to his assignments, unlike many of the other undergraduates who consulted me [A6c]. He would ask academic skills advisers at the university to review his English in written assignments before submitting them [A7]. He was an outstanding student [A8]. So I was astonished to receive a phone call towards the end of the semester by a colleague, Paolo, coordinating another subject that Ashley was enrolled in [A9]. Paolo asked me for advice about Ashley, as *a tutor in the other subject was intending to fail Ashley on the grounds of cheating. The rationale for this was that the tutor considered that Ashley's written work, which was excellent, could not be his own because "he never spoke in class"* [A1]. Clearly the tutor had never met with Ashley as I had [A10a], in discussing his work [A10b] and his scholarly activities related to it [A10c]. I was able to reassure [A11] my colleague Paolo about Ashley's scholarly qualities [A11a] and integrity [A11b] through my extensive contact with him [A11c], and was thankful that someone had sufficient interest to check the assumptions underpinning 'merit' being applied to an Asian student, before creating a monstrous injustice [A12].

Mimi was an international student from South Asia who was enrolled in one of the subjects that I taught [M2]. I was amazed and shocked to be accused (challenged directly) by some 'white',[3] Anglo women students that I was 'favouring' Mimi by 'giving her' Distinction grades because 'I was like her' [M1]. I did not know how widespread these views were amongst the student group [M3]. I also gained the impression that some of these views about Mimi's abilities were because she did not meet the stereotype of Asian women [M4a], as oppressed, inarticulate, poor and not literate or fluent in English. Mimi's first language was English; she came from a wealthy family and enjoyed the material benefits, like expensive clothing [M4b]. The views by students of my 'favouritism' to Mimi were expressed to my 'white' academic colleagues, who also viewed her with suspicion [M5]. It was extremely difficult for me to offer a different view of Mimi because I was seen as 'biased' [M6]. (I was aware that these claims were part of an invisible yet powerful coalition of like-minded 'white' women—students and academics [M7a]—whose perceptions of me as lacking in integrity were thinly veiled [M7b]. The academic women colleagues who espoused feminism [M8a] were participants in gossip [M8b] that I succeeded due to a mixture of flirtation with men [M9a] and lying about my workload [M9b], claiming competence that was 'really' due to others' efforts [M9c]. I had heard about these views of my 'white' women colleagues [M10a] from occasional, unsolicited warnings from two 'friendly others': a 'white' woman and a 'white' man [M10b], but I believed there was nothing I could do about it [M11a], as I had already been told by a senior social work academic that these things were not happening; it was only my perception that they were [M11b].) None of these people was aware of the self-questioning that I engaged in [M12a] when I did assess assignments from 'students like me' as Distinction or higher, a process that I never engaged in with 'white' and/or Anglo students [M12b], as somehow they were always 'deserving' of these high grades [M12c].

'ACTIVISM' AS CONTINGENT ON RECOGNITION AND DISTRIBUTION

The two incidents show contrasting meanings of 'activism': in Ashley's case, 'being a successful activist', and in Mimi's case, 'being an unsuccessful activist'. The incidents are deconstructed as 'representations of reality' through rhetorical devices (Potter 1996)—linguistic resources that are deployed as an intersection of knowledge and power. The meanings of activism are contingent on how I have constructed the identities of participants, particularly Ashley and Mimi as students, and the possible meanings of injustice towards them.

In Ashley's story, the pivotal event [A1] is that an unidentified tutor was going to fail him despite his excellent written assignments, because "he did not speak in class". In re-presenting this incident, my background knowledge to support 'how I know what I know about Ashley' is presented [A2–A8]. My prior construction of Ashley as 'normal' (A2–A4c) is set implicitly against an image of 'the normal social work student' in the Australian context. I took account of his ethnic, cultural and linguistic differences from the dominant group of students. I normalised behaviours that might otherwise be constructed as 'abnormal'. This process of normalisation relies on a three-part list (Potter 1996, 196) to show how Ashley's self-consciousness about 'being Chinese' was managed, and yet given legitimacy because his preferred English first name had been 'legally adopted' and was not a name he used for illegitimate purposes.[4] Further, while I have noticed Ashley does not speak in class, I have attributed this to his lack of confidence in his English-language skills, rather than lack of participation or other abnormalising constructions as 'student',[5] such as lack of preparation or disinterest. I have further normalised Ashley's identity as a competent student by getting to know his abilities when he voluntarily consulted with me about his work; his competence compared favourably, even excelled, that of his peers. These interactions with Ashley also suggest that in a "safe space for coming to voice" (Collins 2000, 100), Ashley is able to do so.

What I say subsequently to Paolo are counter-claims to repair Ashley's identity from abnormal (incompetent and dishonest student) to normal (competent), or even supernormal—(excellent), and honest [A10a—A11c]. It is my prior knowledge of Ashley's competence as a student that allows me to offer an alternative construction of Ashley's apparent incompetence and implied dishonesty. I have also implied criticism of the tutor who had 'clearly never met with Ashley as I had' [A10a], thus undermining his competence and construction of Ashley as 'incompetent and dishonest student'. The overall re-presentation makes a case for 'being a successful activist' in that particular incident on Ashley's behalf [A12].

In the incident about Mimi, the pivotal event occurs almost at the start [M1], where my emotive language ('amazed', 'shocked', 'accused') suggests that something unexpected and disturbing had happened, quite possibly challenging my existing construction of Mimi as a 'normal student', as 'being the same as' her non-Asian peers in regard to her participation and relative successes and failures.

In this re-presented incident, unlike in the previous one, the pivotal event [M1] operates metaphorically, almost tangibly a physical barrier: a wall or gate. It is tricky to negotiate because I became part of the incident about Mimi. It is difficult to separate the 'facts' from the rhetorical purposes, and it poses the problem of reflexivity (Butler 1990, 142–143; Delamont 2009, 58–60).

> If the subject is culturally constructed, it is nevertheless vested with an agency, usually figured as the capacity for *reflexive mediation*, that remains intact regardless of its cultural embeddedness. (Butler 1990: 142–143; original emphasis)

As a rhetorical device it can be seen as an implicit contrast structure (Potter 1996, 194–195), where both Mimi and I as visibly embodied identities—'Asian' 'women', being 'alike'—precludes us from exercising agency and autonomy, this being seen instead as a manifestation of "stake and interest"(Potter 1996, 122–132), as 'bias' [M6].

In addition to the rhetorical features implicit in its construction, the pivotal statement operates much as an actual physical barrier between two spaces: it divides and gives definition to what is on both sides. The point of re-presenting the incident can only continue to have relevance or purpose *because of* the pivotal statement. Otherwise Mimi's 'normality' as a 'student' seems unproblematic.

The remaining statements [M3–M12c] flow from it, simultaneously constructing both Mimi and myself as abnormal identities. Although I did not know whether such views were 'widespread' [M3], a "modalising term" (Potter 1996, 188) to ascertain how 'normal' this assumption was amongst the student group, there appeared to be some commonality of views between 'white' women students and academics [M5]. I offer my constructions of Mimi's 'normality' as a student [M4a–M4b], *and* the possibility that her embodied identity as 'Asian' 'woman' also undermined her normality for (some of) her peers. She could not simultaneously be 'successful' *and* an 'Asian woman student'.

I was unable to be an activist on Mimi's behalf, partly because of perceptions of my 'stake and interest' [M6] as 'being like Mimi' and partly because of my relative powerlessness [M7a–M11b], through constructions of abnormality by my peers [M9a–M9c]. I have placed part of this account [M7a–M11b] into round brackets to indicate that it is 'background' necessary to make sense of the statements preceding (especially M6) and following [M12a–M12c]. While the account can be read by excluding the section in round brackets, after a lot of thought, I decided to include it as it seemed to explain better why I was unable to properly be an activist for Mimi.[6]

I have represented this construction [M7a–M11b] as a perceived 'powerful coalition' where 'white' women academics (and students) 'espoused feminism' [M8a], yet their practices did not appear to meet these expected ideological aims. Their practices, as a three-part list (Potter 1996, 196), are presented as 'typical' of 'non-feminist' practices [M8b; M9a–M9c]. I claim 'facticity' of these constructions, not as characteristics of an abnormal mind (for example, as "just my perceptions" [M11b]), but instead supported by 'occasional, unsolicited warnings by two friendly others' [M10b], a three-part list showing restraint, sufficient distance through being 'unsolicited' and people 'on my side'.

However, despite these apparent coalitions with alternative constructions of my identities as 'Asian' 'woman' 'academic', ultimately, my activism for Mimi was stymied *because* I was unable to be an activist for myself. Although I have constructed myself as an 'unsuccessful activist' in this case, I have justified this within struggles around identities in which a primary issue concerning a 'student' unfortunately implicated me as well.

I repaired my identities (initially privately, to myself, and now in this re-presentation) as an 'Asian' 'woman' *and* 'competent' 'honest' 'academic' [M12a–M12c], through modalising terms ('none', 'never', 'always') and contrasting practices where I make a distinction between how I assess 'students like me' ('Asian', possibly 'women') and 'students not like me' ('non-Asian') as an intersection of academic integrity and competence: 'a process of self-questioning'.

(MIS)RECOGNITION AND (MAL)DISTRIBUTION?

This chapter has aimed to examine activism as a situated social practice, contingent on the situated constructions of identities, with potential or actual "maldistribution" of rewards due to "misrecognition" of identities as students (Fraser 2000), whose ethnicity and/or gender generated particular constructions of "competence" and "merit" (Young 1990).

The methodological approach sits uneasily within strident debates about writing from experience, differentiating between the preferred "autobiographical" to the disputed "autoethnographic" (Delamont 2009; Ellis, Adams and Bochner 2011), and particular definitions of research as planned and systematic (Delamont 2009, 59–60; Ellis, Adams and Bochner 2011, 7, 13–14), leaving little room for emergent epiphanies in lived experience that may be worthy of deeper consideration. In the interests of legitimating the chapter and its aims, I hope I have achieved appropriate scholarship by:

> studying a setting, a subculture, an activity or some actors other than [myself] ... [while being] acutely sensitive to the interrelationship(s) between [myself] and the focus of the research ... [rather than an approach] where there is no object except the author ... to study. (Delamont 2009, 58)

While it is a given that the entire chapter relies on rhetorical devices to present a plausible argument (Potter 1996), special attention has been paid to the two 'critical' incidents as examples of activism in practice. Through a deconstruction of rhetorical devices (Potter 1996), I have shown how I have constructed the situated meanings of 'activism' and identities of participants, as political processes and struggles between versions of normal and abnormal identities, 'entitlement' and 'merit', and, thereby, consequences for distribution.

However, is it enough to recognise the processes in constructing and re-presenting identities, as situated practices, and retold as 'critical' incidents? Does a sociological analysis of micro-practices of how meanings and identities are constructed as social practices of knowledge/power, and with potential or actual material consequences, offer any insights for institutionalised (mis)recognition and 'maldistribution' (Fraser 2000)?

The activism and constructions of identities of all participants seemed to emerge within particular situations, rather than necessarily being determined by pre-existing identity affiliations, such as gender or ethnicity (Butler 1990, 142). I am not aware that my activism for Ashley or Mimi occurred because of our shared identities, yet it became necessary to do so to prevent or mitigate (mis)recognition and its possible consequences. Was it coincidence that Ashley and I are 'Asian', although he is Chinese born and I am not? Our gender differences did not seem to matter as he voluntarily consulted with me in the 'safe space' of my office, unlike the experience related by Kothari (1997) as an Asian woman teaching international development to black men, students from developing countries. Mimi's identities were conflated with mine, by others equating our bodily similarities as deterministic of our identities and as moral judgments. My resistance and activism were limited despite my apparently greater structural power as an 'academic' (Simmonds 1992, 59; Kothari 1997, 160–163).

The analysis does not suggest that Ashley and Mimi experienced monolithic expressions of 'racism'. For both, there were glimmers of awareness and acts of fairness: by Paolo seeking an alternative view to his colleague's perceptions about Ashley, and Mimi's successful graduation from the social work program. However, the analysis also raises questions about 'agency' and 'activism' by individuals who may not be aware of situations in which they are objectified by others, particularly when coalitions are formed against them. Unlike many narratives of activism and resistance which centralise the agency of the rational subject (individually and collectively), these incidents suggest that it is possible to be powerless because of objectification and exclusion, where you may be a topic of others' conversations but not a participant. There is no "parity of participation as a peer" (Fraser 2000, 114–116).

Unfortunately, I became implicated in the re-presented incident about Mimi even if it began as tangential. This was uncomfortable. Nonetheless, as the analysis of rhetorical devices has shown, the re-presentations are 'about me' as much as they are 'about Ashley and Mimi'. An unintended artefact, through this writing, is my insight that my experiences of objectification, marginalisation and abnormalisation by others parallel Mimi's. Yet I was also a participating subject within a coalition of 'friendly others' that reduced my sense of abnormality and powerlessness.

I cannot make any grand claims as an 'activist'. The achievements are small and confined to the situations. The individuals who perpetrated these potential acts of injustice towards Ashley and Mimi were not aware of the activism that prevented potentially unjust consequences. There were no changes in the assumptions made by 'all academics' or 'all students' about embodied differences that mark 'others' as transgressive and 'abject bodies' representing immorality and incompetence, and therefore undeserving of rewards unless they meet apparently neutral, yet implicitly different, standards of 'merit' than those applied to 'white' and/or 'Anglo' groups (Young 1990).

Public policies tend to address legally definable acts of injustice, such as 'sexual harassment' (McDonald and Flood 2012), including 'bystanders' as activists in resistance to assist victims of oppression. However, there is limited acknowledgment of the probably numerous examples of hidden processes of exclusion similar to those re-presented here that have serious consequences; for example, the exclusion from rewards and the damage to reputations. None of these consequences or their processes can be redressed if the affected individuals remain unaware and therefore are denied the opportunity to act. As Fraser (2000) argues, in extending her earlier advocacy of deconstruction (Fraser 1997):

> what requires recognition is not group-specific identity but the status of individual group members as full partners in social interaction. *Misrecognition*, accordingly, *does not mean the depreciation and deformation of group identity, but social subordination—in the sense of being prevented from participating as a peer in social life. To redress this injustice* still requires a politics of recognition, but in the 'status model' this is no longer reduced to a question of identity: rather, *it means a politics aimed at overcoming subordination by establishing the misrecognized party as a full member of society, capable of participating on a par with the rest.* (2000, 113; emphasis added)

Examining situated micro-practices as 'an ascending analysis of power' offers insights into *how* recognition and distribution are accomplished, beyond compliance and regulation. Such analyses offer opportunities to appreciate how these outcomes are achieved, by understanding practices of resistance and subversion between 'entitled and privileged' and 'excluded and subordinated' and the implicit norms of who is 'deserving' and who is not.

'WRITING', 'READING' AND 'ACTIVISM'

Writing *and* reading are not ethically and politically neutral activities (Cranny-Francis et al. 2003, 89–138). As a participant/observer-writer/narrator, I have "reveal[ed] my epistemological assumptions . . . found ways to change those scripts", although not always successfully, and hope "to connect to others" (Richardson 2006, 1–2). The multiplicity of ways in which this text is read and interpreted may generate resistance to the intended 'message' *and* opportunities for activism towards transformative politics. So, how have you read it?

NOTES

1. Versions of these incidents about Ashley and Mimi were included in D'Cruz (2012), but the detailed analysis is specific to this chapter.
2. I have used alphanumeric codes to identify text within each re-presented incident, linked to the deconstruction that follows. The letters *A* (Ashley) or *M* (Mimi) are used, while numbering from 1 onwards identifies the relevant sections of text. The re-presented incidents have been reworked through several versions to best capture my aims in retelling them. While the process

of writing has always aimed to be 'faithful to the facts', like all writing, the invisible processes 'behind the finished product' are also part of the process of construction and of 'representing reality'.

3. I have placed 'white' in quotes to indicate that it is my perception of the identities of others, partly as bodily characteristics and partly knowing of their claimed identities as 'white' when they discussed racism as oppression by 'white' people, their abhorrence of it and championing of oppressed people of colour, particularly Aboriginal Australians. However, 'whiteness' is as fluid an identity as any other, and it is possible to be a "white woman of colour" (Alvarez 2004).

4. In re-presenting this incident about Ashley, I have become aware that I have used the adverb 'legally' to qualify 'adopted' because I do not wish to give the wrong impression that Ashley was doing anything odd or problematic. At the time, I recall noticing his embarrassment if I used his Chinese given names in class, as there were stifled sniggers, and his (and my) awareness of the 'oddness' of its sound in the midst of Anglo and European (and more contextually familiar) names.

5. Treating Ashley's 'not speaking in class' as a sign of his incompetence and as deterministic of his inability to write assignments of high quality was a surprising construction, as undergraduates 'not speaking in class' is often a point of frustration for many academics who want to generate interaction and discussion, and possibly 'evidence' of learning and reading of assigned texts. Marks are often given for 'participation' just to encourage 'speaking in class'.

6. I struggled with whether including this section [M7a–M11b] was an "introspective contemplation of myself" (Delamont 2009, 60) that "allows me the power of being the victim with all the moral righteousness on my side" (Fook 1999, 196). It is interesting as a process of representation of the self, where ethical concerns and political processes intersect.

REFERENCES

Alvarez, J. 2004. "A White Woman of Color." In *Race, Class and Gender: An Anthology*, 5th ed., edited by M.L. Anderson and P.H. Collins. Belmont, CA: Wadsworth/Thomson Learning.

Atkinson, P. 2009. "Illness Narratives Revisited: The Failure of Narrative Reductionism." *Sociological Research Online* 14 (5):16.

Butler, J. 1990. *Gender Trouble: Feminism and the Subversion of Identity*. New York: Routledge.

Collins, P.H. 2000. *Black Feminist Thought: Knowledge, Consciousness and the Politics of Empowerment*. 2nd ed. New York: Routledge.

Cranny-Francis, A., W. Waring, P. Stavropoulos and J. Kirkby. 2003. *Gender Studies: Terms and Debates*. New York: Palgrave Macmillan.

Crinall, K. 1999. "Challenging Victimisation in Practice with Young Women." In *Transforming Social Work Practice: Postmodern Critical Perspectives*, edited by B. Pease and J. Fook. St. Leonards, NSW: Allen and Unwin.

D'Cruz, H. 2007. "Working with 'Diverse Bodies, Diverse Identities': an Approach to Professional Education about 'Diversity.'" *International Journal of Inclusive Education* 11 (1): 35–57.

D'Cruz, H. 2012. *National Anti-racism Partnership and Strategy*, Submission to the Australian Human Rights Commission, Canberra, Australia

Delamont, S. 2009. "The Only Honest Thing: Autoethnography, Reflexivity and Small Crises in Fieldwork." *Ethnography and Education* 4 (1): 51–63.

Ellis, C., Adams, T. E. and Bochner, A. P. 2010. "Autoethnography: An Overview" [40 paragraphs]. *Forum Qualitative Sozialforschung/Forum: Qualitative Social Research*, 12(1), Art. 10, http://nbn-resolving.de/urn:nbn:de:0114-fqs1101108.

Fook, J. 1999. "Critical Reflectivity in Education and Practice." In *Transforming Social Work Practice: Postmodern Critical Perspectives*, edited by B. Pease and J. Fook. St. Leonards, NSW: Allen and Unwin.

Foucault, M. 1980. *Power/Knowledge: Selected Interviews and Other Writings 1972–1977*. Edited by C. Gordon. London: Harvester Press.

Fraser, N. 1997. *Justice Interruptus: Critical Reflections on the "Postsocialist" Condition*. New York: Routledge.

Fraser, N. 2000. "Rethinking Recognition." *New Left Review* 3 (May–June): 107–120.

Gray, M., J. Coates and M. Yellow Bird, eds. 2008. *Indigenous Social Work around the World: Towards Culturally Relevant Education and Practice*. Aldershot, UK: Ashgate.

Kothari, U. 1997. "Identity and Representation: Experiences of Teaching a Neo-Colonial Discipline." In *Knowing Feminisms: On Academic Borders, Territories and Tribes*, edited by L. Stanley. London: Sage Publications.

Lane, M. 1999. "Community Development and a Postmodernism of Resistance." In *Transforming Social Work Practice: Postmodern Critical Perspectives*, edited by B. Pease and J. Fook. St. Leonards, NSW: Allen and Unwin.

McDonald, P., and M. Flood. 2012. *Encourage. Support. Act!: Bystander Approaches to Sexual Harassment in the Workplace*. Canberra, ACT, Australia: Australian Human Rights Commission. Accessed August 14, 2012. http://www.humanrights.gov.au/sexualharassment/bystander.

Morley, C. 2009. "Using Critical Reflection to Improve Feminist Practice." In *Critical Social Work: Theories and Practices for a Socially Just World*, 2nd ed., edited by J. Allan, L. Briskman and B. Pease. Crows Nest, NSW: Allen and Unwin.

Naples, N.A. 2008. *Crossing Borders: Feminism, Intersectionality and Globalisation*. Hawke Research Institute for Sustainable Societies Working Paper Series, Number 36. University of South Australia, Magill Campus, Adelaide.

Nash, J.C. 2008. "Re-Thinking Intersectionality." *Feminist Review* 89:1–15.

Potter, J. 1996. *Representing Reality: Discourse, Rhetoric and Social Construction*. London: Sage Publications.

Richardson, L. 2006. "Skirting a Pleated Text: De-Disciplining an Academic Life." In *Emergent Methods in Social Research*, edited by S.N. Hesse-Biber and P. Leavy. Thousand Oaks, CA: Sage Publications.

Riessman, C.K. 1994. "Subjectivity Matters: The Positioned Investigator." In *Qualitative Studies in Social Work Research,* edited by C.K. Riessman. Newbury Park, CA: Sage Publications.

Roseneil, S., and J. Seymour. 1999. "Practising Identities: Power and Resistance." In *Practising Identities: Power and Resistance*, edited by S. Roseneil and J. Seymour. Basingstoke: Macmillan.

Schiele, J., ed. 2011. *Social Welfare Policy: Regulation and Resistance among People of Color*. Thousand Oaks, CA: Sage Publications.

Simmonds, F.N. 1992. "Difference, Power, and Knowledge: Black Women in Academia." In *Working Out: New Directions for Women's Studies*, edited by H. Hinds, A. Phoenix and J. Stacey. London: Falmer.

Yeatman, A. 1995. "Interlocking Oppressions." In *Transitions: New Australian Feminisms*, edited by B. Caine and R. Pringle. St. Leonards, NSW: Allen and Unwin.

Young, I.M. 1990. *Justice and the Politics of Difference*. Princeton, NJ: Princeton University Press.

16 Politics on a Small Stage
Relationships as a Theatre for the Mis/Performance of Fairness and Respect

Mark Furlong

THE INTERPERSONAL IS THE IDEOLOGICAL

Just as 'the personal is the political', there is a politics in personal relationships. Most obviously, this is seen in the distribution of tasks in a domestic relationship as Chodorow (1978) long ago demonstrated: who does the shopping? the cleaning? and so forth. More subtly, there is also a politics in the intimate aspects of relationships, e.g. is emotional work fairly distributed within traditional heterosexual couples (Hochschild 2003)?

A similar analysis can also be conducted in other examples of sociality. In friendships, peer groups, meetings between strangers, in the workplace, in romances—in every instance of affinity and affiliation—it is possible to identify patterns in how responsibilities and benefits, privileges and disadvantages, are distributed. The key question is not "at this moment did party A do better (or worse) than party B?" Rather, the question is: over an extended period was there a fair distribution of outlays and rewards (to overuse the economic metaphor)?

Of course, there are larger tides which affect how personal relationships are conducted, understood and experienced. These structural currents involve dynamic contexts, configurations which set up inequalities of outcome concerned with variables such as class, gender, sexuality and race. The presence of differentials related to these variables produces an uneven distribution of probabilities around how roles, responsibilities and benefits are allocated in specific relationship examples. This being clear, in the here and now the empirical, and to some extent phenomenological, issue around fairness is observable with respect to particular questions in specific sites. For example:

- Is there a pattern where one party's concerns tend to take centre-stage in this friendship?
- When a work group meets socially, is the division of labour fair with respect to who takes responsibility for maintaining conversations?
- Is there a judgment-making bias that favours one party, or alliance, in this book club?

- Which person, or category of person, is feted and affirmed, respected and acknowledged—and which person, or category of person, tends to receive the opposite kind of attention, in group X?

Like a mobile whose sub-units rotate in contrary but connected arcs, each of us lives within an interdependent matrix of interpersonal associations. This assembly is an aesthetic entity, but it is also a political field or, more precisely, a set of overlapping fields. As with the personal, it is not possible to eradicate this political dimension; nor should it be ignored.

That is, amongst a larger set of interwoven dimensions (the behavioural, the emotional, the symbolic, etc.), there is a politics at work in every relationship—and this is where it gets wondrously interesting: the what, how and why of this politics will have a local and unique biography yet, because the politics of relationships is conducted within a common larger milieu and social vocabulary—a vocabulary whose elements include the everyday experience and expression of power, ethics and ideology—what happens in 'this one-off meeting between strangers', or 'that couple's sexual affair' cannot be partitioned from the abiding, and yet dynamic, larger context (Jamieson 1998; Bauman 2003; Furlong 2009).

That this larger context might condition the locally interpersonal introduces a matter that can be approached by way of an aphorism. An old Arabic saying states that "men resemble their times more than their fathers." Insofar as this is the case, it is presumably also true with respect to personal relationships: just as the personal is interpenetrated by the socio-structural, it follows that the interpersonal, the field of personal relationships, is inseparable from the larger, evolving formations such as gender, ideology and culture.

This interpenetration means that the understanding, representation, experience and conduct of relationships evolve rather than remain timelessly archetypal. Rather, what happens between strangers, between intimates and between known, but not too well-known, associates will be shaped by the conditions within which these exchanges occur. If these conditions are characterised by globalisation, the rise of techno-consumerism and the process of individualisation, this will affect the character of, and the prospects for, personal relationships. Two examples might illustrate this possibility.

First, the twin values of pragmatism and opportunism are currently valorised. Evidence for this claim is illustrated in the uncritical acceptance accorded Giddens's (1991, 2002) template for contemporary personhood: that the well-adjusted self should be both "reflexive" and a "strategizer"—an opportunist whose business is to unsentimentally calculate risks and rewards. Secondly, the contemporary subject increasingly frames their thinking in terms of choice. This phenomenon is associated with the increased infiltration of commercial images and fantasies within the subjectivity of an ever larger number of individuals (Hochschild 2003; Offer 2006).

Both these specifications disrupt the prospects for positive relationships, given the latter inscribes the expectation that one party—the me—should control 'the relationship'. This expectation is incompatible with the logic of relationships as no single person can control any real partnership. The former mind-set is problematic as it antagonises the prospects for just (or stable) relationships as the strategic mode of thought eschews the importance of ethics because goal-directed planning and action is privileged. Mindful that the relational has some vestigial, even uncanny, features, a sensibility that is military and/or commercial is no ally of respectful or ethical partnership.

Given there is such a strong tide running against the prospects for cooperative affiliation, this chapter investigates how personal relationships can be understood as a context within which acts of resistance and recognition can be undertaken. Although a detailed development of this argument is not possible within the limits of the present exercise, an outline will be introduced. Towards this purpose, a vignette from an 'ordinary' social relationship and one from an example of professional practice are used to animate the argument.

In what follows, two related themes are prominent:

(i). The necessity to contest the assumption that any one individual should, or can, be in control of a relationship
(ii). The importance of participants in a relationship being able to distinguish their intentions from the outcomes of their actions.

From this material an optimistic case is made that both disadvantaged and ordinary citizens can reach towards more reciprocal and ethical relationships.

Two particular risks should be acknowledged. Firstly, broad-brush generalisations are inevitable in the current exercise however reductive such stereotyping is. Second, the question of voice is at issue. Putting this crudely, it has to be asked: who is the writer to pontificate about a realm that is so private, so creative, so local: surely, nobody has the right to be holier-than-thou? Although only partial, it can be countered that there is value in the current exercise because the political and ethical dimensions of interpersonal relations tend to be so embedded, so hidden in plain sight, that they amount to "successful ideological effects (which) have no need of words, and ask no more than complicitous silence" (Bourdieu, as quoted by Lorenz 2012, 599). Insofar as this is true, there is purpose in externalising this dimension so it can be better traced and contested.

Qualifications and Cautions

Two additional cautions should be noted. The first relates to the point of view from which this chapter is written. What follows has been formulated from a partisan standpoint: I am committed to contesting the process of individualisation (Bauman 2003; Howard 2007). This general process, I believe, has already significantly eroded the prospects for stable and ethical personal relationships because, at its core, this process is an ideological program that instructs each individual to regard everything in life—lifestyle, identity, location of residence, attitudes, mood, relationships—as items at a smorgasbord: *I am in charge; I can choose only what I want!*

This dream is colonising individual consciousness, as well as the imagination of therapeutic and human service practice: the former is apparent in how the motifs of entitlement, control and freedom have come to increasingly structure contemporary subjectivity (Offer 2006); and the latter glimpsed in the assumption that *the quest for autonomy* (Seedhouse 2002) is a positive title for a 'modern' professional text. This noted, I also wish to contend that there are grounds for optimism in that individuals and groups can engage in 'taking it back' practices (White 2007), actions which can revive old connections, remodel current affiliations and also initiate new relationships based on the values of accountability, recognition and fairness.

Mindful this is a partisan starting point, the presented material is designed to have several levels of relevance. Firstly, what is examined may be useful to practitioners who undertake face-to-face work with clients in therapeutic, health, human service and community settings. General readers may also find what is raised relevant insofar as each of us has an interest in reviewing our own sociality. This ambit may seem unusual yet to do otherwise, to only focus on the practitioner or, alternatively, to only to zero in on the client or the 'lay public', would be to engage in a dividing practice. Such a bracketing would engage in the practice of othering, of establishing an us and a them.

The second qualification relates to a different level of complication: that there are essential contradictions central to the nature of relationships themselves. Relationships are generated and maintained in ways that are both private and public, vestigial and in-the-moment, instrumental and symbolic, unique and patterned, mysterious and materially embodied. *And* they are also inevitably political.

This noted, the relational is a site where reciprocity and recognition can contest asymmetry and exploitation, but it does not always work this way. A practical vignette is now introduced to concretise the hard-to-pin-down dynamic between fairness and recognition in relationships.

VIGNETTES

Amongst a larger set of attributes, being able to approximate fairness requires that participants are able to distinguish their intentions from the effects of their actions.

Vignette 1: The Two Housemates

> Reece had arrived at Hayley's new flat to help her move in. At one point they found themselves struggling to manoeuvre a heavy desk with Hayley grappling with the front half while Reece tussled with the weightier rear end. Without warning Hayley called out, "My hand's caught in the drawer!" Assuming it's what she wanted him to do, Reece immediately dropped his end. Unfortunately, this produced an even sharper pain. "That's made it worse", Hayley shouted, "get it off me please!" Feeling unfairly blamed, Reece retorted, "Stop yelling at me. I am not trying to hurt you." Much in pain, Hayley hissed, "It's not about you! It's my hand that's stuck!" His bile rising, Reece indignantly replied, "I only came here to help"—whilst under his breath thinking, *She's being so unfair. As soon as I can, I'm out of here.*
>
> Struggling on, somehow Hayley's hand was finally released. Reece and Hayley then found themselves staring at each other. Still in shock, Hayley was relieved, but it was an aggrieved Reece who was the first to speak. "It was so unfair when you yelled. You must have known I was not trying to hurt you." More than a little stunned, and before she had the chance to think it over, Hayley then said, "Reece, you're being a complete baby. Do you really want me to apologise because I got hurt?" At this point Reece saw he only had two choices. He could walk right out, which he feared would kiss off the friendship, or he could allow himself to be unfairly silenced (*She's trying to make me swallow my feelings!* he said to himself). Both of these choices, he felt, were aversive. Hayley's thoughts mirrored Reece's, albeit with the names of the culprit and the victim reversed.

Assuming Hayley was not sending him hate mail or medical bills, if Reece remained indignant it seems this would reflect an inability to distinguish his intentions from the effects of his actions. Such an impairment is far from unique as it appears an increasing number of us find it hard to see it from the other's point of view.

Our behaviour can hurt, embarrass or disregard others without this being our intention (and, in the abstract, we mostly know this). In these situations there is no *mensa rea*, no knowledge of anticipated wrong doing, to put it in legal terms. Yet, all this is a nothingness if we, like Reece, harbour enough righteousness to feel unfairly blamed if someone gets upset with what we've done when this effect had not (we say to ourselves) been intended. Most likely, Reece failed to make the distinction between intentions and outcomes because the horizon of his awareness was bounded by his own internally perceived guiltlessness. This failure represents the functional inability to experience the other as a separate being. Simply put, Reece was self-referential and, most likely, so was Hayley if not to the same degree.

Mead (1962) maintained that sociality was predicated on each person developing, and being able to intuitively deploy, what he termed "the generalized other". This internalised entity acts as an informant in the conduct of social relations as we are organised in our actions by imaginatively putting ourselves in the shoes of the other: the stranger who is lost in a new town; the person I have accidentally bumped into. (Developmental psychology frames a similar construct as *the Theory of Mind*; see, for example, McHugh and Stewart 2012.) This faculty can be described analogously repurposing an idea from bio-mechanics. Proprioception is the preconscious capacity to sense the body's part–whole relationships, for example, in intuitively knowing the inclination of our trunk to the angle of our head. These somatic data are available synchronously, in real time, and are used constantly. If the interpersonal field is considered, a parallel capacity is needed: the radar to know about the other as a separately conscious and equally valuable independent entity.

If an awareness of the other as a co-present entity is diminishing, how might this be understood? New attitudes, values and habits associated with the process of individualisation might be implicated (Bauman 2001; Howard 2007). Perhaps, as Greenfield (2008) proposes, human neurology is changing due to its immersion within dense information and communication technology-based environments. However a recession in interpersonal awareness might be explained, the incapacity to put oneself in the other's shoes is becoming more blatant: think of the driver who shouts indignantly, "But *I* had my indicators on!" when called to account for pushing into a line of cars. When the horizon of awareness becomes the subject's intentions or, more generally, their feelings, focus, entitlement—whatever is on their mind—this disrupts other-orientedness. In the imbroglio between Reece and Hayley, missing in action was the generalised other.

Reflection 1: What Promotes or Relegates Fairness?

Continuing with the themes of accountability and perspective taking, a scenario is described. Following this scenario, two different classes of reflection are invited.

Scenario

Parent *A* and parent *B* discussed what should be done in response to their son breaking an important, but not crucial, house rule. In this conversation it was agreed that *A* would communicate to their son that as a consequence of his misbehaviour he would be grounded the following weekend.

A did not pass on this message, nor did *A* proactively communicate to *B* that the agreement had lapsed. Moreover, *A* did not retrospectively communicate that what had been agreed upon had not occurred.

Sometime later *B* discovered the message had not been passed on and decided to politely raise this with *A*. *A*'s response was unapologetic and very clear: *"I thought about it after we spoke and I changed my mind about what should be done."* To this statement, *B* remained mute.

In considering this scenario, a threshold question is the matter of personal accountability: ethical actors who are prepared to be accountable for what they do or do not do.

Step 1: Why Might A and B's Actions Be Right?

There are reasons why the actions of *A* and *B* might be understandable. For example:

- *A* might be in a hierarchically superior position, or in some other material way be advantaged, in relation to *B*. In this event it makes sense for *B* to remain mute.
- The relationship between *A* and *B* might be so clearly understood as fair that *A*'s action might be reasonably understood as a definitely tolerable exception to this pattern. In this event neither *A* nor *B* need do anything.
- The exchange is situated within a culture of passivity, face-saving or conflict avoidance. In this event *A* and *B* have no practical alternatives.

Step 2: What Might Be Said to Avoid Accountability?

Mindful of the reasons *A* and *B* might have had little or no choice, the following statements are likely to function as alibis, as the expression of privilege or as, more generally, that which avoids accountability. This list of statements might be used as a starting point in a process of review.

1. There was no legal contract in place. In this circumstance, *A*—like everybody else—has the right to change his or her mind.
2. Rather than being rigid in their thinking, *B* should be prepared to be flexible.
3. When something goes wrong, it is best not to dwell on this: 'just move on'.
4. *A* might feel harassed, or even worse, embarrassed, if *B* does not immediately accept *A*'s explanation.
5. *B* should immediately accept what *A* has said; otherwise the situation between them might become antagonistic.

If each of these statements is rejected, a general position is established: each of us should be ready to accept a degree of personal accountability for our behaviour in each of our relationships. For example, if each party in a relationship cannot assume that what is agreed upon is what will happen, a quality of instability and provisionality will be generated. In the above example it appears parent *A*'s horizon of awareness was bounded by i-referenced items to the extent that the prospects for accountability—for the recognition of the other—fell away.

A Psychotherapeutic Vignette

Psychotherapy is assumed to result in clients having higher-quality relationships. Yet, the opposite might be true. For example, Bauman contends that traditional psychotherapy socialises clients towards becoming more self-referential. He argues that the therapeutic process:

> advises more self-appreciation, self-concern and self-care, more attention to (my) . . . inner ability for pleasure and satisfaction—as well as less 'dependence' on others and less attention to other's demands for attention and care. Clients who diligently learned the lessons and followed the advice faithfully should from now on ask themselves more often the question 'what's in it for me?'(2003, 57)

Insofar as Bauman is correct, it follows that the psychotherapies, such as cognitive-behavioural theory, will tend to have a negative effect on the relationships of those who are their recipients because the cognitive pattern learned as the precondition for a successful outcome has an inadvertent by-product: a habit of mind which compromises the prospects for secure, moral connections between the client and their significant others.

Although it is an alarming possibility, a broad literature review only identified several relatively marginal psychotherapeutic traditions which practically (White 2007), or theoretically (Greenberg and Mitchell 1983), regard clients as interdependent entities whose interests are vitally correlated with their significant others. Surprisingly, the majority of traditions constructed their clients (and people in general) as a self-serving business—as bounded identities, as republics of self-interest, who had no accountability to, or positive capacity to connect with, others (Furlong 2010a; 2010b).

Borrowing from non-mainstream traditions—particularly narrative therapy (White 2007), Action and Commitment Therapy (Blackledge, Ciarrochi and Deane 2009) and philosophical consultation (Colgate 2004)—an activist approach to encouraging relational ethics within the therapeutic project can be identified. The 'schools' that are sourced to develop this approach are diverse but have at least one element in common: unlike their mainstream counterparts, these alternative traditions dismiss the claim that psychotherapy is a technical, ideologically neutral endeavour.

Vignette 2: Captured by the Game

Taylor is a twenty-nine-year-old web-based games designer. He tells Freya, a private psychotherapist, he loves his work: "It's the high point of modern art, the best possible way to spend my time." He does not see he has "any real issue" and has only agreed to see Freya because his younger sister, Sam, who he has always trusted, arranged the appointment.

Taylor tells Freya he works/plays around the clock in an almost exclusively male environment but does not see himself as "one of those hairy-arsed Neanderthals." Rather, Taylor says he is into "fun, rolling round the globe fun." When prodded a little, he also says he is worried—"just a bit you know"—about the headaches, sleeping problems and preoccupations he is "maybe increasingly" experiencing.

He thinks he is bi, and has had many one-night stands with (mostly) men as well as several short-term heterosexual romances. "I'm not worried about being gay or bi or whatever. That's an old world hang-up, not mine. What I am big on is [and this is a repeated theme] being in control. It's my wheel, my game. I'm not giving that up for anything, or anyone."

Freya thinks she will only see this man once. *He won't come back,* she says to herself. *So can I perhaps seed one line of thought, introduce one provocation, that might resonate with this likeable, self-absorbed and now not-so-young man?* Keeping the tone light she says:

> You have a few worries, but we both know what got you through the door was your regard for your sister. In my trade, we'd call you a window-shopper, so most likely you'll not come back. Given this I want to try and give you something you can't lose. If you decide to come back, we can talk about what you think; if you don't, maybe it can be one of those coins that rolls around in your money box.

Taylor's curiosity is piqued by this pitch. Freya then leans forward and says:

> The theory I work to is that each of us is not as independent as we think. Rather than being a stand-alone entrepreneur, I reckon we are social beings—but there is a twist that makes this hard to see. The trick that makes our inter-dependence hard to grasp is that the energy driving our personal relationships tends to change its focus. For example, at sixteen most people value their connections with their peers the most; as lesbians and gays head north into their lives, feeling part of a tribe is a wellspring; most young mums are super close to their kids; most new couples—gay, bi or straight—get so high on each

other they withdraw from others. And, if someone is twenty-nine and
bi, the challenge is to pioneer, to find a way to customise and protect,
a sustaining network. Do you know what I mean?

On this theme I want to ask you this: when you consider your
network, your mob, now and how you'd like it to look in, say, ten
years, who do you think is meant to be in control?

Use your knowledge as a games designer: who should be in control in the multi-player game of friendship or romance? I really look
forward to discussing this with you if you want to come back. If you
decide not to, no drama. No one is going to chase you.

Somewhat taken aback, Taylor replied, "Yish, that's a lot to take in. What
can I say? Maybe I will think about it. Is that all?"

In the standard therapeutic account, the above would be judged as
not merely inelegant, but as intrusive and manipulative (as if any brand
of therapy is really non-directive). Alternatively, it could be understood as
an example of purposive work. Consistent with the rejection of the myth
of neutrality, Freya could stand behind her work and describe it clearly:
"Ideologically, in my practice I seek ways to contest the interpersonal
thoughtlessness that is atomising clients." In terms of what Freya is trying
to achieve, she would contend:

> I set out to de-centre Taylor's assumption that relationships are a site
> where one person can be in control. Hopefully, if he thinks it through,
> it might become clearer to him that (i) everybody, including him, is
> always 'in relationships', and (ii) rather than ever being able to be in
> control, it is the capacity for uncertainty and tolerance, and the know-
> how to negotiate, that is important.

Rather than espouse a bogus claim to neutrality, it is more honest to declare
one's position, mindful that there can be a paradox here: declaring one's
position can cause 'blow-back', a situation that can at times lead to one's
preferred outcome becoming less attainable (Furlong and Lipp1995).

THE DANCE BETWEEN SUBJECTIVITY AND SOCIALITY

The subject position which most aligns with the current environment is
to be i-centred. Horrifyingly, this disposition disrupts the prospects for
accountable, secure attachments. For different reasons, this is the case for
the two cohorts of most concern in the current work: formal clients of
health and human services, and those who are deemed normally well-adjusted. Members of each group tend to reference what is happening in their
environment, and within their own minds, to themselves and their interests
even if the reasons for this are dissimilar.

The well-adjusted are i-referenced because their habits of mind comply with the specifications for personhood invited by the process of individualisation (Furlong 2009). That is, these people have learned to become "sovereign individuals" (Davidson and Rees-Mogg 1997)—opportunists who incessantly calibrate the costs and the benefits, the risks and rewards, of what is and might be. Insofar as this disposition has sculpted an individual's subjectivity, there is a direct outcome: everything is about me—including my relationships: *Is this relationship working for me, or can I do better? What about my 'need' for affirmation, for sexual satisfaction, for choice, for emotional attention?* Within this framing the other, literally each and every other, is experienced as either a resource or an obstruction. In direct contradiction to Emanuel Kant's categorical imperative—treat each person as an ends, not as a means—the other, in fact all relationships, are instrumentalised.

'Losers', those who have been disconfirmed by the media and/or the competent authorities in mental health, child protection and the like, have a stream of consciousness that is i-referenced for a different reason. If you are one-down, you are likely to be on guard, hot-wired to the prospect you are about to be 'dissed' once again. Shamed, afraid of again being emotionally hurt, you will keep the drawbridge up. This is a protective measure, a defence. Sadly, this has consequences as if someone trusts too little, if they are hyper-alert to the possibility of, let alone to actually receiving, criticism and rejection, this sets up a vicious cycle: if you provide little or no start-up information in your contact with others, if you hedge your bets by exiting relationships first, if you look away or down because you are embarrassed, you lose track of the other in your stream of thought. This is a logical reaction to the experience of social exclusion, but this defensiveness is nonetheless a poignant form of self-harm as it wards off the very relationships that might reverse this cycle.

For those who are successful products of the process of individualisation, and also for those who have been stigmatised and excluded, the point is to contest, to hold against, the habit of being self-referential both subjectively and behaviourally. Conceptually, the principle of decision is to appreciate the existence of, and yet to also be aware of the impossibility of truly recognising, the other.

Levinas (1987) said that the other is a mystery, but before this magic can be appreciated the other has to be conjured up. This is no small challenge because, as discussed above, the other as a sentient, equally important entity is inconsistent with the lore of individualisation. Insofar as civility, modesty, duty, honour, respect for others, etc., have been replaced as the top-of-the-agenda items by an overriding concern with me—my feelings, my interests, my needs, my past, my thoughts, my fantasies—then the other has disappeared as a stand-alone value. Literally, there is no stage upon which it is possible to imagine and animate the other. They have gone, slipped into the wings, disappeared over the event horizon.

In this circumstance, the task is to contest the i-formation. This can be done in many ways. Guerrilla tactics have a place. One might ask, for example, why did William Gadda, an Italian novelist, call "the 'I' the filthiest of pronouns" (as quoted by Calvino 2007; 108)? More philosophical discussions also have their place. In these and other ways—as a tactic in professional practice; as a theme in one's own reflections—the idea is to perturb the established figure and ground structure. This can be furthered by:

- Taking up, talking up, the focus on accountability and fairness
- Concentrating on the importance of, and singling out ways that express and enact, being just and other-oriented
- In discussing the possibility of achieving a balance between the autonomous and the relational self
- In considering the question of the type of reputation you, or the client, wishes to have, or not have

Such exercises disrupt the figure and ground configuration which sustains excessive self-referentiality. Over time, a different figure and ground practice can be worked up (Furlong, 2013b).

REPRESENTING RELATIONSHIPS

Unlike you or I, her or him, relationships have no visual or physical presence. More, different kinds of relationship cannot be identified by voice or colour, smell or taste, nor can they be weighed, packed up or transported. However deliquescent they may be, this does not prevent us from treating relationships as immediate and real. For example, it is not thought mad if someone says "this relationship is not working for me" or, in other circumstances, "you and I, we have a beautiful thing going."

Given this ambiguity, can a relationship be just or unjust? Perhaps, it is only individuals who can be judged as fair or otherwise (as is the practice in violence prevention programs: see, for example, Dunn and Powell-Williams 2007). This is an uncertain point as, on the one hand, attributing responsibility to an abstract entity—a friendship, a business partnership, a romance—is to anthropomorphise a social relation. Courts do not put a relationship in the dock; it is only individuals who are held accountable and judged as innocent or guilty, fair or exploitative. Yet, this common sense can be de-centred. After studying Indian culture Dumont (1986, 9), a French anthropologist, concluded:

> Western ideology grants real existence only to individuals and not to relations, to elements and not to sets of elements.

Putting it crudely, Dumont argues Westerners cannot see or name relationships, cannot put the relational at the forefront of awareness. 'It' just does not seem to be palpable or visible—like all real things are meant to be.

Most likely, we have become entranced by the process of individualisation. This process has been gathering momentum, according to Elliot and

Lemert (2006), for centuries, but has radically intensified over the last two decades. According to Elliot and Lemert (2006), individualisation:

> remains the master idea of modernity for a whole host of reasons, not least because ideologies pertaining to the free and autonomous individual have been essential to the patterning of relations between self and society throughout the capitalist west. (7)

Enchanted by individualisation's heady power, the capacity to apprehend, to experience and consciously respect, relationships has diminished. Yes, the absence of relationships can be felt, sometimes catastrophically, but their nature and needs, variability and character, may be less apparent as the individual—the her or the him, the I-me-my-mine—has come to occupy centre-stage.

If the focus is on relationships, in contrast to personhood, one way to represent relationships is to view examples as specific coordinates in a field constructed by two axes:

- The vertical axis has Giddens's (1992) idealisation of "pure relationships" at one pole and Kipnis's (2003) idealisation of personal relationships as "pure commodity" at the other.
- The horizontal axis has personal relationships as "conscious, technical competence" at one pole and as "spontaneous, vestigial acts" at the other.

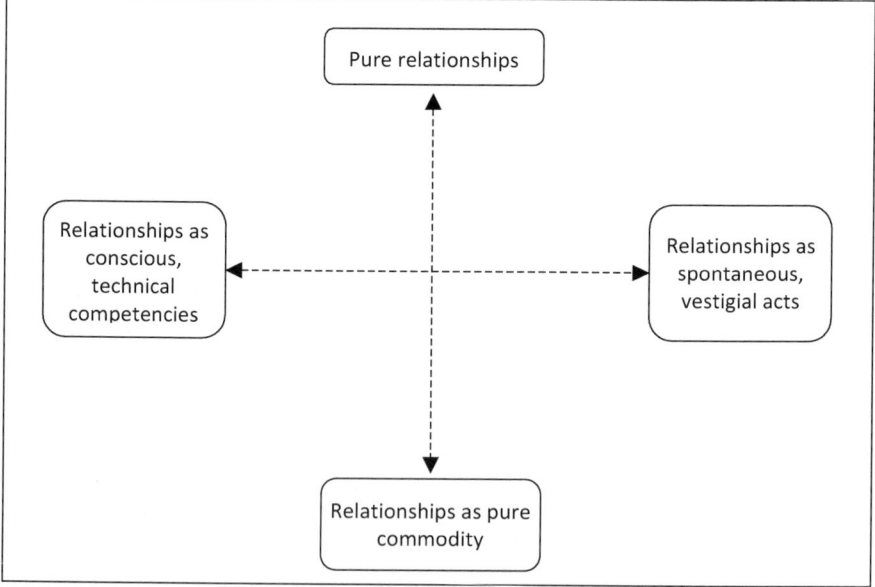

Figure 16.1   Representing relationships.

On these two axes it is possible to locate different understandings of, and assumptions about, personal relationships. Broadly, ethical relationships are more likely to be found in the top left–hand quadrant and their antithesis in the lower two quadrants. On this basis, if the aim is to approximate the ethical, if the plan is to 'move' a relationship towards what is a more ethical configuration, the navigation should be to the northwest.

CONCLUSION

When it comes to relationships, almost everyone wants to do the right thing. This is especially the case with those we care most about and whose respect we seek. Whilst some of us have narrow preoccupations, such as a yen for fame or an aversion to being seen the fool, there are few who are generically psychopathic or determinedly estranged. This leaves a great majority who would be disturbed if they judged themselves, or if they felt their peers judged them, as unjust in relation to their intimates. In a lower register, this allegiance to fairness is also a concern in most people's relationships within their broader circle: with respect to work associates, neighbours or the many with whom there is regular, albeit informal exchange. Even if the category was 'exchanges with complete strangers', only a minority would think it a grace not to be judged disrespectful, damaging or unfair.

It follows that personal relationships can be understood as a small stage upon which participants act out, dramatise in the here and now, the politics of fairness, respect and recognition. In this sense, we are all actors who have an active interest in reviewing our performance—our behaviour and our attitudes—with respect to the reference 'ethics and relationships' even if it is rare that the matter of ethics is at the forefront of awareness.

Mostly, we frame our engagement with the world around other priorities—say, "I'm getting on with it: no navel-gazing for me right now"—but a concern with fairness, with getting a fair shake and with wanting to act properly towards others remains a basic criteria in life. It may even be that reference to this criteria is totemic as the matter of fairness has long been endowed with symbolic significance to those who are participants in a given relationship.

There will remain, of course, differentials with respect to capital and status between, for example, women and men; injustice will be inscribed into biographies with respect to race; narratives about class will echo between generations. These, and more, currents continue to be live contexts for us all, but this does not mean that personal relationships are less of a wellspring of purpose, or less than secularly spiritual, whatever the structural configuration may be. Tuning into, and allowing oneself to be guided by, an internal moral compass in one's affiliations therefore remains a key interest to all of us. It is towards bringing this interest into greater subjective awareness that this chapter has been directed.

REFERENCES

Bauman, Z. 2001. *The Individualized Society*. Cambridge: Polity.

Bauman, Z. 2003. *Liquid Love: On the Frailty of Human Bonds*. Cambridge: Polity.

Blackledge, J., J. Ciarrochi and F. Deane. 2009. *Acceptance and Commitment Therapy: Contemporary Theory, Research and Practice*. Bowen Hills: Australian Academic Press.

Calvino, I. 2007. Six Memos for the New Millennium, New York: Vintage Press.

Chodorow, N. 1978. *The Re-Production of Mothering*. Berkeley: University of California.

Colgate, C. 2004. *Just between You and Me: The Art of Ethical Relationships*. Melbourne: Pan Macmillan.

Davidson, J., and W. Rees-Mogg. 1997. *The Sovereign Individual*. London: Macmillan.

Dumont, L. 1986. *Essays on Individualism: Modern Ideology in Anthropological Perspective*. Chicago: University of Chicago Press.

Dunn, J., and M. Powell-Williams. 2007. "Everybody Makes Choices: Victim Advocates and the Social Construction of Battered Women's Victimization and Agency." *Violence against Women* 13 (10): 977–999.

Elliot, A., and C. Lemert. 2006. *The New Individualism: The Emotional Costs of Globalization*. London: Routledge.

Furlong, M. 2009. "i-dolatry: The Emerging Grammar of First-Person Talk." *Arena* 101:12–14.

Furlong, M. 2010a. "Psychotherapy as Vector for Anomie and Isolation." *Psychotherapy in Australia* 16 (2): 38–43.

Furlong, M. 2010b. "Sovereign Selves or Social Beings?: The Practitioner's Role in Constructing the Subjectivity and Sociality of the Consumer." *New Paradigm* Autumn:50–57.

Furlong, M. 2013a. Calling to the Client as a Relational Being, *Psychotherapy in Australia*, 19(3): 68–75.

Furlong, M. 2013b. *Building the Clients Relational Base: A Multidisciplinary Handbook*, Bristol: Policy Press.

Furlong, M., and J. Lipp. 1995. "The Multiple Relationships between Neutrality and Therapeutic Influence." *Australian and New Zealand Journal of Family Therapy* 16 (4): 201–211.

Giddens, A. 1991. *Modernity and Self-Identity: Self and Society in the Late Modern Age*. Cambridge: Polity.

Giddens, A. 1992. *The Transformation of Intimacy: Sexuality, Love and Eroticism in Modern Societies*. Oxford: Polity.

Giddens, A. 2002. *Runaway World: How Globalization Is Re-Shaping Our Lives*. London: Profile Books.

Greenberg, J., and S. Mitchell. 1983. *Object Relations and Psychoanalytic Theory*. Cambridge, MA: Harvard University Press.

Greenfield, S. 2008. *ID: The Quest for Identity in the 21st Century*. London: Sceptre.

Hochschild, A. 2003. *The Commercialization of Intimate Life: Notes from Home and Work*. Berkeley: University of California Press.

Howard, C. 2007. *Contested Individualization: Debates about Contemporary Personhood*. New York: Palgrave Macmillan.

Jamieson, F. 1998. *Intimacy: Personal Relationships in Modern Society*. Cambridge: Polity.

Kipnis, L. 2003. *Against Love: A Polemic*. New York: Vintage Books.

Levinas, E. 1987. *Time and the Other*. Pittsburgh: Duquesne University Press.

Lorenz, C. 2012. "If You Are So Smart, Why Are You under Surveillance?: Universities, Neoliberalism and New Public Management." *Critical Enquiry* Spring:599–629.

McHugh, L., and I. Stewart. 2012. *The Self and Perspective-Taking: Contributions and Applications from Modern Behavioral Science*. Oakland, CA: New Harbinger.

Mead, G.H. 1962. *Mind, Self, and Society*. Chicago: University of Chicago Press.

Offer, A. 2006. *The Challenge of Affluence: Self-Control and Well-Being in the USA and Britain since 1950*. Oxford: Oxford University Press.

Seedhouse, D. 2002. Total Health Promotion: Mental Health, Rational Fields and the Quest for Autonomy, Hoboken: Wiley.

White, M. 2007. *Maps of Narrative Practice*. New York: W.W. Norton.

Contributors

Georgia Birch has successfully completed her PhD at Deakin University, examining how previous physical activity and motherhood influence activity levels in later life for older Somali women. Georgia has been in the fitness and health promotion industry for over twenty years and has for the past four years become a strong advocate for the local Somali community. She is a board member and consultant for a humanitarian organisation KISIMA in Africa, which works towards supporting the disaster and conflict affected local communities in Somalia through the provision of relief supplies. Georgia is interested in research in marginalised groups and in presenting their views in their words and in a style that allows them to speak.

Heather D'Cruz (Bachelor of Social Work, Master of Social Work (with Distinction), Doctor of Philosophy) was employed in Australian public sector organisations (1979–1996) and as an academic at various Australian universities (1996–2009). More recently, she was an Adjunct Research Associate, Centre for Human Rights Education, Curtin University, Western Australia (2010–2012). Heather's research interests are in child and family policy and practice, and identity, diversity and inclusivity. She is the author of *Constructing Meanings and Identities in Child Protection Practice* (2004, Tertiary Press, Australia), and (with Martyn Jones) *Social Work Research: Ethical and Political Contexts* (2004, Sage, London). She is a co-editor (with Struan Jacobs and Adrian Schoo) of *Knowledge-in-Practice in the Caring Professions: Multi-disciplinary Perspectives* (2009, Ashgate, UK), and (with Margaret Kumar and Niranjala Weerakkody) of *Where are you From? Voices in Transition* (2010, Common Ground Publishers, Altona, Victoria, Australia). A second edition of her co-authored book with Martyn Jones, *Social Work Research in Practice: Ethical and Political Contexts* (Sage, London), is in press. She was an invited Visiting Leverhulme Fellow (2007–2008), sponsored by the University of Salford, Greater Manchester, UK.

Sarah Epstein is currently undertaking her PhD at Deakin University in Melbourne, Australia. Her thesis examines feminist mothers' experiences of raising sons and investigates how feminism's engagement with ideas of gender and masculinity intersect with the mother–son relationship. She is a social worker by trade and has extensive work experience with victim/survivors of sexual assault. Sarah currently provides group supervision and consultation for multidisciplinary teams in Women and Young People's Services.

Stephen Fisher teaches in the Diplomas of Community Development and Services at Chisholm Institute, Dandenong. He is also a PhD candidate at Deakin University, investigating the most effective ways to train men to become advocates for the elimination of violence against women. He has just completed a training handbook to equip men in the Pacific to end violence against women.

Mark Furlong (PhD) teaches in the social work program at Deakin University. Prior to commencing full-time university-based work, for almost twenty years Mark practiced in therapeutic and mental health settings with a focus on relationship-building—a background that included substantial service as a consultant and trainer. He has published in mental health, family therapy, family studies, psychotherapy, social work and primary health professional journals as well as non-academic pieces for *Dissent* and *Overland* magazines. Mark's book, *Building the Client's Relational Base: A Multidisciplinary Handbook*, was published by Policy Press in 2013. His research foci are: (i) the impact on relationships of the process of individualisation, (ii) how practitioners can be assisted to develop their clients' relational base and (iii) how personal relationships are experienced, understood and conducted. Currently, Mark writes a regular column for *Arena* observing "the changing dance between selfhood and sociality."

Sophie Goldingay (PhD) lectures in the School of Health and Social Development at Deakin University, Geelong, Australia, and coordinates the undergraduate social work honours program. She has worked in mental health and criminal justice settings as a social worker for eleven years before becoming a social work educator in 2004. Her research interests include understanding the experiences of young people in custody, especially those serving time in age-mixed settings and those who have disabilities. She is also actively involved in projects which aim to improve the quality of social work education, especially in relation to learning outcomes for students who traditionally would not attend university. Some recent publications include: "Young Women Prisoners in New Zealand: Substance Abuse and Violent Offending," *Te Awatea Review* 6, no. 2 (2008): 17–19; "The Bullying Problem: Exploring Ways Young Women

Prisoners Talk about Prison Bullying," *Te Awatea Review* 5, no. 2 (2007): 9–13; "Jail Mums: The Status of Adult Female Prisoners amongst Young Female Prisoners in Christchurch Women's Prison," *Social Policy Journal of New Zealand: Te Puna Whakaaro* 31 (2007): 56–73.

Norah Hosken is a social work lecturer and PhD candidate in the School of Health and Social Development at Deakin University with thirty years' experience as a practitioner and educator in social work, community work, welfare and women's sectors. Norah has worked in urban, regional, rural and remote locations including the Pilbara in northwestern Australia, demonstrating particular expertise in working effectively with highly discriminated against individuals, groups and communities. Her current PhD research is an institutional ethnography exploring the links between one Australian regional university's gendered, racialised and classed practices and its governance of social justice. Recent publications include: "Developing and Enacting Ethical Frameworks for Cross-Cultural Research," in *Discourse, Power and Resistance—Down Under: Volume 1,* edited by T McKenna, J White and M Vicars (Rotterdam: Sense, 2012); "Social Work and Welfare Education without Discrimination. Are We There Yet?" *Practice Reflexions* 5, no. 1 (2010).

Tina Kostecki, Bachelor of Social Work (University of Queensland), Master of Social Work (University of Melbourne), is a Lecturer in Social Work at Deakin University, Victoria, Australia. Tina has worked for twenty-three years as a social work practitioner mainly with women who have experienced intimate partner violence and also in the fields of child protection, foster care, crisis care and health. She has conducted previous research relating to the analysis and context of policy activism by a group of women's services during the political climate of the 1990s. Most recently, her research interests have been in the field of critical gerontology, in particular, older women's experiences of aging and more broadly, in the application of critical theoretical perspectives to inform social work practice.

Clare Land is an Anglo-identified non-Indigenous person living and working in southeast Australia. Her PhD, entitled "The Politics of Solidarity with Indigenous Struggles in Southeast Australia," was awarded by Deakin University, where she is currently employed as a Research Fellow. Her engagement since 1998 with the history and present of settler colonialism in Australia is inspired by Indigenous struggles and has taken the form of community-based organising. This practice generates questions which Clare has pursued through critical studies in history and sociology. For the last eight years, Clare has collaborated with Gunai/Maar man Robbie Thorpe to co-present a community radio program focusing on colonialism.

Mirjana Lozanovska is a Senior Lecturer at Deakin University. Her research on ways that architecture mediates human dignity and identity through multidisciplinary theories of space includes fieldwork and analysis of the village (of emigration) and the city (of immigration). She is the author of "Abjection and Architecture: The Migrant House in Multicultural Australia," in *Post Colonial Spaces*, edited by G. Nalbantoglu and W.C. Thai (Princeton, NJ: Princeton University Press, 1997); "Emigration/Immigration: Maps, Myths Origins," in *Drifting: Migrancy and the Limits to Architecture*, edited by S. Cairns (New York: Routledge, 2004); "Sacred Time after Emigration: A Study of the Holy Mother Festival in Zavoj, Macedonia," in *Every Day's a Festival! Diversity on Show*, edited by S. Küchler, L. Kürti and H. Elkadi (Wantage: Sean Kingston Publishing, 2011). Mirjana Lozanovska leads the Cultural Ecology Research at the School of Architecture and Building, and is a member of Centre for Memory, Imagination and Invention, a university research centre.

Tania Mataki is of Ngai Tahu, Ngati Mamoe, and Te Whanau Apanui descent. She is currently chief executive of Te Puna Oranga, a social service agency that provides sexual abuse counselling and abuse prevention education and training for Maori by Maori in Christchurch, New Zealand. Tania has twenty years of experience working in counselling programs, women's refuges, sexual violence prevention and women's prisons. She has also been part of a research team that explored young women prisoners' experience of serving time in adult prisons in New Zealand. Her positions have included Otautahi Women's Refuge Program Facilitator, Southern Regional Trainer National Network Refuge and the Southern Coordinator Research for Iwi and Maori Provider Access.

Jack Migdalek has a background in drama, dance and physical theatre. He has worked as a performer, writer, choreographer and director in Australia, the United Kingdom and Japan. In 2012 Jack completed a PhD on Embodied Choreography and Performance of Gender under the supervision of Maria Pallotta-Chiarolli. Currently Jack is a drama lecturer for Trinity College, Melbourne University, and education materials writer for the Arts Centre Melbourne.

Maria Pallotta-Chiarolli is Senior Lecturer in the School of Health and Social Development at Deakin University, Melbourne, Australia. Her primary areas of interest are cultural diversity, gender diversity, sexual diversity and family diversity. Maria is also an External Faculty Member of Saybrook University, San Francisco, and Founding Member of AGMC Inc. (Australian GLBTIQ Multicultural Council). Her books include *Someone You Know* (Australia's first AIDS biography); two collections of young people's voices, writing and art called *Girls Talk* and *Boys*

Stuff; *So What's a Boy: Addressing Issues of Masculinity and Schooling*; *Being Normal Is the Only Way to Be: Adolescent Perspectives on Gender and Schooling* (these last three books with Wayne Martino); *When Our Children Come Out: How to Support Gay, Lesbian, Bisexual and Transgender Young People*; *Tapestry: Five Generations of Women in One Italian Family*; and *Border Sexualities, Border Families in Schools* (a recipient of a Lambda Literary Award, 2011). Her first novel, *Love You Two*, was co-winner of a 2010 Lambda Literary Award.

Bob Pease is Chair of Social Work at Deakin University in Geelong, Australia. He has been involved in pro-feminist politics with men for many years and is a founding member of Men against Sexual Assault in Melbourne. He has published extensively on masculinity politics and critical social work practice, including four books as single author and eight books as co-editor, as well as numerous book chapters and journal articles. His most recent books include: *Working with Men in the Human Services* (co-editor, Allen and Unwin, 2001); *A Man's World?: Changing Men's Practices in a Globalized World* (co-editor, Zed, 2001); *Critical Social Work: An Introduction to Theories and Practices* (co-editor, Allen and Unwin, 2003); *International Encyclopedia of Men and Masculinities* (co-editor, Routledge, 2007); *Critical Social Work: Theories and Practices for a Socially Just World* (co-editor, 2nd ed., Allen and Unwin, 2009); *Migrant Men: Critical Studies of Masculinities and the Migration Experience* (co-editor, Routledge, 2009); *Undoing Privilege: Unearned Advantage in a Divided World* (Zed, 2010); and *Men and Masculinities around the World: Transforming Men's Practices* (co-editor, Palgrave, 2011).

Julie Peters has come from the Biological Sciences and Creative Writing to be confirmed as a Doctoral Candidate at Deakin University. Her thesis uses autoethnographic method to examine the conflicts and confluences between non-conformity to dichotomous gender performance norms and the forces of normative gender coercion. Peters has been published in *Gay and Lesbian Issues* and *Psychology Review* of the Australian Psychological Association, as well as presenting numerous papers, submissions to government and presentations to as diverse groups as Victoria Police, the Victorian Equal Opportunity Commission, the University of Melbourne Department of Psychiatry, AIDS Nurses, public health professionals and undergraduates from a number of universities. Peters has also appeared on prime-time television and radio and performed in comedy debates to raise awareness on a number of public health issues.

Russell Shuttleworth, a medical anthropologist and social worker by training, is currently Senior Lecturer in Social Work at the School of Health and Social Development, Faculty of Health Sciences, Deakin University.

Dr. Shuttleworth's research and scholarly interests include sexuality and disability, masculinity and disability, impairment-disability across cultures, disability ethnography, critical disability studies theory and sexuality and aging. Involved in the Disability Rights Movement since the mid-1980s, he also worked for many years as a personal assistant for disabled men in the San Francisco Bay Area. Recent relevant journal articles include "What's So Critical About Critical Disability Studies?" (2009) in the *Australian Journal of Human Rights* and "The Sociological Imaginary and Disability Enquiry in Late Modernity" (2013) in *Critical Sociology*, both co-written with Helen Meekosha; and "The Dilemma of Disabled Masculinity, Men and Masculinities" (2012), co-written with Nikki Wedgwood and Nathan Wilson. Dr. Shuttleworth also recently co-edited with Teela Sanders the book *Sex and Disability: Politics, Identity and Access*, published by the Disability Press (2010), which included his chapter "Toward an Inclusive Sexuality and Disability Research Agenda."

Index

An environmentally friendly book printed and bound in England by www.printondemand-worldwide.com

PEFC Certified

This product is
from sustainably
managed forests
and controlled
sources

www.pefc.org

This book is made entirely of sustainable materials; FSC paper for the cover and PEFC paper for the text pages.

#0037 - 160114 - C0 - 229/152/16 [18] - CB